T0294200

# GREATEST GAMES
# ABERDEEN

# GREATEST GAMES
# ABERDEEN

## THE DONS' FIFTY
## FINEST MATCHES

### KEVIN STIRLING

First published by Pitch Publishing, 2023

Pitch Publishing
9 Donnington Park,
85 Birdham Road,
Chichester,
West Sussex,
PO20 7AJ
www.pitchpublishing.co.uk
info@pitchpublishing.co.uk

A CIP catalogue record is available for this book
from the British Library.

ISBN 978 1 78531 302 8

Typesetting and origination by Pitch Publishing
Printed and bound in Great Britain by TJ Books, Padstow

# Contents

To Bernadette, my loving wife of 37 years, who has always been there for me through everything

My son Kevin who has followed my passion for Aberdeen FC

My daughter Joanne who has given us the greatest gift of all, our grandson Jacob.

# Foreword by Joe Harper

FROM THE moment I signed for Aberdeen way back in 1969, little did I think it would be the start of something special; a relationship that has lasted to the present day. My career at Pittodrie over two spells was my happiest days as a player and my relationship with the supporters has endured.

One of them of course is Kevin Stirling whom I got to know several years ago. We first met in Largs in 2002 when Kevin interviewed me for his first book, *Aberdeen FC A Centenary History*. As far as I recalled that was the first occasion our paths had crossed but Kevin reminded me of the time that I was coaching youngsters at the Duthie Park in Aberdeen in 1971. Along with several other Dons team-mates we were training the aspiring youngsters and putting them through their paces. Unknown to me, I was showing the young lads how to volley the ball when I hit a screamer past an up and coming young goalkeeper – a young Kevin Stirling, no less.

We have since met up at various events and games through the years and Kevin is now on his fifth book on Aberdeen FC. I can confirm that Kevin has no equal when it comes to knowledge on the Dons, an encyclopaedic mind on all things Aberdeen. His work over more than 20 years for the Aberdeen match programme has been outstanding, picking up yearly awards.

His latest work on the Dons' 50 greatest games must have been a tough choice. In my time Aberdeen have enjoyed some fantastic matches and Kevin has captured the essence of the club from his choices from 1908 to 2015. All the memorable cup wins are in there along with some of those famous European nights that the club has become famous for. These games have been covered in detail and are a credit to Kevin and his work.

I was delighted to see some of the games I was involved in covered. The Scottish Cup Final of 1970 remains one of my best matches, and so memorable. Scoring the penalty to open the scoring in front of that huge crowd was incredible. My late friend Derek McKay scored twice as we beat all the odds that day. The return to Aberdeen the following day and all those supporters coming out to welcome us was unbelievable. From Stonehaven to the Town House, incredible.

I was delighted to see Kevin cover our win at Celtic in December 1970. That was the day I outwitted Billy McNeill and scored the winning goal after a rehearsed move from the training ground. It was another victory that should have taken us to the title.

I enjoyed some great European nights with the Dons as well, and scoring in front of that Beach End on such occasions will never leave me. The Juventus UEFA Cup tie was one of the most difficult I have ever played in and I think I still have the marks to prove it! Being up against those Italian defenders was an experience. I still managed to score against them though.

In my second spell at the club the 1976 League Cup Final was a fantastic achievement and again we beat Celtic in the final. That win set up Aberdeen for a golden era, of which I was proud to play a part in the early period before I retired from playing in 1981.

I remain so proud of my career with Aberdeen. In my eight years at Pittodrie I managed to score 205 goals, which works out at around 25 goals a season. It is a record that will never be beaten and that is something so special for me. I was a record transfer for the club in 1969 and again when I was sold in 1972; hard to imagine what value a 25-goal-a-season forward would command these days. To become part of Pittodrie folklore is something that will never leave me.

I do hope you enjoy reading through these great games that have defined what a great club Aberdeen FC are. Stand Free!

# Introduction

HAVING FOLLOWED Aberdeen FC for the best part of 57 years, I have been fortunate enough to see the Dons through the best of times. The golden era of the 1980s remains the greatest period in Aberdeen's history; a period that brought success at home and in Europe that has defined the club.

To select the 50 greatest games was, on the face of it, a relatively straightforward task. The major trophies, league wins and classic European nights and it's job done. However, when researching through the archives it was anything but an easy task.

There is so much more to Aberdeen's history than their proud record of trophies and league flags. I have tried to include a wider range of games, even the odd defeat, so that the club is covered in the proper way.

The story begins in 1908, just five years after Aberdeen came into being, through to 2015, a period of more than 100 years and two world wars. Some of the Dons' greatest ever players are featured and many more included in some of the best teams that have taken pride in wearing the black and gold and red shirt.

From Donald Colman to Niall McGinn, some of the finest players to play for the club include Harry Blackwell, Matt Armstrong, Willie Mills, Frank Dunlop, Willie Cooper, Archie Baird, George Hamilton, Chris Anderson, Stan Williams, Fred Martin, Jimmy Mitchell, Archie Glen, Jackie Allister, Alec Young, Graham Leggat, Harry Yorston, Teddy Scott, Joe O'Neil, Bob Wishart, Jackie Hather, Charlie Cooke, Bobby Clark, Martin Buchan, Jimmy Smith, Henning Boel, Joe Harper, Arthur Graham, Jim Hermiston, Dave

Robb, Zoltán Varga, Jim Forrest, Drew Jarvie, Stuart Kennedy, Steve Archibald, Willie Miller, Alex McLeish, Jim Leighton, Doug Rougvie, John McMaster, Doug Bell, Neale Cooper, Neil Simpson, Gordon Strachan, Peter Weir, Eric Black, John Hewitt, Mark McGhee, Frank McDougall, Stewart McKimmie, Billy Stark, Theo Snelders, Hans Gillhaus, Charlie Nicholas, Brian Irvine, Jim Bett, Paul Mason, Eoin Jess, Scott Booth, Stephen Glass, Billy Dodds, Duncan Shearer, Dean Windass, Bobby Connor, Hicham Zerouali, Arild Stavrum, Russell Anderson, Kevin McNaughton, Scott Severin, Jonny Hayes, Adam Rooney, Scott McKenna, Kenny McLean, Andy Considine, Lewis Ferguson, Calvin Ramsay and Graeme Shinnie.

These games are certainly not the greatest played by Aberdeen, far from it. They do cover some near escapes as the Dons retained their proud record of never having been relegated in their history. For the younger generation of Aberdeen supporters, they may not be aware just how close the club have come to being demoted; 1959, 1976 and 1995 rank among what our great manager famously stated as 'squeaky bum time'. Sir Alex Ferguson of course features and I make no excuse for condensing several of the games within that glorious period of the 1980s. I was fortunate enough to follow the Dons throughout that period; a team that Ferguson boasted could go anywhere in the world and get a result. Who would argue? Aberdeen went to the likes of Munich and Hamburg and did not concede a single goal. Twenty of the games are within that wonderful period and I could have selected 20 more with justification. The one game that stands out above all others is of course the 1983 European Cup Winners' Cup Final against Real Madrid. Every year it seems that we Dons supporters must remind the football world that the last team to beat Real Madrid in a major European final was – Aberdeen.

The European era is well represented with 12 matches featured, from the Dons' debut against Reykjavík in 1967 through to that wonderful balmy evening in Croatia as Rijeka were defeated on their own patch. In between times the 1983 double European success of winning the Cup Winners' Cup and the European Super Cup are of course included. European football is what defines Aberdeen

Football Club. It is the success of 40 years ago that endures and is an achievement that 'sticks in the craw' of opponents and those who choose to dismiss what Aberdeen have achieved.

The four occasions Aberdeen have won the league are all included: 1955, 1980, 1984 and 1985.

The Dons' 1985 league win remains the last occasion that a side outside of Glasgow has won the title, such has been the impact of richer resources and finance making it more difficult to break that sequence.

To win major honours in Scotland, any side invariably must defeat the two Glasgow clubs. It was Alex Ferguson who brought that siege mentality to Aberdeen. No matter how good, how talented, how determined any Aberdeen team was, they had to have that resolve going into these big games that the whole world was against them. With that in mind my selections do include several unforgettable clashes against both Celtic and Rangers. Most are in domestic cup ties and finals. Long before winning any league championship took priority over the domestic cups, it was the glamour of the cup that caught the imagination and had the crowds turning up in their droves. Some of Aberdeen's most memorable successes have come in the domestic cups. From their first appearance in the Scottish Cup Final of 1937 through to their last success in the League Cup in 2014, the first eight games in this book are all cup matches.

Also included are some firsts and significant matches: the first Scottish Cup Final, record win, first European tie, record Pittodrie attendance, first league championship, first Scottish and League Cup wins and the Dons' first European Cup tie.

If I had to select one friendly that was worthy of inclusion it would be the wonderful dismantling of Manchester United at Pittodrie in a 5-2 win in 1972. However, the manic events during that balmy summer of 1967 when Aberdeen clashed with Wolves in the aptly named LA Coliseum in the USA just had to be included.

Many great Aberdeen matches did not quite make it, so it's worth mentioning that several of those are referenced in subsequent games. The 5-1 defeat of Rangers in the 1976 League Cup semi-final would usually make the shortlist but as Aberdeen went on to win the trophy, the final was included. That was repeated in 1995 when Aberdeen again beat Rangers before going on to lift the prize. The famous Eoin Jess 'keepy-up' routine from one of our own earned Jess legendary status at Pittodrie.

There have been many famous European nights at Pittodrie. Lots of them were worthy of inclusion but the line had to be drawn. I always remember John McRuvie of Northsound Radio many years ago saying that you could 'smell' those nights at Pittodrie. He got it, just like so many others who have been fortunate enough to see the old place on such occasions. Pittodrie, at some point in the future, will be consigned to the past as discussions on a new stadium have been going on for several years. For me, Pittodrie will always be the beating heart of Aberdeen Football Club.

Kevin Stirling
February 2023

# Aberdeen 0 Celtic 1

21 March 1908
Scottish Cup semi-final
Pittodrie Park, Aberdeen
Attendance: 20,000

| Aberdeen | Celtic |
|---|---|
| Rab Macfarlane | Davie Adams |
| Donald Colman | Alex McNair |
| Jock Hume | Jim Weir |
| Alex Halkett | Jim Young |
| Jim McIntosh | Willie Loney |
| William Low | Jimmy Hay |
| John McDonald | Alec Bennett |
| Jim Muir | Jimmy McMenemy |
| Tom Murray | Jimmy Quinn |
| Charlie O'Hagan | Peter Somers |
| Willie Lennie | Davie Hamilton |
| *Manager:* Jimmy Philip | *Manager:* Willie Maley |

'WE KNEW the significance of the game. It was the biggest occasion the club had been involved in since it came into being just five years ago.' The words of Aberdeen legend Donald Colman, the former player, trainer and Scotland international who invented the first dugout in British football.

Colman was looking back on his career in the *Aberdeen Daily Journal* before his benefit game in 1912 as he recalled the Dons' first Scottish Cup semi-final, 'Looking back it was a great occasion and although it ended in disappointment we gave it everything and were unlucky not to take it to a replay. Manager Jimmy Philip was keen to see the club develop and progress and reaching the last four of the Scottish Cup was a landmark for Aberdeen FC. From a personal point of view, I was proud to have played my part in that side. It was a great pity we didn't reach the final as we deserved to.'

After being formed in 1903 following the amalgamation of the three major clubs in the city, Aberdeen, Orion and Victoria United, the current Aberdeen Football Club entered the top division in Scottish football in 1905, a position they have never relinquished. The progression was as much expected as it was surprising. The authorities insisted that any application to join the Scottish leagues would only be looked upon favourably if the three major clubs in the city joined forces. Following a difficult and prolonged period of negotiating, the new club eventually came into being on 14 April 1903. Those efforts were rewarded with progression in the Scottish Cup in 1908. Gone were the days of heavy defeats in the qualifying rounds when several smaller Aberdeen-based sides were outclassed against more experienced and streetwise opponents. The progress in 1908 perhaps vindicated that the combined strength of the established clubs meant that Aberdeen and the north-east was well represented on the national stage.

Aberdeen progressed to the last four after wins over Albion Rovers, Dundee and Queen's Park. The quarter-final victory over Tayside rivals Dundee was significant. It took three games for the 'stripes' (early reference to the black and gold strip) to prevail in a second replay that was played at Hampden Park. The venue of course was the national stadium in Glasgow and attracted interest in the west with two east-coast teams playing. Willie Lennie had been a doubt and the train journey south, as the Dons' party were housed within their own carriage, would not be beneficial for the Aberdeen winger. Lennie played and scored a sensational goal in 75 minutes as Aberdeen went on to win 3-1. Looking back this result proved significant in terms of Aberdeen showing up well on a national stage. There was also the fact that one of the most vociferous backers of Aberdeen's bid to gain admission to the Scottish leagues was the Dens Park club. Dundee had sent letters to the authorities claiming that professional football should be taken to the Aberdeen area and that the resources and supporter base would make Aberdeen a great asset to the mainstream of Scottish football.

Semi-finals were not played at a neutral venue until 1912. Celtic arrived at Pittodrie as cup holders and had gained a reputation for being a tough, uncompromising side that had an impressive record in the Scottish Cup, against opponents who were in uncharted territory.

On the eve of the game both sets of players and officials were treated to a performance at the Palace Theatre in Aberdeen. Celtic were staying at the old Murtle Hydro.

The club directors anticipated a record crowd, such was the interest in the tie. In advance of the game parts of the ground were built up to accommodate the large crowd that was expected. Pittodrie regulars were confident their side could overcome the Glasgow outfit and reach their first Scottish Cup Final. Football was the game of the working man, but it was reported in the *Aberdeen Daily Journal* that the Celtic tie attracted 'hundreds of occasional patrons, most who had never seen a first-class game. Elderly gentlemen, clergy, lawyers, doctors, merchants and so on; ladies old and young, many of them fashionably attired and wafting choice perfumes around.'

It was reported that special trains from all over Scotland brought spectators to the Granite City. Two from Glasgow conveyed a large travelling support for Celtic while others also arrived from Montrose, Dundee and Edinburgh, such was the interest in the game. The gates of Pittodrie were opened at 2pm, almost two hours before kick-off. The Pittodrie enclosure and stand was full of around 12,000 within that area and by 3.30pm the rest of the ground was packed as more than 20,000 filled every vantage point.

The First Aberdeenshire Royal Engineers pipe band entertained the huge crowd ahead of referee Ferguson from Falkirk coming on to the field to inspect the playing surface. Shortly after it was the black and gold of Aberdeen that took to the field as they left the Pittodrie pavilion to rousing cheers from the home support. Several minutes later Celtic, in their green and white strips, entered the fray to more muted calls from their own support.

Aberdeen won the toss and played towards the sea in the first half. Conditions were near perfect, and it was noted that several of the Celtic players were of a 'burly' nature. Celtic were first to attack in the opening minutes, but Jimmy Quinn's effort was blocked by Colman. Aberdeen responded when Jock Hume set up winger Willie Lennie, but he could not get the better of Young. There was little to choose between the teams in what were tense opening exchanges although Lennie looked the more likely for Aberdeen as did Quinn for the visitors. Indeed, it soon became clear that Quinn, the Celtic centre-forward, was their most dangerous threat and after the Aberdeen keeper saved from a 20-yard effort the defenders looked to close the dangerman down at every opportunity. On one occasion Wilf Low went in hard on Quinn, who jumped clear of the challenge. Before half-time Quinn was again in the wars as he was challenged heavily by Aberdeen keeper Macfarlane, the Celtic player falling to the ground clutching his head. Donald Colman was showing all his experience as he rallied the home defence, bringing an assured calm to proceedings. Aberdeen were attacking on occasion with their threat coming down the left where the Charlie O'Hagan and Lennie combination almost brought the opening goal. O'Hagan and Lennie were the first capped players for Aberdeen. O'Hagan was a regular in the Ireland side while Lennie became the first Aberdeen player to play for Scotland in 1908.

The home side were lucky not to concede when a rare slip by Macfarlane saw the ball fall to Somers, whose effort went over the bar. It was a reprieve for Aberdeen at that point as on reflection it was the visitors who were creating the better opportunities. Alex Halkett then set up Murray but his effort from 15 yards was saved by Adams. Some of the Celtic tactics were not to the supporters' liking, such was their robust approach to the game. The referee was hardly doing the Dons any favours: on one occasion when O'Hagan remonstrated after being fouled no fewer than six times in five minutes the official threatened to send the Irish international off!

The first half was a nervous affair as both sides looked to gain what would almost certainly be a crucial advantage. Aberdeen gave little away at home and Celtic proved to be an excellent side on the road. The stage was set for an intriguing second half. Aberdeen centre-half Wilf Low had been the outstanding player in that first period. Latterly known as the 'Laughing Cavalier', Low was Aberdeen-born and as hard as the city's granite. He would later join Newcastle and played for Scotland on five occasions. Low remained on the payroll at Newcastle as he took over the position of head groundsman after retiring from playing.

Aberdeen opened the second half on the offensive when O'Hagan took advantage of a mistake by McNair, but his effort went wide. Halkett then tried his luck from long range when he should have set up Lennie, who was clear in on the Celtic goal. The game was turning more physical with hard 'charges' from both sides resulting in some heavy challenges. Celtic gradually fell back and became more defensive as Aberdeen kept up the pressure. For a 15-minute period in the second half Aberdeen dominated the tie and passed up several chances that would have surely taken the Black and Golds through to their first cup final. Lennie, Murray and McDonald all came close to scoring as Celtic defended in depth. Then Low went upfield and came close with a fierce drive from outside the penalty area. At this point reference was made to the crowd producing 'an almost continuous roar of encouragement' as Aberdeen threw everything at Celtic.

Seven minutes from time a rare Celtic attack resulted in a corner. It was McMenemy who went upfield and his header from that cross deceived Aberdeen keeper Macfarlane to give Celtic an undeserved lead. Aberdeen responded with a late rally and continued pressing up until the final minute but they just came up short. The last chance came from a McDonald corner that caused mayhem in the Celtic defence but as the ball ended up on top of the net the final whistle sounded moments later.

The consensus afterwards was that Aberdeen were desperately unlucky not to at least take the tie to a replay and that referee Ferguson found few friends in the city after some poor decisions.

The total gate money amounted to £586 (19,294 paying at the turnstiles). The total receipts from the grandstand was £129. That included season ticket holders and ladies, who were admitted free and estimated to amount to about 1,500 in number. Such was the interest in attending matches at Pittodrie that the club decided that ladies would no longer be admitted free of charge as of the following season.

The Celtic party departed Aberdeen station at 7pm from the East Dock platform. However, their exit from Pittodrie was anything but cordial. It was reported that the Celtic players, officials and referee were pelted with stones as they left the field. As local officials took steps to prevent this, it proved futile. The local press was sympathetic to the club, but Aberdeen were braced for further action from the authorities.

Manager Jimmy Philip was never slow in confronting the authorities. On one occasion Philip proposed the very first foreign tour by a Scottish international team, informing the authorities that he would foot the bill if there was a loss. Philip did, however, take Aberdeen to Bohemia, Moravia and Poland in the summer of 1911, the club's first overseas tour. He had been a driving force behind the club's efforts to gain admission to the Scottish leagues and was often lobbying other member clubs to get their support. This was essential as the fate of any club hoping to gain admission to league football was down to members. Philip was Aberdeen-born and appointed in a part-time role in 1903. A wood turner by trade, he was also a first-class referee and was invited to officiate at the Olympic Games of 1912 in Stockholm.

The defeat to Celtic was the start of a difficult period for Aberdeen against the Glasgow club in the Scottish Cup. A further defeat, this time at Celtic Park in 1911 at the same semi-final stage, was only avenged by a first Scottish Cup success over Celtic in 1935.

In the meantime Aberdeen's progress to the latter stages was an indication they were progressing in the right way. A sustained challenge for the league championship followed three years later and with three of their players now established internationals, the foundations were set for establishing the club as a major force in Scottish football.

However, events on 28 June 1914 in Sarajevo would bring conflict in Europe that was to bring an end to football for several years.

# Aberdeen 13 Peterhead 0

10 February 1923
Scottish Cup third round
Pittodrie Park, Aberdeen
Attendance: 3,241

| Aberdeen | Peterhead |
|---|---|
| Harry Blackwell | Drysdale |
| Jock Hutton | J.K. Allan |
| Matt Forsyth | Jock Hume |
| Bert MacLachlan | F. Thomson |
| Vic Milne | J. Buchan |
| Arthur Robertson | G. Slessor |
| Billy Middleton | W. Hutcheson |
| Doug Thomson | G. Allan |
| Walter Grant | A. McRobbie |
| Andy Rankine | Sandy Hall |
| Jimmy Smith | W. Milne |
| *Manager:* Jimmy Philip | *Manager:* Sandy Hall |

ABERDEEN HAD emerged from the troubles of the Great War in a perilous state. Their finances had been decimated by years of warfare that had a profound effect on the country. When Aberdeen played their final game of the season on 28 April 1917, competitive football did not return until August 1919.

In an era when cup-tie venues could be switched for various reasons, more so for financial gain and crowd safety, it was in 1923 that Pittodrie witnessed one of the most incredible games ever played in the city. When the draw for the third round was made the Dons were due to travel to Recreation Park in Peterhead. It was the Aberdeen directors who approached the Blue Toon club to see if they would agree to taking the tie to Pittodrie. It was a local derby in the true sense; Peterhead was only 30 miles up the north-east coast from Aberdeen. As the only major club in the city, Aberdeen through their history have never had to face a local derby as such. That was very different before the amalgamation of the original Aberdeen, Orion and Victoria United in 1903. In the obscure days of the local Northern League, derby clashes were frequent and the Chanonry, Cattofield and Recreation Park were the scene of some fiery encounters at the end of the 19th century.

Negotiations took place on the assumption that the Highland League side would simply be there to make up the numbers and make a tidy sum in the process. It must be said that any acceptance that Peterhead had no chance of beating Aberdeen all emanated from the Highland club's own directors. On reflection it was perhaps that line of thought that grated with the Peterhead players, who believed they had a chance of making a real game of it. The directors from both clubs then arranged a meeting and it was agreed that Peterhead would give up ground rights in exchange for a £250 cash guarantee. Also included was travelling expenses for the players and directors and that Aberdeen would agree to a friendly at Peterhead before the end of the season. The deal seemed to have been agreed but when news of the switch reached the Peterhead players, they were livid to a man. They immediately demanded to be paid £10 each for taking part. Their club stood fast and agreed to pay the players but only if they won the tie. No fewer than eight Peterhead players refused to play, which left the Highland League club in turmoil ahead of what was without doubt their biggest game so far.

Panic ensued and the Blue Toon did manage to secure former Aberdeen full-back Jock Hume from Arbroath on the eve of the game. However, the rest of the side was scraped together. Among the players secured were C.P. Murray and J.T. Wiseman, secretary and captain of the local Aberdeen University team. Both were listed on the team line-ups under false names. As it was a Scottish Cup game such behaviour was frowned upon back then as it is today. Both had also been cup-tied, having already played for the university in the competition – against Peterhead! Even under the unlikely event that the makeshift Peterhead side were to win, the Aberdeen captain Bert MacLachlan was ready to put in a protest.

Aberdeen had been going well in the First Division and were serious contenders to go far in the Scottish Cup. Progress was made after defeating Forfar Athletic and Airdrie and by the time the clash with Peterhead finally came around there was more farce to come. On the eve of the tie torrential rain hit the north-east and subsequent blizzard conditions on game day compounded matters. The *Aberdeen Daily Journal*'s description of an 'easterly hurricane' may have been extreme but the Pittodrie pitch was flooded in parts, although in those days very much 'playable'. For context it was reported that the spectators who did bother to turn up 'laughed heartily when Peterhead players found themselves diving after the ball into pools of water'.

It was no surprise that the game was as one-sided as can be imagined. Aberdeen won the toss and elected to play with the strong gale behind them. Peterhead had the experience of Jock Hume in their side but despite some heroic efforts he could not stem the flow as Aberdeen set about reaching a club record tally. After Walter Grant opened the scoring following some incessant pressure the Dons went three goals ahead with a brace from Doug Thomson. Before half-time a Milne penalty and an Andy Rankine header made it 5-0. Any thoughts that Aberdeen may ease up in the second half as they faced the elements were dispelled when Vic Milne scored a sixth for the home side. Milne was a huge favourite at Pittodrie and an interesting character. He was the son of Aberdeen's first chairman and a registered doctor during his time at Pittodrie. Born in Aberdeen in 1897, he went on to sign for Aston Villa in 1923 and played as an amateur. He went on to become Villa's club doctor between 1930 and 1933 after he retired from playing.

Aberdeen continued to dominate the tie and when Grant 'walked through' the Peterhead defence to add a seventh goal, Milne completed an unlikely hat-trick soon after. Further goals came as Grant took his personal tally to four before Doug Thomson completed his hat-trick. Before the end Middleton and Smith brought up an unlucky 13 for an outclassed Peterhead side. Grant was never a prolific scorer for the club, making 100 appearances in a ten-year spell that was interrupted by the Great War. Grant served in the forces and upon his release from the army he signed for Aberdeen on a permanent deal on 16 June 1920.

Thomson's career at Pittodrie came to an end a few weeks later after he was convicted of theft. After scoring against Third Lanark the inside-forward went out on the town to celebrate. Some heavy drinking in the Bon Accord Hotel along with some football friends led to Thomson returning to the hotel where he was later caught by police with bottles of alcohol and food. Thomson appeared in police court in March 1923 and pleaded guilty to theft. He was fined 30 shillings, and never played for Aberdeen again.

Goalkeeper Harry Blackwell was a virtual bystander in horrendous weather conditions. It was in this game that the famed 'Blackwell's Brolly' was seen. The Aberdeen custodian had borrowed a raincoat from a spectator, and it was only taken off once when he was called into action during the game. The umbrella offered additional protection from the elements as he watched his team-mates cruise to victory.

Sheffield-born Blackwell was a real character at Pittodrie, joining from Scunthorpe in 1921. He went on to make 252 first-team appearances between 1921 and 1930. He also received a benefit from the club in 1926, and later played for Orient and Preston after leaving Pittodrie.

The blizzard conditions were indeed as bad as it got. Two Peterhead players, Buchan and McRobbie, left the field before full time suffering from the effects of the cold. Across at Advocates Park not far from Pittodrie towards the town centre, Aberdeen Junior club Richmond were playing host to Port Glasgow in the Scottish Junior Cup. Midway through the second half the visitors conceded the tie to prevent their players any further suffering due to the weather.

On reflection the decision to switch the game from Peterhead to Aberdeen was an error of judgement from the Highland League side. Due to the weather the crowd was kept down to 3,241 hardy souls but they did witness a piece of club history. The drawings were £181 which meant Aberdeen certainly lost out financially, but it seemed the 'magic' of the cup was clearly missing from what were farcical circumstances.

In an era where football finances were not as crucial as in the modern day, there was still stern criticism of Peterhead following their Pittodrie mauling. There was a general belief among their regular first-team players that if the tie had been played at their Recreation Park ground then they would have had a real opportunity to knock Aberdeen out of the competition. Their directors took that chance away from them in pursuit of cashing in. Peterhead keeper Buchan also stated that he took the attitude he would not go to Aberdeen even if he was given the entire £250 the club secured for the switch. Such sportsmanship was to be admired but the general feeling was that money came before sporting integrity and the hostility towards the Peterhead directors following the game was substantial. Even the local businessfolk were livid. The shopkeepers, hotel and bar owners and others were not shy in voicing their indignation at the club, especially when the country at that time was in a deep recession. There were also fears that Aberdeen would report the ineligible players to the Scottish Football Association and that sanctions would follow for Peterhead. As it turned out the matter was never raised.

Another story emerged from this game concerning Peterhead player-manager Sandy Hall. Born in Peterhead, he decided against a life at sea and opted for cutting granite in Aberdeen. It was in 1901 that he travelled to Canada in search of a new adventure. His stone-cutting work took him to Galt just outside of Toronto where he joined the successful local football team. It was in 1904 that Hall played his part in an incredible achievement; winning an Olympic gold medal in St Louis representing Canada. Hall became Scotland's first homegrown Olympic champion. After returning to Scotland, Hall had a trial with Aberdeen but he eventually signed for St Bernard's. After spells with Newcastle, Dundee, Motherwell and Dunfermline, it was at Peterhead that he finished a remarkable career. It is also known that not long after the Aberdeen game he emigrated to Toronto with his family. It is not known if the Aberdeen result was a factor in that decision, but he faded into history and even up until his passing in 1943 he was never that well known in Scotland.

Aberdeen for their part moved on to the fourth round but were beaten 2-0 by Hibernian at Easter Road to end their Scottish Cup interest for that season.

# Aberdeen 3 Celtic 1

9 March 1935
Scottish Cup quarter-final
Pittodrie Park, Aberdeen
Attendance: 40,105

| Aberdeen | Celtic |
|---|---|
| Steve Smith | Joe Kennaway |
| Willie Cooper | Bobby Hogg |
| Charlie McGill | John Morrison |
| Bob Fraser | Chic Geatons |
| Eddie Falloon | Malky McDonald |
| George Thomson | George Paterson |
| Jackie Beynon | Jimmy Delaney |
| Paddy Moore | Willie Buchan |
| Matt Armstrong | Jackie McGrory |
| Willie Mills | Charlie Napier |
| Ritchie Smith | Hugh O'Donnell |
| *Manager:* Pat Travers | *Manager:* Willie Maley |

'WE ARE hopeful, but I really can't say what the team will be yet.' This short statement came from Celtic manager Willie Maley as the Glasgow club settled into their overnight stay in the Caledonian Hotel in the centre of Aberdeen ahead of their clash with the Dons, as reported in the *Evening Express*.

Welcomed by a small crowd on their arrival, it was no surprise that Maley was confident. In all previous six Scottish Cup meetings, Aberdeen had yet to succeed. En route to the quarter-final Aberdeen had seen off Falkirk, Albion Rovers and old rivals Hibernian. There were memorable scenes at Brockville following the thrilling success over Falkirk as Willie Mills was carried off shoulder-high by the Aberdeen supporters at full time. The win in Falkirk was the Dons' 100th Scottish Cup tie. One hundred ties in 25 years of competing in the Scottish Cup represented a consistency that had rightfully earned Aberdeen the reputation of being a 'cup tie team'. Despite that tag, Aberdeen had still to reach a final.

Against Hibernian it took a second replay to see off the Easter Road side, and their reward was a home tie and the opportunity to lay their Celtic bogey. Recent form suggested that Aberdeen would be at last ready to make their breakthrough against the Parkhead side.

The Black and Golds had been playing with a style and panache that on their day could take on any side. The Dons may not have had the consistency to win a league championship but in any cup tie, they were formidable opposition. Aberdeen captain Bob Fraser was clear in his mind, 'We are going to win. The team has shown great resolve this season and it is about time we had a win over them [Celtic]. The fight we showed at Easter Road will serve us well for what should be a magnificent occasion.' Fraser was a tough competitor; signed from Albion Rovers in 1931, he was made Aberdeen captain in 1934. He got his break after several Aberdeen players were banned from the first team following the 'Great Mystery' betting scandal that saw five players never appear for the club again. He emigrated to South Africa in 1938 a year after he was part of the Aberdeen party that toured the subcontinent a year earlier.

Interest in the tie was high and the anticipated record attendance did materialise as the Pittodrie gates were closed ahead of kick-off with more than 40,000 spectators crammed into the enclosures. The crowds came early as trains arrived from as far off as Dundee and an estimated 5,000 coming from the outlying areas in the north-east. There were even arrivals by sea. Three young Glasgow men walked to Leith, where they volunteered to help an Aberdeen trawler in return for safe passage to the Granite City. The most popular method of transport in the city was by tram. All morning trams operated throughout the city taking supporters to Pittodrie. The city corporation added additional runs from the city centre to Pittodrie as the huge crowd began to gather.

Aberdeen had previously defeated Celtic 2-0 at Pittodrie in the league and there was further encouragement with the Glasgow side having failed to score at Pittodrie in three seasons.

The home team began well and immediately put Celtic under pressure. The huge crowd were certainly playing their part and after eight minutes Aberdeen took the lead. Matt Armstrong latched on to a Beynon head flick and was brought down inside the penalty area. Referee Martin gave the penalty and Armstrong went on to score from the spot even though Kennaway did get a hand to the ball. Twelve minutes later Aberdeen scored again after a spell of constant pressure. Napier of Celtic was having a torrid time of it and his foul on Moore allowed captain Fraser to set up Willie Mills to head a second goal for the Black and Golds. Tempers frayed as Celtic were losing their composure in what was proving to be a hostile atmosphere. It seemed like years of disappointment against the Glasgow club was being wiped away by this Aberdeen team full of pace and power and playing without fear. In 22 minutes, the tie was effectively over as Aberdeen were awarded a second penalty. It was Mills this time who was brought down, and his front partner Armstrong was again entrusted with the spot kick. On this occasion Kennaway managed to save Armstrong's effort but the centre-forward followed up on the rebound to score and put Aberdeen out of reach.

Celtic reduced the deficit just before the break when McGrory scored after a clever pass from Napier. Half-time came too soon for Aberdeen, who had simply swept Celtic aside. For some observers though it was the Aberdeen defence that was at their best. Eddie Falloon, the Irish centre-half, may have been small in stature, but it was his tenacious marking of Celtic legend Jackie McGrory that provided a platform for Aberdeen to dominate the game. Goalkeeper Steve Smith gave a safe and assured display and he was well protected by Cooper and McGill. Aberdeen have been well served over the years with player combinations that were so popular at Pittodrie, from Lennie and O'Hagan before the Great War to the defensive trio of Smith, Cooper and McGill and the Mills and Armstrong front pairing from that black and gold era of the 1930s.

During the half-time interval, a man in the crowd took a carrier pigeon from a basket and released it with a message of the progress of the game with a destination of 'Somewhere in Buchan'. A second pigeon was later seen off carrying news of the result.

Aberdeen continued to control the game in a second half that lacked more goals but had enough incidents to keep the huge crowd enthralled. Celtic's Napier was involved in a clash with Bob Fraser that almost resulted in blows before both ended up shaking hands after the referee stepped in to prevent an escalation of tensions. It was clear that the atmosphere and the inspired display from Aberdeen were getting to the visitors and as the game ended it was the hosts

ABERDEEN 3 CELTIC 1

who looked the more likely to add to their tally. Aberdeen were best served by Armstrong and Mills, the front pairing that matured into one of the most prolific in British football. Their almost telepathic understanding made it an uncomfortable afternoon for the Celtic defence. Kennaway was their best player with several outstanding saves, and he had no chance with any of the goals. As the Aberdeen players left the field at full time the noise from the crowd was deafening in appreciation of their efforts. The Celtic bogey in the Scottish Cup had been crushed.

Matt Armstrong was a native of Newton Stewart, and provisionally signed for Celtic in 1930 when he was attracting attention as a free-scoring forward with Port Glasgow Juniors. However, the Parkhead club failed to take up their option and Aberdeen manager Pat Travers stepped in to take him to Pittodrie. Travers himself was a former Celtic player for one season in 1911 in between his two playing spells with Aberdeen.

As an understudy to the legendary Benny Yorston and latterly Paddy Moore, Armstrong had to bide his time before establishing himself in the first team. In fact, that process was accelerated by the unfortunate events of November 1931 when several Aberdeen players were involved in the 'Great Mystery' scandal, which hastened Yorston's departure in 1932. When Moore left to return to his native Ireland, Aberdeen turned to Armstrong to take over as the main striker. In the opening game of the 1933/34 season Armstrong scored five goals in an 8-0 rout of Ayr United and a year later he was the top scorer with 39 goals from only 43 competitive games.

The outbreak of war in 1939 put a hold on his remarkable career and during the subsequent years Armstrong guested for Chelsea and West Bromwich Albion among others before returning to Pittodrie for one season in 1946 after being demobbed. A short spell in Dumfries with Queen of the South preceded a return to the north where he took up a post as player-manager with Elgin City for the final three years of his playing career. In 1952 he set a Highland League scoring record at the age of 42.

Armstrong returned to the area after his playing days and took up employment with SMT garage in Aberdeen. Latterly he returned to Pittodrie to run the successful club pools in the 1970s. He passed away after a lengthy illness on 4 October 1995 at the age of 83.

The large crowd that filled Pittodrie was proving difficult to manage by the police and stewards. Before the game finished a barrier collapsed which resulted in several supporters being thrown to the ground. Several people were crushed and trampled on. Fortunately nobody was seriously hurt but two men were taken to Aberdeen Infirmary. It was also reported that several hundred late arrivals were jostling for a view of the game but turned back as their efforts were futile. Others remained and relied on 'running commentary' from those with a better view.

As the crowd dispersed after the game there was minimal disruption, although it was reported that there were traffic jams in the Castlegate area. A group of Celtic supporters were not so fortunate as it emerged later that night a furniture van returning to Glasgow from the game in Aberdeen overturned on the notorious new road at Dunblane, crashing through a wooden barrier and slipping down an embankment. About 30 occupants were thrown about in a scene of total confusion and concern. Three people were taken to Stirling Hospital with minor injuries.

Aberdeen were to join Hamilton, Rangers and Hearts in the last four. After being drawn against the Accies in the semi-final and following their win over Celtic, hopes were high that Aberdeen could reach their first Scottish Cup Final. Alas it was to end in another bitter disappointment as the tag of 'bridesmaids' for the Dons began to stick. After defeating cup favourites Celtic, the expectation levels were raised, understandably, only for another semi-final loss to dampen spirits. Unlike in the modern game where winning is everything, reaching a cup final back then was viewed as a 'success'. The Scottish Cup Final was the biggest game on the country's football calendar and taking part brought accolades that are certainly not apparent in the modern era.

# Aberdeen 1 Celtic 2

24 April 1937
Scottish Cup Final
Hampden Park, Glasgow
Attendance: 146,433

**Aberdeen**
George Johnstone
Willie Cooper
Bob Temple
Frank Dunlop
Eddie Falloon
George Thomson
Jackie Beynon
Johnny McKenzie
Matt Armstrong
Willie Mills
Johnny Lang
*Manager:* Pat Travers

**Celtic**
Joe Kennaway
Bobby Hogg
John Morrison
Chic Geatons
Willie Lyon
George Paterson
Jimmy Delaney
Willie Buchan
Jackie McGrory
John Crum
Frank Murphy
*Manager:* Willie Maley

THE UNCERTAINTY in football was perhaps never more apparent than at Pittodrie during the 1930s. Ever since a new Aberdeen side emerged from the 'Great Mystery' betting scandal of 1931, under Pat Travers they evolved into one of the best footballing teams in Britain. The fact that they never achieved tangible success makes it one of the most disappointing and frustrating spells in club history. The nearest they came was in the 1937 Scottish Cup Final, when the Black and Golds went down to Celtic. Aberdeen at that time were littered with talent, and many observers believed they were the complete footballing team. The 'Aberdeen Way' may have been for the purist and that side was delightful on the eye. If there was a criticism it was that they were guilty of playing too much football, whereas a more direct approach may have paid a higher dividend.

Aberdeen reached their first final after failing at the semi-final stage on no fewer than six occasions, and their route to Hampden was far from glamorous. After receiving a bye to the third round, the Dons accounted for Inverness Thistle, Third Lanark and Hamilton, before disposing of a stubborn Morton in the semi-final. Inverness Thistle were looking forward to a big 'gate' for their tie at Pittodrie at the end of January. Aberdeen showed no mercy to their Highland visitors and routed them 6-0. The Pittodrie pitch was covered in snow, and the freezing temperatures kept the attendance down to complete a miserable day for the Highlanders.

The semi-final was to be played at Easter Road in Edinburgh and although Aberdeen were favourites to progress past Morton, the local press perhaps increased the pressure on the Dons to finally end their cup final bogey. In the build-up to the match it was clear that Aberdeen expected to prevail, and that Morton would surely not have enough class against a team that had been playing with great confidence. Eventually the Black and Golds' quality shone through the Edinburgh mist, and goals from Armstrong and Strauss in the first half were enough to see Aberdeen through to their first final.

Having finally broken their disappointing sequence of defeats in Scottish Cup semi-finals, the fact that Aberdeen had reached their first Hampden final brought massive interest in the area. The only real concern was the fitness of winger Billy Strauss, who had scored the goals that had taken Aberdeen to Hampden and his influence in the side was a huge one. Concerns were raised after Strauss was injured in the win over Morton and the fact that he had not trained all week in the build-up to the final suggested that he would not make it. With Johnny Lang on standby, it would be a cruel blow for Strauss and Aberdeen if their talisman was not fit for the final. Nevertheless, Aberdeen were feeling positive going into the game against Celtic. It was in forward areas that they had a ring of confidence with a better all-round attack that had goals across the front line.

Strauss was with Aberdeen for over a decade between 1935 and 1946 but his 87 appearances (and 45 goals) were limited due to the war. His omission from the cup final team was a hammer blow for the Dons. Strauss later played for Plymouth, and Aberdeen played Argyle in his benefit match in 1951. The South African was also a decent cricketer and scored a century at The Oval playing in the Minor Counties Championship for Devon in 1950.

There were unprecedented scenes in Aberdeen as the city was gripped by cup fever; an estimated 30,000 departed with high expectations. With all modes of transport leaving the north-east, some intrepid fans began to hitch-hike to Glasgow a day before the final. It was an early start for the bulk of the biggest supporter exodus ever seen in Aberdeen when the first of 17 special trains rolled out of the Aberdeen Joint station at 4.25am on the day of the final. Many supporters had travelled down to Aberdeen on the Friday to catch the trains leaving the city the next morning.

The team went by train on the Friday evening in preparation for the final. On the moment of their departure a black cat was presented to Eddie Falloon as a gesture of good luck and as more than 1,000 gathered at the station to see the team off, buses and coaches from all over the north were winding their way down to Aberdeen to be part of the massive following. The station had proved to be a busy place all day as hundreds gathered and remained all day to see off the supporters lucky enough to be on their way to Hampden. It had become a focal point for Aberdeen as the team always travelled by train and on their arrival back in Aberdeen there was always a fantastic support present to greet them after any famous victory. While most of the fans made it by train, Aberdeen supporters overwhelmed the Buchanan Street area as they arrived in Glasgow and the whole station area was turned into a mass of black and gold favours.

Glasgow was preparing for the coronation of King George VI and Queen Elizabeth some three weeks later, but that was of little consequence to the Aberdeen support as they anticipated more than most that Hampden would be filled to the rafters for the game. Meanwhile, the Aberdeen party had enjoyed a restful night at the St Enoch's Hotel in the city centre. Two Rangers players, Bob McPhail and Alan Morton, visited the group the night before the game and wished the players the best of luck against their great rivals. Back then the cup final was the pinnacle of the Scottish season and deemed more prestigious than winning any league flag.

On the day of the final there was a great movement of Aberdeen supporters from the city centre to get to Hampden. Every four minutes a train was arriving in Mount Florida packed with northerners, eager to get their first sight of Hampden Park. More than 44 buses every hour left for Hampden. Trawler owners even instructed their skippers not to land catches on the Saturday, so keen was everyone to get to the game. It is staggering to recall but the final itself was not all-ticket. The previous week, Hampden hosted the Scotland v England international before an incredible 149,000 spectators. The SFA noted that no serious incidents were recorded on that day and that it was beyond them to arrange for two all-ticket matches in a week. One Aberdeen supporter speaking to the *Press & Journal* at the time recalled the bedlam outside of Hampden before kick-off, 'There was about 20,000 or so around the streets of Hampden and countless others who turned back at the train and bus stations when they would have realised the futility of trying to get to the game. In Somerville Drive the spectacle was terrifying as the street was packed with people and they were getting nowhere. Just then we could see the gates close and there were howls of rage.' Another 20,000 were locked outside and around 30,000 inside could not see any of the action.

Missing from the side was the influential Billy Strauss, who had not recovered from the injury sustained in the win over Morton. An intriguing battle was in prospect; Aberdeen were noted for their skilled approach, while Celtic were renowned for strength and pace. If the Scottish Cup were to come north for the first time then it was a popular belief that Aberdeen would have to 'peak' as it would take a real team effort to see off the Celts. Alas, Mills and Thomson were a massive let-down. Willie Mills in particular, was the jewel in the Pittodrie crown, and it was his partnership with Matt Armstrong that was the main reason Aberdeen got to Hampden.

Despite losing an early goal when Crum scored after a fine save from Johnstone, Aberdeen came storming back when Welshman Jackie Beynon crossed to Mills, whose snap shot was saved, only for Armstrong to level the tie. The second half began with Celtic pressing, but Aberdeen were up to the challenge and hit back to dominate for long spells. Kennaway denied Beynon before Mills hit the bar. In a very even game, play was uninspiring for long spells, and it looked like both sides would have to come back for a second game. However, despite Lang missing two good chances for Aberdeen, there was controversy as Celtic took the lead. McGrory bustled past Temple and used an arm to control the ball, and as the Aberdeen defence hesitated and waited for the whistle, Buchan scored off the post to 'hand' the cup to Celtic.

Despite a rousing finale from Aberdeen as they swamped the Celtic goal, it was not to be, and time ran out for the gallant players. Although the black and gold camp was bitterly disappointed initially at their own display, and latterly at the manner of how the winning goal was allowed, further blows were to follow.

Tragedy struck the club when Aberdeen director William Hay died suddenly the day after the final at the age of 50. Mr Hay had been a Don for ten years, seven of which were on the SFA Council.

While the Glasgow press in the aftermath of the game had talked about a 'great final' and one of the best ever seen at Hampden, the Aberdeen view was somewhat different in that it was one of the poorest displays by the Dons all season. While the plaudits from the west were perhaps influenced by the fact that the cup had stayed in Glasgow, the reality was that Aberdeen on the day fell far short of what was expected. Although Eddie Falloon was a colossus in defence, it was in the forward areas that Aberdeen were badly let down. Willie Mills, often described as the complete footballer by many, just failed to show any of his undoubted talent on the day. Billy Strauss was sorely missed, and his replacement Johnny Lang missed several great opportunities. Jackie Beynon looked the most dangerous forward and he was unlucky on several occasions. On reflection the Aberdeen side of 1937 was perhaps a formidable one built on a strong teamwork ethic, but on the day they simply did not rise to the occasion and the club's first major final was to end in bitter disappointment.

Weeks after the final, Aberdeen embarked on a tour to South Africa and six games in tragedy struck once more. Jackie Beynon and Billy Strauss were hospitalised with flu and appendicitis respectively. Beynon then developed peritonitis, and on 26 June 1937, he died in a Johannesburg hospital. He was buried in an emotional ceremony in South African. One can only imagine the feelings of the touring party, as the trip had to proceed. Beynon joined Aberdeen from Doncaster Rovers in 1932 and soon became a firm favourite at Pittodrie.

The group left for Southampton to board the *Stirling Castle* ship, which would take them to Africa. There was no airliner in those days and the voyage would take at least two weeks to reach Cape Town. It was common for the players to be stripped and ready for training on one of the decks daily. During the voyage the club made sure that the players would be great ambassadors by dressing appropriately for dinner each evening with formal dress required. They were not the only well-known faces on board; also travelling was billiards world champion Joe Davis and the USA's world featherweight boxing champion Petey Sarron, who was on his to Africa for a series of exhibition fights.

# Aberdeen 3 Rangers 2

11 May 1946
Southern League Cup Final
Hampden Park, Glasgow
Attendance: 135,000

| Aberdeen | Rangers |
|---|---|
| George Johnstone | John Shaw |
| Willie Cooper | Dougie Gray |
| Pat McKenna | Jock Shaw |
| Frank Dunlop | Charlie Watkins |
| Andy Cowie | George Young |
| George Taylor | Scot Symon |
| Alex Kiddie | Willie Waddell |
| George Hamilton | Willie Thornton |
| Stan Williams | Billy Arnison |
| Archie Baird | Jimmy Duncanson |
| Willie McCall | Jimmy Caskie |
| *Manager:* Dave Halliday | *Manager:* Bill Struth |

FOLLOWING THE end of the Second World War, the Scottish League had been keen to get football back and the hastily arranged Southern League Cup complemented the first national league since 1939. This competition was the forerunner to the current Scottish League Cup which commenced in 1946. The authorities were keen to get football back to some kind of normality. Season 1945/46 saw a full fixture list which was duly completed but it was never classed as official by the authorities. Aberdeen competed favourably in the league, finishing in third place and scoring 76 goals from 30 matches. However, it was in the cup competition that the Dons excelled.

The new competition was played immediately after the completion of the league fixtures. The Dons had a tough run to Hampden, playing in no fewer than eight ties before coming through a replayed semi-final against Airdrie. Captain Frank Dunlop recalled his pride to the *Press & Journal* about how his side made the big day, 'To be honest we were happy just to get back playing football. It had been a terrible time and a lot of players have missed many years of playing due to the war. We had been playing a lot during the hostilities and we were aware that we had to play our part to keep spirits up. Once we began to put together a few great results we knew we could be on the verge of something special.'

Sporting red shirts for only their second season, Aberdeen had performed well during the various competitions that were played during the war years. Although they were regional, the Dons began to get used to lifting silverware, unofficial as it was, and they went into the final in confident mood.

On 11 May 1946 Aberdeen faced Rangers before a huge 135,000 crowd as rank outsiders. There was no real issue with that; Rangers had been perennial winners on the national stage while the Dons were mere gatecrashers. Manager Dave Halliday spoke in the *Press & Journal* and embraced their position, 'We accept that we are not expected to do well at Hampden. However, I have confidence in my players. It has been a tough time for all, but we have prepared well and anyone writing us off would be foolish. Some of our players have lost years from their careers due to the recent events and for some these games do not come around that often. We intend to make the most of it.'

Undaunted, there were high hopes from within the Aberdeen camp and that confidence spilled out on to the Hampden turf. As early as the first minute Aberdeen stamped their authority on the game by taking the lead. Andy Cowie, the right-back with a potent long throw, hurled the ball deep into the Rangers box. The move had taken the defence by surprise and it was the diminutive figure of Stan Williams who flicked the ball on for Archie Baird to head home past Shaw. By half-time it looked as though Aberdeen were well on course for victory, going in two goals ahead, but Rangers came back strongly to level the tie. Aberdeen had been on top for so long they had not legislated for Rangers' sheer will to battle their way back. There was no doubting the quality of the Dons, it was a tough mentality that was required, and they answered their critics in style by scoring a dramatic winner in the last minute. George Taylor, so often used as a utility player, popped up to convert another Kiddie cross to make it 3-2. There was no way back for Rangers this time and Dunlop proudly held the trophy high after being presented with the silverware on the Hampden pitch.

George Taylor was born in Aberdeenshire and went on to play 82 games for the Dons. His career, like so many others at that time, was interrupted by the war. After making his debut in March 1939 he resumed his career at Pittodrie in 1945. A former Junior with Hall Russell United, Taylor had the distinction of being a double cup winner with Aberdeen after he played in the 1947 Scottish Cup Final win over Hibernian. In 1948 he was transferred to Plymouth and took up a role as trainer where he remained for ten years before becoming chief scout for Argyle in 1966.

Alex Kiddie recalled the final many years later, 'Playing at Hampden in front of a 135,000 crowd was a great experience. We were up against Rangers and were not expected to win. I suppose that suited us as we had been in good form that season although we were a relatively new team. It was a warm day at Hampden and the crowd was barely settled when we took the lead. A long throw from Andy Cowie was knocked on to Archie Baird whose header put Aberdeen ahead.

'[For the winning goal] I managed to win the ball and set off down the wing. I could see we had support in the middle, so I was keen to get the ball over. It was almost time up when I got the ball on the right. I made one last effort to get to the byline. I crossed the ball over into the box and fortunately George Taylor was in a good position to score. It was an incredible feeling. The ball returned to the centre circle and after Rangers restarted the referee blew for full time.

'Playing in front of such a huge crowd was the highlight for me. I was not that aware of it at the time. It was only when I went over to take a corner kick that I noticed the crowd. When you are in the game you tend to be so wrapped up in that, you don't really notice these things.

'As an amateur, I was not entitled to any cash bonus. After the game the Aberdeen chairman William Mitchell expressed his gratitude at my performance and told me that the club would see about rewarding me for my efforts. That came in the shape of a watch that was given to me by the club and engraved on the back, "A.A Kiddie Southern League Cup 1945/46". Like I said, that watch has remained with me ever since and is still keeping perfect time all these years later!'

On the players' triumphant return to Aberdeen they could hardly have anticipated the frenzied scenes at the Joint station. Thousands of supporters congregated at the station to welcome their heroes home, a welcome usually only afforded to the returning soldiers from the armed forces.

The club always travelled by train in those days, often staying overnight for the longer trips to the west of Scotland. First-class travel was the way and Aberdeen never shirked on looking after their players. The station had often seen chaotic scenes of celebration as supporters would congregate to welcome the team home from successes away from the city. The first occasion was in 1904 when Aberdeen won their first trophy on the national stage – the Scottish Qualifying Cup, a trophy still being played for in Highland League circles. Aberdeen defeated Renton in Dundee, a famous name from the early days of Scottish football.

While all the euphoria that had surrounded the Dons' success was centred in the city, it all added to the feelgood factor that prevailed at the time. The Southern League Cup was also on display for those who did not make it to Hampden in the local *Aberdeen Weekly Journal* shop at 319 Union Street along with photos from the game and souvenirs from the day. The cup was placed in the shop window by the Marchioness of Huntly, a director of Aberdeen Journals. In attendance were Aberdeen chairman William Mitchell, manager Dave Halliday, director William Philip, and William Veitch, the managing director of Aberdeen Journals.

Aberdeen citizens were gradually getting back to normal but there was still some military work to be carried out; both Stan Williams and George Hamilton had little time to dwell on their success as they were whisked away to fulfil military obligations shortly after the game.

The Southern League Cup was not the only piece of silverware the Dons lifted in what was a remarkable season. The regional Dewar Shield was won after defeating Falkirk at Pittodrie, and the Mitchell Cup (donated by Aberdeen chairman William Mitchell) was won after defeating Dundee at Dens Park. A unique treble in what were unprecedented times.

Those who wanted to get a glimpse of the cup had to be quick as after several days the Scottish FA requested that the trophy be returned to Hampden. The hastily arranged Victory Cup was then played to a conclusion in May 1946. Aberdeen were eliminated by Clyde in the quarter-final. The authorities were left somewhat embarrassed as they did not have a trophy to present to the winners. With silver being in such short supply following the war, Aberdeen had to return their trophy as ironically it was then presented to Rangers as they beat Hibernian 3-1 at Hampden on 15 June 1946.

For Aberdeen it was in many ways a watershed season. They had finally managed to win on the national stage after dominating the regional competitions and they were now seen as serious contenders for all the major honours.

# Aberdeen 2 Hibernian 1

19 April 1947
Scottish Cup Final
Hampden Park, Glasgow
Attendance: 82,100

**Aberdeen**
George Johnstone
Pat McKenna
George Taylor
Joe McLaughlin
Frank Dunlop
Willie Waddell
Tony Harris
George Hamilton
Stan Williams
Archie Baird
Willie McCall
*Manager:* Dave Halliday

**Hibernian**
Jimmy Kerr
Jock Govan
Dave Shaw
Hugh Howie
Peter Aird
Sammy Kean
Gordon Smith
Willie Finnegan
Jock Cuthbertson
Eddie Turnbull
Willie Ormond
*Manager:* Willie McCartney

ABERDEEN INSIDE-FORWARD and former prisoner of war Archie Baird declared it was a long-standing joke in the north-east that any prospective bride to be would get her wishes, 'Once the Dons win the Cup.' Such were Aberdeen's previous attempts to win the elusive Scottish Cup.

Since the club came into being in 1903, Aberdeen had lost out in six semi-finals in 1908, 1911, 1922, 1924, 1926 and 1935. That sequence was broken in 1937 but the Black and Golds went down to Celtic in the final. Ten years on the club finally secured their first Scottish Cup win.

As the country began to recover from the Second World War, Aberdeen made it to the first final for eight years after a steady and unspectacular road to Hampden.

The Dons opened their campaign with a home tie against Partick. At that time Thistle were highly regarded and Aberdeen would have to be at their best to see off the Firhill challenge. A huge 34,000 crowd gathered at Pittodrie for the first Scottish Cup tie to be played there since March 1939. Partick arrived with an impressive front line and it would be down to the likes of captain Frank Dunlop and his defence to keep the lively Thistle forwards at bay.

44

The game itself was never a classic as Dunlop quelled the danger of Mathie while Tony Harris put the shackles on Jackie Husband to great effect. Botha made some progress down the wing and his clever pass set up George Hamilton, who crossed for the inrushing McCall to beat Steadward from close range. Partick levelled the tie in 67 minutes after Dunlop clashed with Mathie. The Partick forward managed to get up from the challenge and beat George Johnstone. Dunlop could not continue after that and that paved the way for Aberdeen to adopt some offside tactics which were fraught with danger. Nevertheless, Aberdeen rallied with a man down and increased the pressure on Partick, scoring a dramatic winner from the most unlikely source with four minutes left. Stan Williams's deep corner fell to Willie Cooper, who met the ball first time to crash it into the net. Cooper was the veteran of the Aberdeen side and he answered the call when a replay looked likely. While some suggested that Aberdeen were fortunate to win, Partick hardly did enough to take anything from the tie. The gate receipts were £2,042, the 34,000 crowd being the third highest of the day.

Aberdeen swept aside the challenge presented by lowly Ayr United in the next round at a windswept Pittodrie. However, they took their time to turn their pressure into goals; all they had to show for their first-half endeavour was a George Hamilton effort a minute before the break. Some inspired saves from Barbour defied the Dons but in the second half and with a strong wind at their backs, the Dons ran riot with a seven-goal salvo that left Ayr reeling. That second half did not get going until referee Bobby Calder had returned to the dressing rooms to get the match ball! Perhaps the Ayr players wished he hadn't as Ray Botha was given a special cheer after he scored his first goal for the club and Tony Harris weighed in with a spectacular hat-trick.

Aberdeen were fortunate to be drawn at home again in the next round but found Morton a tough prospect. With Botha missing from the team, his replacement Willie Millar scored the Dons' only goal after 25 minutes. Despite having their fair share of possession, they could not hold out and a McKillop equaliser in the second half took the tie to a replay.

It was at Cappielow in the replay that Aberdeen showed their quality. A 2-1 win was deserved and it showed that this side had a resilience that many thought beyond them. The *Daily Record* reported, 'Aberdeen made the game look like a game of draughts; always one step ahead of the Morton players.' Despite the home side trying everything to break down the Dons, two first-half goals from McCall and Hamilton put Aberdeen in control. Stan Williams was the catalyst for all the good attacking moves and when the wily winger went off on his trademark runs down the wing, four Aberdeen forwards would be up in support, weaving and bobbling their way into position. Williams made both Aberdeen goals. The first came after the Springbok 'sand-danced' in the penalty area before setting up McCall to score. The second goal was simplistic in approach and his superb run was finished off by a classic downward header from George Hamilton. An eye injury to McLaughlin forced Aberdeen into a tactical switch in the second half as McCall went to right-half with the injured Don making a nuisance of himself on the left wing. That meant a more defensive Aberdeen approach but they never looked in danger as Dunlop and co. snuffed out the Morton threat.

As dreams of a Hampden appearance were now a distinct possibility, the Dons drew Dundee at Dens Park in the quarter-final which prompted great interest in the city. A huge travelling support followed the Dons on the cup trail and they were treated to a classic tie that took 129 minutes to settle. Dundee scored in the first half through Ewen, whose fine solo goal was scored while the Dons were down to ten men with McKenna off the field being treated for a head injury. It was that man Stan Williams who brought Aberdeen level on the hour as he took full advantage of a mistake from Ancell to whip the ball past a stunned Lynch in the Dundee goal. The game went into extra time and Williams was the toast of Aberdeen as he popped up with a winning goal in the third period of extra time, in the 129th minute. With the Dundee defenders leg-weary, Williams summoned enough energy to run in to the area and crash an unstoppable shot past Lynch.

Aberdeen went into the semi-final and a quick return to Dens Park to face Arbroath, who had defied the odds to reach the last four. While the Gayfield side had enough fight in their make-up, they were no match for a classy Dons team who imposed themselves on the game from the start. Williams was fast becoming a hero with the Aberdeen support and he scored in each half to take the Dons through to their second Scottish Cup Final, which was to be played only seven days later.

Aberdeen had little time to prepare for the meeting with Hibernian at Hampden. With Williams and Hamilton perhaps playing at their peak the Dons knew that they always carried a goal threat.

Hibernian captain Dave Shaw, who later moved to Pittodrie as a player, trainer and manager, won the toss and elected to play into the stiff breeze and strong sunshine. Referee for the day was Bobby Calder, who went on to become the Dons' renowned scout between 1949 and 1981. The ritual handshakes before kick-off took place between three men who were and then became huge parts of the club's history – Frank Dunlop, who was about to become the first Aberdeen captain to lift the Scottish Cup, Shaw, and Calder, who was responsible for taking the likes of Charlie Cooke, Jimmy 'Jinky' Smith, Arthur Graham and Willie Miller to Pittodrie, all poached from the Glasgow area where he was based.

After 25 seconds there was a sensation and a shock for Aberdeen as they went behind. A long clearance from Finnigan went deep in to their penalty area. George Taylor was in an unfamiliar left-back role and he opted to pass the ball back to keeper Johnstone. The Dons keeper anticipated the move and went to collect the ball. Johnstone then looked back in disgust as the ball slipped out of his grasp and Hibernian forward Cuthbertson had the easy task of scoring. The Aberdeen response was swift and Stan Williams hit a shot from 25 yards that Kerr just managed to tip over the bar.

Aberdeen were clearly stung in to action and where previous teams had failed on the big occasion, this group had a tough mentality that was to bring a greater reward. McLaughlin, Dunlop and Waddell were all forcing the Hibernian defensive line back as Aberdeen pressed for the equaliser. It took some desperate defending from the Easter Road side to keep Aberdeen out but their luck did not hold. In

35 minutes Aberdeen scored a deserved leveller. A long ball from the Dons' half deceived the Hibernian defence and the livewire Williams was on to the ball as he made his way towards goal. Williams looked up and flicked the ball across goal to George Hamilton, who beat Kerr to it and headed into the empty net. Although Hibernian fought back when Willie Ormond brought out a fine save from Johnstone, their respite was temporary as Aberdeen hit a hammer blow four minutes before half-time. It was South African winger Williams who was causing the most damage and as he collected a long ball down the right wing he was soon closed down by two Hibernian defenders. Williams slipped the ball through them and cut in towards goal. As the Aberdeen forwards lined up for the expected cut-back, Williams cleverly slipped the ball past Kerr at the near post. It was a goal of pure genius and worthy of winning any final.

The expected response from Hibernian in the second half was never allowed to gain momentum as Aberdeen continued to dominate possession, and on the hour the Dons had a glorious chance to finish the tie when they were awarded a penalty. Williams, who had tormented the Hibernian players all afternoon, was brought down by Hibernian keeper Kerr. George Hamilton took the penalty but his effort went straight at Kerr and he saved easily. While that may have offered Hibernian an incentive, the Aberdeen defence managed to close the game down and led by Dunlop the Dons held out with ease to win the Scottish Cup for the first time in their history. The trophy was presented on the field following a fire inside Hampden.

The Aberdeen squad enjoyed the celebrations at the end and it was not until the Monday evening that they eventually arrived back in Aberdeen from their Largs base. More than 15,000 turned up to welcome their heroes home at Aberdeen Joint station. The pouring rain did not diminish the excitement. Lord Provost Thom Mitchell was first to congratulate Dunlop and his players. As the victorious team made their way out of the station on top of a coach, it slowly worked its way past thousands of supporters who lined Guild Street, Trinity Quay, Union Street and Marischal Street. The Caledonian Hotel awaited the players for a civic reception and Dunlop was a proud man, feeling humbled by the reaction from the citizens of

Aberdeen as he spoke to the *Evening Express*, 'I am sure the boys feel that they could travel far and wide and still not find a club like Aberdeen. Personally I feel it an honour to be at Aberdeen.'

Full-back Willie Cooper, who had been with the club since 1927, missed the final due to injury. Cooper was in his 'civvies' as he joined his team-mates at full time. Aberdeen received permission to get an extra medal struck for him, such was the high regard they held him in.

# Aberdeen 3 Hearts 0

13 March 1954
Scottish Cup quarter-final
Pittodrie Park, Aberdeen
Attendance: 45,061

**Aberdeen**
Fred Martin
Jimmy Mitchell
Dave Caldwell
Jackie Allister
Alec Young
Archie Glen
Graham Leggat
George Hamilton
Paddy Buckley
Joe O'Neil
Jackie Hather
*Manager:* Dave Halliday

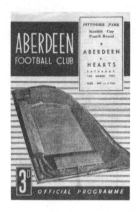

**Hearts**
Jimmy Watters
Bobby Parker
Jock Adie
Dave Laing
Freddie Glidden
John Cumming
Jim Souness
Alfie Conn
Willie Bauld
Jimmy Wardhaugh
John Urquhart
*Manager:* Tommy Walker

IT WAS during the 1950s that both Edinburgh sides, Hearts and Hibernian, enjoyed the best periods in their history. Certainly, when it came to winning the league championship it was an exciting era for Scottish football with no fewer than five different winners – Aberdeen, Celtic, Rangers, Hearts and Hibernian – during that decade. For Aberdeen it proved to be a period where they came so close but ultimately fell short. Three Scottish Cup finals were reached in 1953, 1954 and 1959 but all were lost in what was a frustrating time for the club.

Although league champions were rightly revered back in the 1950s it was cup football that captured the imagination and was afforded more stature, in stark contrast to the modern game. Finance, or lack of it, was never an issue as it is today and the cut and thrust of knockout football attracted some huge crowds. Aberdeen under manager Dave Halliday had gained a reputation of being a 'cup side', a reference to a team that thrived in the now-or-never nature of the game as opposed to a consistency level required to achieve league success. There were no arguments on the Dons' cup exploits down Edinburgh way. Between 1951 and 1958 Aberdeen faced the capital clubs on six occasions in knockout ties and won the lot. Indeed, it was not until 1996 that Hearts recorded their first win over Aberdeen in the Scottish Cup. Back in 1954 the Dons looked unbeatable at Pittodrie in the cup and Hearts visited the north more in hope than expectation, despite being favoured by the national bookmakers.

Interest in the Hearts tie was unprecedented; originally the club had thought that tickets for the ground would not be necessary but following the initial enquiries the game was made all-ticket. It was reported that there would have been around 60,000 sold such was the demand. The last enclosure tickets went quickly, and the ground tickets went on sale at a reserve game against Falkirk. This meant that the Pittodrie attendance record would certainly be broken; the previous best was 44,414 for a Rangers visit on 3 April 1948. Reports at the time suggested that crowd was far more as some ticket holders were not included in the official attendance. Whether or not that would have pushed the total above the 1954 record will remain a mystery.

As the tickets went on sale there then developed the unusual sight of two queues, one for purchasing tickets and another to leave the ground, presumably to make their way to nearby Linksfield for a Scottish Junior Cup tie as local side Sunnybank were playing.

Local interest in the Junior game was as high as it ever had been. Aberdeen quite often signed players from Junior clubs with Sunnybank and Banks O' Dee being the two big clubs in the city. Both were winners of the Scottish Junior Cup; Sunnybank in 1954 and Banks O' Dee in 1957. They remain the only Junior clubs from the north who have won the competition. One signing Aberdeen did make from that Sunnybank side was a young Teddy Scott, who may have only made one first-team appearance but his association with the club was incredible for more than 50 years. Teddy served as a player, trainer, coach and eventually kit man, his efforts being rewarded when he was inducted into the Aberdeen FC Hall of Fame in 2005.

In those days there was no segregation of supporters. Hearts had received an allocation of 8,000 tickets for the tie and although Aberdeen had hoped some would have been returned, it was announced that the Edinburgh club had sold their full allocation.

The game attracted an official attendance of 45,061 and £3,928 receipts but the reality was that many more got in by other means.

Most supporters made their way from the city and down to Merkland Road East to get to the ground. It was at that end where some of the more intrepid fans would try to gain access. With any stewarding being carried out inside the ground due to the large numbers, it was an opportunity for some to scale the walls at the King Street end and gain entry. It was also known that certain turnstiles would not be against a 'two for one' situation as some younger fans would be lifted over the turnstile with only one click registering. Crossing palms with additional silver was not unheard of.

Goals from Leggat, O'Neil and Hamilton eased Aberdeen through to the last four; Hearts had started the game as slight favourites, but the Dons had become a formidable force at Pittodrie and were hard to contain. Graham Leggat's goal was the 19-year-old's 16th of the season, more than any other winger in the 'A' Division.

Certainly, the backing of the huge support was a factor. Joe O'Neil, the towering inside-forward, recalled in the *Aberdeen Press & Journal*, 'The Aberdeen support was the best I ever played in front of. They appreciated good skill and knew the game inside out. That day was one of many great occasions we enjoyed. Most of the boys loved playing at home. We never made it easy for any visiting side and we knew that if we gave everything the support was always there behind us. The manager [Dave Halliday] really bought into that and we used it to great effect. We also had some fantastic front players to get the supporters excited. We feared no side at Pittodrie.'

That Aberdeen were now being talked up as potential challengers for the league suggested they were not that far away from being a potent combination. Halliday's work ethic was built around teamwork and Pittodrie was now becoming a tough place to visit. A combination of these factors was to bear fruit at a later stage, but if Aberdeen were still involved in the cup then that remained the only talking point among the support. Tensions were high during the Hearts game and there was even a mini pitch invasion after visiting hardman Bobby Parker was involved in a fracas with Jackie Hather. It looked as though Parker had kicked Hather while he was on the ground, although the Hearts captain later denied this. It made little difference to the Pittodrie support, who gave Parker a torrid time of it from that point on. One fan did make it on to the pitch to confront him, but the timely intervention of Paddy Buckley meant the incident was defused. From that point on Parker was relentlessly jeered every time he touched the ball. The general belief was that the defender should have been ordered off; however, in that incident the referee went with what his linesman saw and Parker escaped further sanction.

Hather was quite unique in the Aberdeen side. The only English-born player in the squad, Hather emerged from the tough coalmining area of County Durham, joining Aberdeen in 1948. What made Jackie unique was that he played his entire career with only one lung, a disability that he shunned on countless occasions. The club of course were very careful with him but Hather was determined to enjoy his career to the full. It was incidents like the attentions of Parker that often sparked reactions from the terraces. Hather was known for his lightning pace and became known as 'The Hare'. Former Don Bob Wishart recalled his team-mate with fondness when speaking in the *Evening Express* in 2018, 'Jackie was some player. I played as an old-style inside-left so I lost count of the times I set Jackie on his way. I was aware of how quick he was so that made my thinking different in some ways. Jackie was unstoppable when he tore down the left wing. Gareth Bale was not the first wide player to run outside the lines of the pitch. Jackie used to do it all the time to save being brought down. A great player and should have been honoured by England; he was that good.'

The whole game had an unfamiliar look about it as both sides changed from their traditional strips. The Dons turned out in blue shirts and white shorts while Hearts wore white and black. Aberdeen rarely had to change their colours and it was only when they came up against Hearts and Third Lanark that they had to use their second option. They did not have a 'second strip' as such. Apart from the blue kit they used in the cup tie they were also seen in white shirts and black shorts on occasion at Tynecastle.

After the Dons' impressive victory, the *Press & Journal* was fulsome in its praise of Aberdeen and Paddy Buckley in particular, 'The Dons' forwards were led by "mine papa" Paddy Buckley, full of the joy of Hampden in the spring.' The *Evening Express* exclaimed,

'Buckley and his mates spurted in a straight line for goal like scalded cats whipped off a hot plate. Hearts had more lines than any pools coupon,' an obvious reference to the visitors trying to 'dribble' their way out of trouble as opposed to the slick play from the lively Dons. Buckley's reward was a call-up to play for the Scottish League against the Irish in Dublin four days later, after Hibs' Lawrie Reilly pulled out through illness.

The record Pittodrie crowd came in for some praise as well. Pittodrie at that time was an open ground apart from the grandstand and the cover over the King Street end, which traditionally housed the more vociferous Dons supporters. The only other features were the half-time scoreboard, which was situated at the back of the southern terracing towards the King Street end, and the imposing *Green Final* board further along near the corner. The *Green Final* had been an institution in the north-east ever since it first emerged in 1928. Providing generations of Aberdeen supporters with the first news on all things Aberdeen, the Saturday evening sports paper sadly ceased production in the summer of 2002. For many it was essential reading on a Saturday in the pub. Sellers would be on the streets by 6.30pm as the first reports of the games provided many a topic of debate. By 8pm the Dundee equivalent the *Sporting Post* was also available in the city. There was also the 'half-time' edition of the local *Evening Express*, which was sold as supporters left the ground at the King Street end as the paper included the half-time scores from around the country.

Just minutes after the stadium was empty it was reported that the crowd had been on 'orderly behaviour throughout' and Pittodrie was the scene of 'miles of terracing steps hardly without a paper and occasional bottle' as the clean-up was about to commence.

# Aberdeen 6 Rangers 0

10 April 1954
Scottish Cup semi-final
Hampden Park, Glasgow
Attendance: 111,000

**Aberdeen**
Fred Martin
Jimmy Mitchell
Dave Caldwell
Jackie Allister
Alec Young
Archie Glen
Graham Leggat
George Hamilton
Paddy Buckley
Joe O'Neil
Jackie Hather
*Manager:* Dave Halliday

**Rangers**
Bobby Brown
Eric Caldow
John Little
Ian McColl
Willie Woodburn
Sammy Cox
Willie Waddell
Derek Grierson
Billy Simpson
John Prentice
Johnny Hubbard
*Manager:* Bill Struth

IN THE modern era of Scottish football one of the most bitter rivalries comes when Aberdeen are up against Rangers. Before the Ibrox club went into liquidation in 2012, the general belief was that the rivalry originated from some ferocious battles in the late 1970s. Looking back it was anything but; from reports from a Scottish Cup tie in 1906 when Rangers launched a protest against Aberdeen forward Paddy Boyle through to the Dons' 1953 Scottish Cup Final defeat, games against Rangers were always combative and controversial. It was during the late 1970s that the rivalry was taken to a new level. Doug Rougvie was sent off in the 1979 League Cup Final when Rangers' Derek Johnstone feigned injury, then John McMaster was trampled on by Willie Johnston in 1980, and it all culminated when Rangers' Ian Durrant suffered a serious injury in 1988. It is a rivalry that lasts to the present day.

Aberdeen reached the semi-finals of the Scottish Cup in 1954 after seeing off non-league Duns, Hibernian and Hearts. Before the draw for the last four was made the SFA announced a change in the format of the competition. The top two divisions – both the 'A' and 'B' leagues – would not enter the cup until the fifth round, while in the first four rounds clubs would be guaranteed against financial loss with gate money divided equally. The home club would be liable for all match expenses and the SFA would guarantee the visitors against loss. The governing body would take a five per cent cut from all ties to meet these expenses. Aberdeen came out against Rangers, a side they had yet to defeat in the Scottish Cup. Not surprisingly there was now an expectation that Aberdeen would go all the way that year.

For the first time the semi-finals would be played on alternative Saturdays and Aberdeen had to cancel a friendly they had lined up against Admira Wien due to the Hampden clash against Rangers. Prior to the big game the Dons lost the services of the emerging Joe O'Neil, who was injured in a league game against Falkirk, sustaining a depressed fracture of the skull. O'Neil's apparent omission was a big setback; he had been instrumental in the Hearts tie, a tall gangling figure with a deft touch and the ability to spray passes all over the park. Meanwhile, Aberdeen had fixed up young Sunnybank pivot Eddie Scott, who had been starring for the Junior club in their cup run. Teddy, as he was soon to become known, was to play a far more significant role with the club in the future. If ever there were evidence needed of the lure of the cup, then the two meetings with Hearts at Pittodrie in March 1954 pointed to the competition being all-important. A record crowd of over 45,000 turned up for the cup game but seven days later only 18,000 attended for the 1-0 win over the Tynecastle side in the league.

Before the game against Rangers the Dons had a free Saturday due to the Scotland v England international, and days before that they took up an invitation from Leeds United to play a friendly 'under the lights'. Floodlit football had been the latest development in the game and although it had yet to catch on in Scotland it was flourishing down south. On 29 March 1954 a 3-1 defeat at Elland Road was the Dons' first floodlit game, before a crowd of only 7,500. It also marked the debut of centre-half Jim Clunie, who deputised for Alec Young. Clunie was up against John Charles, the legendary Welsh forward, and although he tired in the second half, young Clunie acquitted himself well.

Not for the first time Aberdeen were installed as favourites to beat Rangers and make it to their second cup final in succession.

The Dons clearly were the side in form but Rangers' proud fighting tradition and their uncanny knack of grinding out results in the big matches would mean that Aberdeen would have to peak.

There was a major surprise before the game when Joe O'Neil was in the starting line-up. Less than three weeks earlier he had been lying critically ill in hospital and his remarkable recovery gave the Dons a massive boost. Joe took up the story, 'I had pestered Dave Halliday to let me play. Halliday told me that if the surgeon clears me then I could play, and I was sent off to the neurosurgeon. The doctor told me that the only way I could play was to have a metal plate inserted into my head! I went back to Dave Halliday and said the doctor had given me the all-clear! The boss was furious when he found out after the match. We had no special preparations for the game but the hat-trick I scored was something special. A left foot, a right foot and a header made it complete.'

O'Neil certainly was the hero as Aberdeen took Rangers apart in a record 6-0 win. The inside-forward also suffered a clash of heads with Rangers hardman Willie Woodburn and at one point he was taken off as a precaution. O'Neil was desperate to play having been shunned by Rangers as a young boy.

It was during his days with Bridgeton Waverly in Glasgow that O'Neil had attracted the attentions of several big clubs. Speaking back in 2001, Joe recalled, 'A few clubs were asking about me. I could have joined Manchester United as they wanted me. I would have become part of the side that was to be called the "Busby Babes" but I wanted to stay in Scotland. I knew Rangers had been watching me for some time and they followed that up with an offer to sign for them. It was only after they found out that I attended the Church of Sacred Heart school that their offer was withdrawn.' In the days when this was accepted practice in the west, O'Neil was left with bitter resentment at the way he had been treated. Rangers as a club adopted the stance of not signing Catholic players, such were the religious divisions that prevailed in the west at that time. Playing for Aberdeen and free of any prejudice, O'Neil went on to develop into an old-fashioned inside-forward of great promise and would battle it out with Bob Wishart for a first-team place. The inside-forward role would be the modern number ten, a link between the midfield and front players. In the 1950s they were often the unsung heroes, hard-working and a vital part of any side.

Nowadays such an approach towards injury would be frowned upon by medical staff but in an age when it did not seem so important, playing for the team was everything. It was the Dons' first Scottish Cup win over the Ibrox club and to this day remains Rangers' worst defeat in the national competition. Much was made of the cracked skull that big Joe suffered and the *Evening Express* made light of Rangers in the aftermath, 'If this is what a fractured skull does to you then Rangers' Jimmy Smith should start cracking the Light Blues with a mallet as they leave the dressing room. He would have to take the 56lb weight off their ankles as well. For this was a Rangers team trying to get the piano round a bend in the stairs. They were anxious. Strained and laboured. Jock Shaw [brother of Aberdeen trainer Dave] once said to a young Ranger who confessed to being nervous before a game, "Whit? Think black burning shame on yersel; when you go oot there in a Rangers jersey it is the ither felluhs that should be nervous!"' Aberdeen blew away that tradition – and with it 50 years of frustration.

It can be argued that this result instilled a belief among the Aberdeen players that was to ultimately bring further reward a year later. The signs had been there in patches; on their day Aberdeen were well capable of beating any side. It remained to be seen if they could do so on a regular basis. For the record the Dons' other scorers were Leggat, Buckley and Jackie Allister with a penalty. Although all the talk was centred on the team's scoring exploits, goalkeeper Fred Martin was subsequently talked up as a possible for the Scotland team. His breathtaking save in the first half from Simpson was pure class; centre-half Alec Young explained, 'When a corner came over I thought Archie [Glen] was getting it, then there was Simpson meeting the ball perfectly with his head to send the ball downwards a yard from the post. I don't know how the big 'un got down to it, but he saved the ball with his fingertips. We knew then that Fred was putting the shutters up.'

No doubt the Aberdeen support went home happy but the scenes in the dressing room after the final whistle were astonishing. The players were so happy that they were dancing around the room playing pranks and singing. The singing was divided in to two with one half bellowing, 'Glesca [Glasgow] belongs to me' while the northern contingent, sang 'A Gordon for me'. It was clear just how much that victory over Rangers meant to the players; they had laid a ghost to rest.

The directors announced after the game that the players would be taken to Switzerland for a holiday after the season as a thank you for their efforts. The trip would coincide with the World Cup, which was being held there. Aberdeen had prepared for the game in Gleneagles and it was not until after midnight that the train carrying the victorious side rolled back into the station. Much to their delight there were several hundred supporters waiting to greet their heroes. Any sympathy that was directed towards Rangers was soon quashed after it emerged that several Aberdeen players were nursing injuries after some harsh treatment from the Ibrox men. Trainer Dave Shaw revealed the secret behind the success in the *Press & Journal*, 'Nothing like hard work in training. It was the inside-forward blend which broke the Rangers. The long passes of Geordie Hamilton and the running through of O'Neil to link up with Paddy Buckley. You must have a contrast in those roles.'

Joe O'Neil eventually left Aberdeen in 1956 and joined Leicester City, teaming up with former boss Dave Halliday. Joe moved to Bath City in 1959 where he later became manager and settled there after retirement.

The Aberdeen party went through to Switzerland to take in the World Cup. Both keeper Fred Martin and George Hamilton were included in the threadbare 13-man squad that Scotland took to Berne. The Scots were ill-prepared and even with Hamilton, who was carrying an injury, the squad was woefully inadequate for their three matches. They could have learned a lot from Aberdeen, who by tradition made sure their players were well looked after.

# Clyde 0 Aberdeen 1

9 April 1955
Scottish League Division A
Shawfield Stadium, Glasgow
Attendance: 15,000

**Aberdeen**
Fred Martin
Jimmy Mitchell
Dave Caldwell
Joe O'Neil
Alec Young
Archie Glen
Graham Leggat
George Hamilton
Harry Yorston
Bob Wishart
Jackie Hather
*Manager:* Dave Halliday

**Clyde**
Ken Hewkins
Albert Murphy
Harry Haddock
Ralph Granville
Tommy Anderson
Davie Laing
John Divers
Archie Robertson
Ally Hill
George Brown
Tommy Ring
*Manager:* Pat Travers

*Aitken's Beer*
*JUST WHAT I WANT !*
*Nearest to Shawfield . . .*
THE PARK BAR
962 MAIN STREET, BRIDGETON
—The Sportsman's Rendezvous—

**CLYDE F.C. LTD.**
Season 1954-55            No. 19
SCOTTISH LEAGUE - DIVISION A
CLYDE
*versus*
ABERDEEN
SATURDAY, 9th APRIL 1955
OFFICIAL PROGRAMME · THREEPENCE

CLUB SECRETARIES, PLEASE NOTE:—
THE WOODEND
120 HAMILTON ROAD, MOUNT VERNON, GLASGOW, E.2

THE MOST remarkable factor in the Dons' first league title success in 1955 was that there had been no new additions to the playing staff in the summer of 1954. Although Aberdeen had finished ninth in the previous season, that was not as bad as it seemed. Had Aberdeen won their final game of the campaign at Easter Road they would have climbed to third, such was the parity in the league at that time. Manager Dave Halliday and trainer Dave Shaw were happy enough with the players at their disposal. The Dons had lost out in the Scottish Cup Final against Rangers in a replay, so the foundations for a serious challenge were certainly there.

There were no clear favourites before the season started. Certainly, the two Glasgow clubs would be there, but the challenge from both Hibernian and Hearts was a realistic one. All the big-city teams could command crowds in excess of 40,000, and with clubs paying their players more than they could earn in England, it was more of a level playing field. Whether Aberdeen could breach the top four remained to be seen, but history tells us that seven different clubs won the title between 1947 and 1965. It was a window of opportunity in Scottish football that had never been seen before and has not been repeated since.

Halliday resisted the temptation to bring in any new faces. Fred Martin was the established goalkeeper having been a regular in the side since 1951, taking over from George Johnstone. Jimmy Mitchell was signed by Halliday from Morton in a record £10,000 deal and he was immediately installed as captain. Halliday looked upon Mitchell as a vital factor in the side and his leadership qualities would be vital in the months ahead. At left-back it was a straight choice between Billy Smith and Dave Caldwell. The contrast in style between these two made it a difficult choice; while Caldwell adopted a more methodical approach, Smith was very much in the face of opponents, a tough competitor. The half-back line may not have been as straightforward as legend would have us all believe. The renowned trio of Allister, Young and Glen will go down in Pittodrie folklore. Halliday and Shaw only decided how they came about after some considerable time. Jack Allister was brought from Chelsea and in January 1954 in a friendly against Wolves at Pittodrie he was handed the inside-right role; it was a problem area for the Dons at that time. The idea was soon changed due to an injury in that game to Alec Young. Allister reverted to his right-half role and established himself in the side. Allister was a tenacious player and one description was typical as he would be in among a melee of players with boots flying all over the place, and out he would come with the ball at his feet. Young was plucked from successful junior side Blantyre Vics and regarded by many as too small for a centre-half, but Halliday had a good feeling about him when he went to watch him play. Young's famed sliding tackles were turned into almost an art form. Archie Glen completed the half-back line and he added the grace and composure to the side. Glen was another player who was brought from the Junior ranks, spotted by George Hamilton on a chance visit back to his native Ayrshire.

Perhaps Aberdeen's most potent weapon was their pace in attack. This went against the norm in Scottish football as speed, although an asset, was not essential. The stereotypical defender was one of a bustling, no-nonsense type who took no prisoners. Coming up against players with pace frightened them. Aberdeen in 1955 had that in abundance. Graham Leggat had emerged from the reserve team as a youngster of vast potential and he saw off the challenge of Alan Boyd and others to stake a claim for regular starting place on the right wing. On the left it was Jackie 'The Hare' Hather, the only Englishman in the squad, played his entire career with only one lung. In 1955 there was little doubt that Hather was the quickest player in the game. The spearhead of the front line was Paddy Buckley, signed from St Johnstone by Halliday. Buckley was the original livewire; a cheeky smile disguised a burning desire to succeed. Buckley had the lot and he would take some tough treatment from defenders, his numerous injuries through the years bearing testimony to that.

The link between the forward line and the defence came with Harry Yorston on the right and Bob Wishart. Yorston was perhaps never fully appreciated by the support and was often criticised but he endeared himself with his fellow pros. Wishart was the more cultured of the two and offered a fine balance on the left.

Aberdeen were the most-travelled club in the First Division at the time and the long hours spent away also helped build team spirit. The club always went to games by first-class train. If they were down in Glasgow, then the journey would be made on the Friday night with a top-class hotel booked and a possible theatre visit. What many will find hard to believe was the fact that Aberdeen players were the highest-paid in Britain at one point. In England a wage ceiling was in force and the top Scottish clubs set their wage structure slightly higher with a view to keeping their top players at home. Aberdeen's first-team players were on £18 per week with the reserves picking up £14. There was also the bonus of £2 for a win. Only Rangers could come close to matching those amounts. There was also a loyalty payment made by Aberdeen with £750 coming each player's way after five years' service. National service had also to be considered as players were often away doing their duty in the prime of their footballing careers. Throughout the 1950s Aberdeen had shown up well in the cup competitions but consistency in the league was missing. That all changed in 1955 as Aberdeen closed in on a first league championship.

It all came down to the Dons' game at Shawfield in Glasgow against Clyde on 9 April. The Aberdeen objective was clear; three points from their final three games would take the title. A win over Clyde would put Celtic out of the running whatever they did and if Hearts did not win at Ibrox that same day then Aberdeen would be champions. Hearts' challenge was disappearing in each passing game. They would have to win their last six games and win them with a lot to spare to catch Aberdeen on goal average. It was a long shot at best, but still mathematically possible. Celtic were the main challengers; if Aberdeen lost at Clyde then the following week they were due at Parkhead for what many had hoped would be a title decider. That was the last thing that the Dons wanted so the Clyde game was massive.

To add spice to the occasion it was Clyde who had ended the Dons' Scottish Cup interest only days previously with a 1-0 win in a semi-final replay. While the Dons failed to rise to the occasion in that one the focus was now on two precious points at Shawfield. The Clyde ground was not typical of others in that the stadium had a huge running track around the perimeter, which hosted regular dog racing. The massive scoreboard at one end restricted access to the crowd, who were a long way away from the action. The almost eerie atmosphere did not help the Dons. Clyde were enjoying the most successful period in their history and boasted three Scottish internationals in their side. They also had former Aberdeen manager Pat Travers in charge, and he knew enough about the Dons to know that his team could cause them problems. Aberdeen were also badly hit with injury as both Paddy Buckley and Jackie Allister were ruled out.

There was no doubt that Aberdeen's players were nervous; they knew what was at stake. The game reflected that apprehension and was fragmented and littered with errors, but it was settled in the 13th minute when Aberdeen gained a penalty. Graham Leggat's deep corner found George Hamilton at the back post. His header was then cleared off the line as keeper Hewkins came for it and missed. The ball bounced up invitingly for Bob Wishart, whose header looked goalbound. It was then that Clyde defender Murphy punched the ball clear. Archie Glen and Jackie Allister used to take alternate penalties, but Glen had no doubt suffered a crisis of confidence as he had missed his last two efforts. Allister had then taken on the responsibility but as he was not in the side that day it fell on Glen's shoulders. Glen had done his homework though and noticed that South African keeper Hewkins was weak on his left side. Glen opted to hit it hard to Hewkins's left-hand post, the ball flew into the top corner and Aberdeen had the vital lead. It was an advantage they would hold on to despite some nervy moments. Jimmy Mitchell and co defended in depth towards the end of the match and held out. For George Hamilton, playing in his final game, it was a fitting end to a glorious career. When news came through that Hearts had lost at Ibrox the Dons could not be caught and were now champions.

It was in the confines of the dressing room that the champagne was in full flow and the realisation that Aberdeen had won the title for the first time dawned. When the party arrived back at Aberdeen Joint there were no thronging masses to greet their heroes. It was late that Saturday night that around 30 diehard Aberdeen supporters were present. In hindsight this was new territory for the club; there was never the same glamour and excitement attached to the league as there was with a cup success. That did not change until the mid-1970s in Scotland.

Aberdeen claimed the championship after winning 24 of their 30 league games, with only one defeat at home.

While there was so much to look forward to with new horizons in European football, things were about to change at Pittodrie as manager Dave Halliday decided to take up a new challenge with Leicester City. It was a shock for the Aberdeen board as Halliday seemed to have been so content at Pittodrie. That was certainly challenged when there was a row over a cash bonus for the players after they won the title. It left a sour taste on what was such a milestone for the club.

The Dons' last home game of the season was on 23 April against Raith Rovers. The 3-2 win only attracted a crowd of around 10,000; hardly the reception the new league champions would have expected. With the departure of Halliday and the final game being played by George Hamilton it was certainly the end of an era at Pittodrie.

## Scottish League Division A 1955

|                    | P  | W  | D | L  | F  | A   | Pts |
|--------------------|----|----|---|----|----|-----|-----|
| Aberdeen           | 30 | 24 | 1 | 5  | 73 | 26  | 49  |
| Celtic             | 30 | 19 | 8 | 3  | 76 | 37  | 46  |
| Rangers            | 30 | 19 | 3 | 8  | 67 | 33  | 41  |
| Hearts             | 30 | 16 | 7 | 7  | 74 | 45  | 39  |
| Hibernian          | 30 | 15 | 4 | 11 | 64 | 54  | 34  |
| St Mirren          | 30 | 12 | 8 | 10 | 55 | 54  | 32  |
| Clyde              | 30 | 11 | 9 | 10 | 59 | 50  | 31  |
| Dundee             | 30 | 13 | 4 | 13 | 48 | 48  | 30  |
| Partick Thistle    | 30 | 11 | 7 | 12 | 49 | 61  | 29  |
| Kilmarnock         | 30 | 10 | 6 | 14 | 46 | 58  | 26  |
| East Fife          | 30 | 9  | 6 | 15 | 51 | 62  | 24  |
| Falkirk            | 30 | 8  | 8 | 14 | 42 | 54  | 24  |
| Queen of the South | 30 | 9  | 6 | 15 | 38 | 56  | 24  |
| Raith Rovers       | 30 | 10 | 3 | 17 | 49 | 57  | 23  |
| Motherwell         | 30 | 9  | 4 | 17 | 42 | 62  | 22  |
| Stirling Albion    | 30 | 2  | 2 | 26 | 29 | 105 | 6   |

# Aberdeen 6 Hibernian 2

10 September 1955
Scottish League Division A
Pittodrie Park, Aberdeen
Attendance: 17,367

| Aberdeen | Hibernian |
|---|---|
| Fred Martin | Tommy Younger |
| Jimmy Mitchell | Jock Paterson |
| Dave Caldwell | George Muir |
| Bobby Wilson | James Thomson |
| Jim Clunie | Jackie Plenderleith |
| Archie Glen | Tommy Preston |
| Graham Leggat | Gordon Smith |
| Paddy Buckley | Eddie Turnbull |
| Harry Yorston | Lawrie Reilly |
| Bob Wishart | Des Fox |
| Jackie Hather | Willie Ormond |
| *Manager:* Dave Shaw | *Manager:* Hugh Shaw |

ABERDEEN MANAGER Dave Halliday made it a triple success for the Dons with the Southern League Cup, Scottish Cup and then the Division A title in 1955, completing an impressive haul of silverware. Considering the club's formative years and the time before the Second World War were bereft of success on the national stage, it seemed Halliday was making up for lost time.

It is well enough documented that Aberdeen took their bow in European football in 1967 against Icelandic side KR Reykjavík. That 10-0 win was a memorable beginning to what has become an incredible European adventure for the club over 50 years. It could have been very different had that great side from 1955 been allowed to enter the first European Cup competition. The European Cup was very much in its infancy and the new concept was not met with widespread approval from some sceptical clubs. That left the inaugural competition open to manipulation as there was no set criteria in place.

It was not until the following season that the respective league champions of all European countries were invited to compete in the competition. As it was, the initial event in 1955/56 was open to a selection process by any country to put a team forward. Despite Aberdeen being league champions in 1955, the SFA under the guidance of president Harry Swan put Hibernian forward to represent Scotland. Swan was also chairman of Hibernian and the decision reflected badly on the authorities as Aberdeen were treated badly in the whole affair. Hibernian were eventually outclassed in the semi-final by Stade de Reims who in turn came up against that wonderful Real Madrid side who made the formative years of the European Cup very much their own.

For Aberdeen it left a bitter taste. Halliday had spoken openly to the *Sunday Post* before his move to England on how the game was changing, 'Football is developing, and we all have to look forward and beyond our borders. We saw how good the Hungarians were at both Wembley and against Scotland at Hampden [Hungary became the first European team to defeat England at Wembley in 1953 and followed that up with a 7-1 demolition in Budapest a year later]. The Europeans bring some wonderful technique and flair to football. For too long we have only looked at the game in this country. That would be wrong in my opinion.'

Inside-left Bob Wishart recalled the disappointment when speaking at a club event in 2003, 'It was all very new and we were never really made aware of what was happening. We talked a lot about the new European competition and how it would work. It was an exciting prospect that we could play European teams abroad. It was that fantastic Hungary national side that gave the country a real wake-up call. Up until then just about every player in Scotland and England had rarely played against European players. That was all changing and we were in there at the start. I remember Honvéd coming over and playing a few games in England. It would have been a great experience to play in Europe but the "bigwigs"in Scotland denied us that opportunity. We saw that Hungary side at Hampden in 1954 when they played Scotland. The club took all of us down for the game. Fred [Martin, the Aberdeen keeper] was a busy lad that day. The Hungarians' movement and passing was something else.'

It can only be imagined how well Aberdeen would have fared in that first competition had they been allowed to represent their country as champions. Back then Hibernian had no little flair and they were keen exponents of a passing game that would have perhaps been arguably more suited for European football. However, the Aberdeen side was as tough as the city's granite and the methodical and tactical approach by Halliday and trainer Dave Shaw made them one of the most complete teams in British football. Pittodrie was a virtual fortress and away from home goals were hard to come by playing against Aberdeen.

As a marker, Aberdeen made it quite clear who should be flying the flag for Scotland in Europe in 1955 when Hibernian came north for the opening game of the league season. On 10 September the Dons hammered Hibernian 6-2 with a display of pace and power that made a mockery of the SFA decision to overlook them for the European Cup. The sides were also drawn together in the League Cup sections and Aberdeen won both matches.

Included in the Aberdeen side were youngsters Bobby Wilson and Jim Clunie. Both had shown up well in the League Cup group matches as the Dons were missing more experienced players through injury. Clunie was up against Scotland centre-forward Lawrie Reilly and apart from one occasion the Hibernian player was kept quiet. Wilson deputised for the injured Jackie Allister and he showed enough to suggest he would be a regular in the first team despite his youthful years.

Once again it was Paddy Buckley who was a thorn in Hibernian's side. His three-goal haul brought delight from the Pittodrie terraces as they watched their side make the best possible start in defence of their league title. Buckley relished playing against the Easter Road side. He was brought up in Leith and supported Hibernian as a boy. He always hoped they would come in for him, but it never happened. It was Halliday who spotted something special in Buckley when he was at St Johnstone; Buckley was signed in 1952 in a £7,500 transfer and he went on to become a firm favourite at Pittodrie. Seen by many as too small to be a senior centre-forward, Buckley defied his doubters and used his speed and strength against the burlier Scottish defenders to great effect. His 28 goals from all matches in 1954/55 made him the Dons' top scorer in that historic championship-winning season. Buckley's career at Pittodrie, however, ended in controversy in 1957 as after suffering a knee injury there were issues over his insurance after he turned out for Inverness a year later.

There was also the return to form of Pittodrie 'Golden Boy' Harry Yorston, whose late free kick consigned Hibernian to a heavy defeat and sent the Aberdeen supporters home delighted with their team's efforts. Yorston was a local lad, brought up a stone's throw from Pittodrie, and he signed from local side St Clements in 1946 before going on to become one of the Dons' greatest forwards. One of the 1955 champions, he was perhaps the first Aberdeen 'pin-up boy'. Yorston scored 141 goals from his 277 Aberdeen appearances. Capped for Scotland and the Scottish League, Yorston resisted the temptation to join the trail to England and shocked the football world by retiring from the senior game in 1957 to take up employment as a fish market porter, where the pay was superior to what top international players could earn back then. In Aberdeen the thriving fish market was the main industry in the city at that time, long before oil was discovered in the North Sea in the early 1970s. It was also the most lucrative. Aberdeen was the leading port in Scotland, and on a par with Hull and Grimsby in England.

While Aberdeen were celebrating their first championship in 1955, there was also a first for Chelsea as they won the English title. At that time they were by no means one of the top clubs, but they took the English championship in style led by captain and top scorer Roy Bentley, who was Chelsea's answer to Aberdeen legend George Hamilton. Bentley was a prolific scorer and a majestic header of the ball in his day. Not unlike Aberdeen, the Chelsea side of 1955 was a relatively ageing one, built on a shoestring by Ted Drake. The similarity to what Aberdeen faced was mirrored by Chelsea's plight with the FA. The English authorities steadfastly refused to allow Chelsea to enter the first European Cup, a decision which by today's standards seems absurd.

That Chelsea side began to break up and they were never allowed the opportunity to grace the European stage, so both Aberdeen and Chelsea had to content themselves with a 'Championship of Britain' clash at Pittodrie in September 1955. It was on the traditional Aberdeen holiday and the game attracted a lot of interest as the best team from each side of the border locked horns. Aberdeen emerged victorious with a fantastic 4-3 win as the Dons' own Paddy Buckley outshone the talented Bentley, scoring a hat-trick. On reflection it was small comfort to both sides, who really should have been battling it out on foreign fields for the first time in serious competition.

In 1967 both teams were runners-up in their respective national cup finals, the Dons losing to Celtic while Chelsea went down to Tottenham. Three years later Aberdeen and Chelsea won the Scottish and FA Cups respectively. The Dons defeated Celtic 3-1 while Chelsea saw off Leeds after a replay at Old Trafford. Even all the way back in 1905 Chelsea were admitted into the English league for the first time, just as Aberdeen were admitted to the First Division in Scotland. Also, neither Aberdeen nor Chelsea also managed to win a major honour before the Second World War.

# Aberdeen 2 St Mirren 1

22 October 1955
Scottish League Cup Final
Hampden Park, Glasgow
Attendance: 44,100

**Aberdeen**
Fred Martin
Jimmy Mitchell
Dave Caldwell
Bobby Wilson
Jim Clunie
Archie Glen
Graham Leggat
Paddy Buckley
Harry Yorston
Bob Wishart
Jackie Hather
*Manager:* Dave Shaw

**St Mirren**
Jim Lornie
David Lapsley
Jim Mallan
Jackie Neilson
Willie Telfer
Bobby Holmes
Jim Rodger
Davie Laird
Jackie Brown
Tommy Gemmell
Brian Callan
*Manager:* Willie Reid

WINNERS' MEDALS remain part of the climax to all major football competitions in the modern era. The everlasting memento for competing players endures throughout their careers and beyond. When Aberdeen won their first League Cup in October 1955, the club were disappointed to discover that no winners' medals were to be presented. Aberdeen later sought permission from the authorities to get medals struck for the players and the backroom staff. In the aftermath of the game the players were told that they could keep their jerseys as a lasting memento, and they were also given a £10 bonus.

Aberdeen had been due to meet cup final opponents St Mirren at Paisley on league duty seven days before the big game. Under normal circumstances it would be feasible to change the team around in an attempt not to give too much away to your opponents and protect your best players from injury. However, the shadow side that turned out at Paisley was down to necessity given the now-critical injury problems. Manager Dave Shaw reported to the *Evening Express* that he was keen to have his strongest side out for the final, 'We are hopeful that Buckley, Leggat and Caldwell will all make it and we will look at how they are next week. To be honest it has been a really difficult time, but the players who have come in have been magnificent.'

For the trip to Paisley, Shaw handed Norman Davidson a first-team debut at centre-forward and he also included Ian Macfarlane and George Mulhall. Jim Clunie continued at centre-half in the absence of Alec Young, as did the promising Bobby Wilson at right-half. The relative success of what was essentially a makeshift Aberdeen side was attributed to a work ethic that suggested that there was no fitter team in Scotland. Captain Jimmy Mitchell told the *Press & Journal*, 'We find our easiest day of the week is a Saturday. Our training routines have been stepped up which always include a full-scale practice match every Tuesday morning, which lasts for two hours. On Wednesday it was another game in sand shoes and in between the vigorous sprinting and stamina work was necessary.'

In the build-up to the final there were more problems with Ian Macfarlane and Dave Caldwell both struggling to fill the left-back slot. Caldwell had been injured playing in a representative game for the RAF but was hopeful of making the final. Aberdeen were firm favourites to win the League Cup; there was little indication to suggest otherwise. The Dons were the only undefeated team in the British Isles and a weakened side comfortably cruised to a 3-0 win at Paisley the week before. Shaw adopted a policy that had stood the club well under Dave Halliday's principles, 'At the start of the season I decided that if a first-team player was injured, then the fellow playing in that position in the reserve team would step up.'

Further evidence of just how professional the Aberdeen setup had become emerged when the Dons' reserve squad would now travel to away games by first-class rail. There was one awkward moment in Glasgow when the first-team players of a top Scottish side stepped out of their third-class seats only to look aghast at the young Dons making their way from their first-class compartments. It later emerged that one player, who was not named, protested so vigorously at his treatment that he was duly dropped by the club directors. It seemed that Aberdeen had been getting to the opposition off the field as well as on it.

Shaw had quite rightly earned a formidable reputation as a trainer in his time and Charlie McCaig had taken up the methods introduced by him. Invariably these 'new' approaches attracted interest from the press but Shaw was having none of it. A report by Peter Black in the *Weekly News* explained, 'What goes on behind the scenes at Pittodrie is not the easiest thing to find out. If you aren't a signed Aberdeen player, you have as much chance of horning in on their day sessions as you have of getting past the guards at the Palace. Despite this "Iron Curtain" it is possible to suggest that Dave Shaw's formula for brighter football has been drawn freely from his namesake at Hibernian. The speculative long ball, so long the bane of my sporting life, is getting short shrift. While it would be an exaggeration to say the Dons have mastered their short game as the Hungarians and Brazilians have done, everything is moving towards that desirable end.'

Certainly, the game had evolved some way in a relatively short timescale. This was, of course, hastened by the influence from across Europe. The suggestion that the Aberdeen ethic was built around an Easter Road influence was simply not true; the 'Aberdeen Way' was built on speed of thought and mind and quick passing which was totally alien to the game in Scotland. The great Hibernian side of the early 1950s was built on possession in any area of the pitch and a more thoughtful build-up. The contrasts were stark and it was a matter of opinion over which was the more successful.

There was no doubt that Aberdeen were keen to get their 'big' players back for the final. Paddy Buckley, who was such a huge influence on the side, was desperate to play. Bob Wishart explained, 'Most of the recognised first-team players wanted to play. After all, it was a big occasion and not to be missed. It was not uncommon for some to play through injuries. The truth behind us struggling in the final for long periods was because some of the guys were not 100 per cent fit. In those days the team more or less picked itself and quite often it was up to the player himself to declare himself fit. That was certainly the case in the final, no doubt about that.'

As was traditional before big games, lucky mascots emerged; Jim Clunie, who had enjoyed a meteoric rise to first-team football, celebrated his call-up to the Scottish League squad by announcing that although he was not superstitious he would be carrying his lucky football boot on his key chain. Before the players caught their train from Aberdeen station the night before the game, they were seen off by the mascot, Blackie the Alsatian, who was adorned in club colours for the occasion. Blackie was a regular visitor to Joint station and never failed to see off the team before they made their way to games.

The match itself was frustrating for the Dons although they took the trophy with a 2-1 victory. It took an outrageous winner from Graham Leggat 11 minutes from time to finish off a brave and plucky St Mirren side. Although the performance was sluggish it did not detract from the celebrations which were far more jubilant than what followed their league success earlier in the year. Jimmy Mitchell was celebrating his 31st birthday on the day of the final and he proudly lifted the League Cup after the presentation at full time.

Much of the debate following the game was centred on Leggat's winning goal; was it meant or was it a fluke? Former Don Tommy Pearson, reporting for the *Daily Mail* at the time, asked Graham, 'Did you really try to score?' Paddy Buckley chipped in his own inimitable style, 'Of course he did. He has been practising that kind of shot for ages.' Leggat's goal was either the sublime act of genius or a pure fluke; taking the ball in from the right wing, he rolled it from right foot to left foot and shot at goal, all in one sweet movement. St Mirren keeper Lornie was as bemused as the others as he was helpless while watching the ball fly into the top corner.

On the players' return to Joint station they were taken aback by the reception afforded to them. More than 15,000 packed in to the tight confines of the concourse as the players emerged with the trophy. The team did not arrive back in Aberdeen until near midnight by virtue of their official dinner in Glasgow. Jimmy Mitchell was carried shoulder-high through the thronging crowds as the jubilant crowd swamped the rest of the players. 'We want Leggat,' the fans cried. They were to be disappointed as young Graham was still in unassuming mood as he made his way back to Jordanhill College in Glasgow to continue his PE studies, oblivious to the hero worship in Aberdeen. The *Press & Journal* reported some frenzied activity, 'A roar that could be heard half a mile away reverberated through the station as Jimmy Mitchell stepped from the train carrying the cup. Police reinforcements called in for the occasion had to clear a way through the seething mass of people as the players were chaired to the bus waiting inside the station to take them home.' Dave Shaw was amazed, 'I played for Hibs when they won trophies, but it was nothing compared to this. The support has been quite incredible.' Shaw had continued the great work undertaken by Dave Halliday and on the face of it the transition was seamless. There were, however, some concerns that were soon to emerge.

The last word on the final goes to Bobby Wilson, who made only his ninth first-team appearance for the Dons, 'The League Cup Final was undoubtedly the highlight of my career. I remember Tommy Pearson, the ex-Dons player who was later manager, at that time was writing for the *Daily Mail,* saying to me in the Glasgow hotel after the game that I was a lucky young man to be a winner so early in my career. Tommy went on to say that many players would go through a whole career and not win anything like this. I also remember Dave Shaw telling us before the semi-final against Rangers that when we run out on to the pitch to take a few seconds to look around all the way up the huge terraces. When I would take an early throw-in it would not come as such a shock to see just how big the crowd is. I was also lucky enough to go with Aberdeen on tour to Canada a year later which was a fantastic experience, a trip of a lifetime. Had Aberdeen not won the league and then the League Cup I doubt if the club would have received such an invitation.'

# Rangers 1 Aberdeen 2

18 April 1959
Scottish League Division One
Ibrox Stadium, Glasgow
Attendance: 40,000

| Aberdeen | Rangers |
|---|---|
| Fred Martin | George Niven |
| Dave Caldwell | Bobby Shearer |
| Jimmy Hogg | Eric Caldow |
| Ken Brownlee | Harold Davis |
| Jim Clunie | Willie Telfer |
| Archie Glen | Willie Stevenson |
| Dickie Ewen | Alex Scott |
| Norman Davidson | Ian McMillan |
| Hugh Baird | Max Murray |
| Bob Wishart | Ralph Brand |
| Jackie Hather | Andy Matthew |
| *Manager:* Dave Shaw | *Manager:* Scot Symon |

ABERDEEN REMAIN one of only two clubs in Scottish football who have never been demoted from the top division, an unbroken spell that was only ever interrupted by two world conflicts in the 20th century. They did compete in the old Second Division in 1904/05 after they were admitted into the mainstream Scottish leagues. A year later they were voted into the top division; at that time there was no automatic relegation. Aberdeen had to rely on the member clubs as opposed to sporting merit. Automatic promotion and relegation did not come into force until 1922.

That incredible record has on occasion been tested as the Dons have flirted with relegation in some of their more difficult periods. Just four years after they became champions, season 1958/59 proved to be one of the most disappointing in their 120-year history. A run of only four wins from 22 league games plunged Aberdeen into a relegation battle. Progress was made in the Scottish Cup and after a semi-final replay win over Third Lanark at neutral Ibrox their entire season came down to the final week. The Dons' success in reaching the cup final had almost masked their wretched league form and the *Evening Express* suggested they had concentrated everything on the cup, 'While the Dons have to be congratulated in reaching another cup final it is vital they do not slip out of the league. Aberdeen's proud record is under real threat and unless Dave Shaw and the players get their act together it is likely the club will be a Second Division side next season. Such a situation would have a real impact on the club finances. It is true that doing well in the cup brings in more money through the gate but the thought of playing lower-division teams next season will not appeal to many Dons supporters.'

With St Mirren due to be faced in the Scottish Cup Final to conclude the season, the Dons' final league game a week beforehand was against Rangers at Ibrox. The task was clear; if Aberdeen gained at least a point they would not be relegated. In contrast Rangers were looking for a draw to claim the league championship. The Ibrox side had only dropped two points at home all season and remained undefeated. On the face of it the odds were stacked against the Dons. Their form away from Pittodrie was hardly inspiring; Aberdeen had lost their five previous away games in the league. Rangers were hot favourites to see off Aberdeen and secure the championship in front of their own fans.

Dave Shaw had found the transition from training ground to manager's office a difficult one. Shaw had thrived in his trainer role during the club's most successful period to date. He was the obvious choice to take over from Dave Halliday, who moved to Leicester City after the championship success in the summer of 1955. Halliday's departure came as a shock to the directors. The most successful manager at that time was perhaps unsettled by a pay dispute after the Dons won the title as a promised bonus payment was not forthcoming. Halliday was tempted to try his luck in England as he was clearly upset in the aftermath of the title success and Aberdeen not being put forward to represent Scotland in the new European Cup.

As the league-winning team began to break up it proved a difficult task for Shaw to keep the Dons challenging for honours. Patience was never a given for Aberdeen managers but at least Shaw had taken the team to the Scottish Cup Final. Would relegation be a price to pay for cup success? Shaw spoke to the *Press & Journal* ahead of the trip to Ibrox, 'We know what we need to do. It will not be difficult to focus the players on what we need to do, despite looking ahead to the final. It has been a difficult period and we have had a few injury problems which has not helped us get any consistency. Our recent form in the league has been poor but we can't afford to dwell too much on that. I trust the players to achieve a result.'

Shaw also had to contend with some player unrest. In an era where players could request to be transfer-listed, both Ken Brownlee and Dave Caldwell had asked to leave and those requests were granted. This was always a gamble on the players' part. With no freedom of contract and no agents, players were effectively on their own when it came to their career paths. With no offers coming in for either man it was business as usual at Pittodrie. They had only 18 appearances for the first team between them, but both played a crucial part in the victory over Rangers. Caldwell had reverted to his favoured right-back role for the semi-final win over Third Lanark and Brownlee came in to replace Ian Burns; both were in line for a starting place at Hampden for the final.

The league campaign came to a dramatic conclusion as Aberdeen held on for a famous win at Ibrox which concluded with the Rangers players being roundly jeered from the stands at full time. The mood changed when news came through that arch-rivals Celtic had come from behind to beat Hearts at Celtic Park. Effectively Celtic had handed the league title to Rangers.

The team that had capitulated in the closing weeks of the season turned everything around in a sensational result. Even after the Dons fell behind to a Brand goal in 24 minutes, they shocked Rangers with two Norman Davidson goals either side of half-time. Fred Martin, the Aberdeen and Scotland keeper, was winding down his career and his heroics were crucial in the success. Martin was speaking at a club event many years later when he recalled, 'It is not until after your career is finished that you can fully appreciate what was achieved. We had some great times in the '50s and many huge occasions but that day at Ibrox was more a relief than anything else. Relegation back then was not looked upon as such a disaster as it is these days. For one thing the financial downside was not as important. Ibrox was always a difficult place to go but in my time, we fared well there and that game in 1959 was one of our best down there. I recall having to make a few saves, but we defended well that day. When we equalised the Rangers players got nervous and when Norman [Davidson] popped up to score the winner we knew we were safe. There were no wild celebrations either, just relief.

'Looking back in the late '50s we did not keep up with other sides who were improving all the time. We always had a strong reserve team back then but some of the lads who came in when needed were perhaps not as good as we had hoped. From my own position I was coming to the end of my career as a keeper and never wanted to finish playing anywhere than Pittodrie. Mind you, I believe no less than nine keepers were given their chance in 1960 after I retired so I must have been doing something right!'

As results came in from around the grounds it emerged that Falkirk had been relegated along with a doomed Queen of the South, whose own demotion had been confirmed several weeks earlier. Aberdeen were hoping that Partick Thistle may have done them a favour but the side who defeated the Dons at Pittodrie in January capitulated at Dunfermline and went down 10-1.

In the *Evening Express* report it was suggested that there were wholesale changes needed in the Aberdeen squad. With 38 players on the books it was expected that there would be several moving on. What was not expected was that Shaw himself later decided to step down in November and revert to his previous position as the trainer. Tommy Pearson, in his regular *Daily Mail* column, was appointed as the new man in charge. It is hard to imagine a manager standing down and carrying on as effectively an assistant to the new man coming in, but Shaw thought he was far better suited to getting back to the training ground and working with the players.

The Dons' Ibrox hero was Norman Davidson, whose goals saved the club from certain relegation. Davidson was born in Kintore, just a few miles from Aberdeen, and 'Norrie' – as he was better known – went on to score 84 goals from his 146 first-team appearances after signing in February 1955. It was in the post-championship era that Davidson enjoyed the most successful part of his career. In season 1957/58 he scored 27 goals in a side that was struggling in mid-table. Even the arrival of Hugh Baird from Leeds did not deter Davidson and he continued to serve the Dons until his transfer request in 1960 after he was dropped from the first team. Norrie went on to win the League Cup with Hearts in 1962.

Of the five remaining Aberdeen players who had been a part of the championship side of 1955, all were in the twilight of their careers. Fred Martin, Dave Caldwell, Archie Glen, Bob Wishart and Jackie Hather were all soon to leave the club as the 1960s was to herald a new era at Pittodrie.

## Scottish League Division One 1959

|  | P | W | D | L | F | A | Pts |
|---|---|---|---|---|---|---|---|
| Rangers | 34 | 21 | 8 | 5 | 92 | 51 | 50 |
| Hearts | 34 | 21 | 6 | 7 | 92 | 51 | 48 |
| Motherwell | 34 | 18 | 8 | 8 | 83 | 50 | 44 |
| Dundee | 34 | 16 | 9 | 9 | 61 | 51 | 41 |
| Airdrie | 34 | 15 | 7 | 12 | 64 | 62 | 37 |
| Celtic | 34 | 14 | 8 | 12 | 70 | 53 | 36 |
| St Mirren | 34 | 14 | 7 | 13 | 71 | 74 | 35 |
| Kilmarnock | 34 | 13 | 8 | 13 | 58 | 51 | 34 |
| Partick Thistle | 34 | 14 | 6 | 14 | 59 | 66 | 34 |
| Hibernian | 34 | 13 | 6 | 15 | 68 | 70 | 32 |
| Third Lanark | 34 | 11 | 10 | 13 | 74 | 83 | 32 |
| Stirling Albion | 34 | 11 | 8 | 15 | 54 | 64 | 30 |
| Aberdeen | 34 | 12 | 5 | 17 | 63 | 66 | 29 |
| Raith Rovers | 34 | 10 | 9 | 15 | 60 | 70 | 29 |
| Clyde | 34 | 12 | 4 | 18 | 62 | 66 | 28 |
| Dunfermline | 34 | 10 | 8 | 16 | 68 | 87 | 28 |
| Falkirk | 34 | 10 | 7 | 17 | 58 | 79 | 27 |
| Queen of the South | 34 | 6 | 6 | 22 | 38 | 101 | 18 |

# Aberdeen 3 Hibernian 0

22 March 1967
Scottish Cup quarter-final replay
Pittodrie Park, Aberdeen
Attendance: 44,000

| Aberdeen | Hibernian |
|---|---|
| Bobby Clark | Thomson Allan |
| Jim Whyte | Bobby Duncan |
| Ally Shewan | Joe Davis |
| Frank Munro | Pat Stanton |
| Tom McMillan | John Madsen |
| Jens Petersen | Alan Cousin |
| Jimmy Wilson | Pat Quinn |
| Jim Storrie | Colin Stein |
| Ernie Winchester | Alex Scott |
| Harry Melrose | Peter Cormack |
| Dave Johnston | Eric Stevenson |
| *Manager:* Eddie Turnbull | *Sub:* Jim O'Rourke |
| | *Manager:* Bob Shankly |

'JUST WAIT until we get them back up the road to Pittodrie,' Eddie Turnbull exclaimed in the aftermath of the Scottish Cup quarter-final with Hibernian at Easter Road in March 1967. The Aberdeen boss and Hibernian legend, part of the much-heralded 'Famous Five' forward line of the 1950s, was clearly annoyed at the treatment his players received in a brutal cup tie. It took a late header from Jimmy 'Jinky' Smith to level the tie at 1-1 and force a replay at Pittodrie in midweek.

Turnbull was cutting his coaching teeth at Queen's Park when Aberdeen decided he would be the ideal fit for them. He recalled his first impressions when he took over at Pittodrie, 'There was an overwhelming lack of confidence about the place. Aberdeen had been ejected from the Scottish Cup by East Fife. They had also been humiliated 8-0 by Celtic at Parkhead. Avoiding relegation was my sole aim. On my arrival at Pittodrie I met the trainer who was none other than Dave Shaw who was once my captain at Easter Road. His assistant was a fine lad called Teddy Scott, who over the years played a great part in developing young players at Aberdeen. I discovered the training gear was a mess so that had to change. I also found the ground only had six footballs for the entire squad. I sent someone to Peter Craigmyle's excellent sports shop in King Street to buy new training gear and enough footballs so each player would have one. The trainers knew then that I was not messing about and that was important.'

Aberdeen reached the quarter-finals after some sensational wins over Dundee and St Johnstone. The opening tie saw the Dons crush Dundee 5-0 at Dens Park. Davie Robb made his debut against his hometown club as Aberdeen scored four in the second half. In the second round Aberdeen went nap again against St Johnstone at Pittodrie to set up the clash with Hibernian.

This was the season that the 'Turnbull Tornadoes' were scoring for fun. The swashbuckling style had the Aberdeen support turning up in their thousands; an estimated 12,000 travelled to Edinburgh for the first meeting and they rallied to the cause on the back of Turnbull's plea to get behind his players. An estimated crowd of 44,000 turned out to see Aberdeen go through after a whirlwind start that was enough to earn a place in the semi-finals against Dundee United. This was cup fever, very much like the halcyon days of the 1950s when Pittodrie housed crowds in excess of 40,000 on numerous occasions.

Turnbull had two problems before the replay as he recalled, 'Bobby Clark, our keeper, was due to sit an exam at Jordanhill College in Glasgow that day. This was going to give Bobby no chance of making the game in time. Clark was vital for me, I had total trust in him, and he was a calming influence in our side. Also, Ernie McGarr, my reserve keeper, was untried, and it would be a gamble throwing him into such a huge game. Fortunately, the course chief was Roy Small who was deeply involved with the SFA and the coaching at Largs. He arranged for Bobby to sit his exam an hour earlier and his father was waiting to drive him to Aberdeen so he could make it in time. Jim Smith was also unable to play so I turned to Ernie Winchester, no longer a first-choice player and looking for a transfer. I recalled him giving Hibernian defender John Madsen a torrid time of it in a previous game. I suggested to Ernie that Madsen would not take too kindly to being given the "treatment". Ernie duly obliged and he was all over them that night.' Winchester relished the physical side of the game and he was never content until he had made his mark on an opponent.

The Aberdeen tie made front-page news in the *Press & Journal* the morning after. 'Pittodrie Bonanza' was the headline with 'Gates Closed' and 'Thousands locked out' subheadings with many Aberdeen and Hibernian fans having been denied entry. The report continued, 'Miraculously no one was seriously injured when crush barriers at the south-east end of the ground collapsed under the weight of spectators. Red Cross volunteers had to give attention to 14 people throughout the game and five were taken to hospital. Charles Forbes, the Aberdeen director, declared after the game, "The stewards and police were overwhelmed for a time. We are sorry that so many were unable to see the game but with so many turning up late there was no guarantee of getting in."'

The kick-off was delayed, allowing those who had tickets entry into the ground. The cash turnstiles were overwhelmed. Ten minutes before the start of the game the police ordered the gates to be closed on safety concerns. It was clear that this fixture should have been made all-ticket but with only four days between the ties the club were never that keen to make ticket arrangements at such short notice. And while there was chaos inside the ground it was not much better outside and in the city. An AA spokesman reported that from 5pm the Ellon to Aberdeen road was blocked with more than 900 vehicles moving towards the city every hour.

As the teams took to the field it was discovered that fan favourite Jimmy Smith had failed a fitness test and his place had been taken by Ernie Winchester. The bustling centre-forward was a bit of an enigma in the red of Aberdeen. Winchester was a ferocious opponent and so often the saviour, but on the downside he was also liable for the odd glaring miss which often attracted derision from the terraces. He joined Aberdeen in 1959 and despite being top scorer in 1964 and 1966 he found himself out of favour with Turnbull. The manager based his whole team structure around teamwork and every player had their role and had to stick with it. Winchester would only play two more league games for the Dons before he moved to the USA and joined Chicago Spurs, and he was overlooked for the Scottish Cup semi-final as Smith had recovered from injury. Winchester returned to Scotland in 1968 and had short spells with Hearts and Arbroath before retiring in 1973.

Despite being on the transfer list, Winchester responded to his recall by opening the scoring in three minutes, almost as if to prove a point to his manager. When Jim Storrie added a second 12 minutes later the Dons were well on their way to an impressive victory.

The visitors were clearly rattled in what was as hostile an atmosphere as Pittodrie had seen for many years. It was a game-management exercise from the Dons; they did have to defend some Hibernian efforts late in the first half, but they were fully in control as they went in at half-time two goals ahead. Despite Pat Stanton and Colin Stein missing chances at the start of the second half, Aberdeen completed a marvellous night when Frank Munro scored at the far post as his header crept past Allan.

Munro was an inspired signing by Turnbull, who was never shy in approaching the board for transfer funds and he was determined to get Munro from rivals Dundee United. The Dons paid £10,000 in October 1966 for his services. Munro went on to become an integral part of the side and had the distinction of scoring Aberdeen's first goal in European competition. It was during the Dons' tour of the USA in the summer of 1967 that Munro caught the eye of Wolverhampton Wanderers manager Ronnie Allen, who went on to prise him away from Pittodrie in a £55,000 transfer in October 1968. That coincided with an alarming dip in Aberdeen's fortunes. Munro went on to score in both legs of Wolves' 1972 UEFA Cup semi-final against Ferencváros and was capped for Scotland on nine occasions between 1971 and 1975.

Munro later joined Celtic in 1977 and was Jock Stein's final signing.

Turnbull was delighted at full time as he spoke to the *Press & Journal*, 'We played as a team and what pleased me the most was the absence of Jimmy [Smith] did not affect our team spirit. I maintain that every player at Pittodrie is a cog in the machine and tonight's performance proves the argument. This is the spirit that brings success. We came through a tough game in Edinburgh and there was enough going on in that game that we felt went against us. We were determined to do something about that tonight.'

There was no doubt that the appointment of Eddie Turnbull in 1965 was a positive move from the Aberdeen board. Scottish football in 1967 was arguably enjoying its finest year. Celtic and Rangers reached the European Cup and European Cup Winners' Cup finals respectively; Dunfermline and Kilmarnock were doing well in the Inter-Cities Fairs Cup (later the UEFA Cup and now the Europa League), and the Scotland national team defeated world champions England at Wembley.

Aberdeen were progressing and although they went on to lose out to Celtic in the Scottish Cup Final, there were plenty of reasons to be optimistic. The defeat at Hampden had the consolation of confirming European football for Aberdeen for the first time. Turnbull's side were playing a positive brand of football that saw them score 113 goals from their 50 competitive outings. With a groundbreaking trip to the USA in the summer to come, these were exciting times at Pittodrie.

# Aberdeen 5 Wolverhampton Wanderers 6 *(in overtime)*

14 July 1967
USA Presidents Cup Final
Los Angeles Coliseum, USA
Attendance: 17,824

| Aberdeen (Washington Whips) | Wolverhampton Wanderers (LA Wolves) |
|---|---|
| Bobby Clark | Phil Parkes |
| Jim Whyte | Gerry Taylor |
| Ally Shewan | Bobby Thomson |
| Frank Munro | John Holsgrove |
| Tom McMillan | Dave Woodfield |
| Jens Petersen | Dave Burnside |
| Jim Storrie | Terry Wharton |
| Jimmy Smith | Ernie Hunt |
| Dave Johnston | Derek Dougan |
| Martin Buchan | Peter Knowles |
| Pat Wilson | Dave Wagstaffe |
| *Manager:* Eddie Turnbull | *Manager:* Ronnie Allen |

'ELEVEN GOALS, two hat-tricks, three penalties, one red and several punch ups … it was the greatest final ever played on American soil,' as claimed in *The Summer of 67*, an account of what was a remarkable period in Scottish football. Aberdeen had just lost the final of the Presidents Cup in 'overtime' as the Americans struggled to come to terms with 'soccer'.

For six long weeks over the summer the Dons, or Washington Whips as they were known for the duration, faced a hectic schedule of games. After finishing fourth in the league, reaching the Scottish Cup Final and the last four in the League Cup, Aberdeen were certainly improving. It was on 23 May that Aberdeen flew out to the United States to compete in what was a novel tournament. The American model was to invite 12 clubs from across the world. Each would embrace an adopted name and the clubs were split into two sections with the winner of each to meet in the final. Washington (Aberdeen) did not start well, going down 2-1 to Cleveland Stokers (Stoke City) in their opening game in the District of Columbia Stadium in Washington. After a narrow win over Scottish rivals Hibernian, the 'Whips' drew with Italian side Cagliari and defeated Cerro of

Uruguay both at their Washington base. The first of three clashes with Wolves ended in a 1-1 draw but the game was to be replayed after the Black Country team used three substitutes instead of the two permitted. That set the tone between the sides, which was to escalate in the final. Prior to that Aberdeen had defeated Wolves 3-0 in the replayed game in Washington to earn their place in the final.

Aberdeen had always relished coming up against English opposition. The cross-border rivalry may often seem to be more intense north of the border as the game has changed so much in the modern era, but in days gone by clashes against English sides were fiercely competitive.

In the build-up to the final, Wolves manager Ronnie Allen claimed, 'In meeting Aberdeen, the Washington representatives, we know we are up against a formidable foe in the championship game. In fact, they are the best side we have faced all season. The game will be far more interesting as we are playing a team from another country. They are also like how we play, more offensive, hard-tackling and aggressive.'

Allen was right on all counts. The first half was as bizarre as it was enthralling. With an American referee who had little or no experience officiating 'soccer' matches and English and Scottish opponents going at it from the start, that first period remains the most brutal Aberdeen have ever been involved in. Feuds from previous games were not forgotten. Ally Shewan, the Dons' left-back, was nicknamed the 'Iron Man' by the American hosts and commentators due to his combative style and heavy tackling. Shewan was as hard as they came, and he had a running battle with Wolves' Derek Dougan throughout. Jim Whyte was up against Dave Wagstaffe, the talented but flawed winger, and they were both involved in some horrendous clashes. On one occasion Wagstaffe committed such a brutal assault on Whyte that the defender chased his opponent across the perimeter track and up part of the terracing. The game was televised in the USA and the commentators were shocked at what was happening as mayhem broke out all over the pitch. In the first half alone, the Dons conceded 20 free kicks. Many more fouls went unpunished by the inexperienced referee.

In between the fouls and feuds there was some action. American observers predicted a tight game with few goals; so much for local soccer knowledge. After just three minutes Wolves went ahead through Knowles. Up until the final the Whips had only conceded 11 goals in 12 games. The extent and passion of Wolves' celebrations laid the belief that this match was not being taken seriously. They were up for it, for sure.

The fouling continued as Pat Wilson went for it in a clash with Thomson after he was thrown to the ground. Then Tom McMillan hauled back Dougan as he was through on goal. Jimmy Smith was always in the thick of it and with his renowned temperamental style he was soon involved. In between times some football was played, and Johnson brought out a great save from Parkes before Whyte stopped the flying Wagstaffe by almost ripping his shirt off. Then Jens Petersen came close with a long-range effort that Parkes did well to keep out. Aberdeen kept up the pressure and were rewarded when Smith scored an equaliser from inside the box with a clever finish before Parkes could close him down.

In previous games the poor quality and leniency of the refereeing had been highlighted, which in turn led to some outrageous fouls. After 32 minutes referee Giebner finally lost the plot or his patience when he sent off Smith. It later emerged that Wagstaffe came upfield and spat in Smith's face, which resulted in him being kicked by Jinky for his troubles. Giebner later declared that he was wrong to send Smith off.

That certainly changed the dynamic of the game, as Aberdeen had to play for more than an hour in energy-sapping heat with a man short.

The second half began with little or no foul play as football broke out. The goals began to come at regular intervals as the teams traded scores rather than blows. Aberdeen's play was inspired as they seemed to thrive on their disadvantage and the sublime Frank Munro orchestrated a move that ended with Jim Storrie putting the Whips 3-2 ahead. The North American public, and probably the rest of the world, had never seen anything to rival this. The loss of Smith was undoubtedly having its effect as the Whips struggled to keep their opponents out and a flurry of goals in the final eight minutes made for a dramatic finale. The game ended 4-4 after Munro levelled with a header in the last minute. With another 30 minutes to come there was more drama. It was hard to imagine that the Whips could muster the energy and determination to play for a further half an hour with only ten men against a team playing at home and equal to everything that Aberdeen could throw at them.

It was no surprise to see the Whips defend in extra time, conserving energy in what were difficult conditions. When Dougan scored late on to make it 5-4 it seemed that was the game decided. It certainly looked that way when Wolves were awarded a penalty after 119 minutes. Wagstaffe floated the ball past Bobby Clark and a goal looked certain until 'Iron Man' Shewan punched it over the bar. There were no dismissals for such trivial infringements in those days. With seconds left it looked all over, until Bobby Clark pulled off a fantastic save from Wharton's penalty. As the large clock ticked towards full time Aberdeen launched a final desperate attack and Whyte was impeded in the box. Going by what happened earlier it was tame; only an inexperienced referee would award a penalty under such circumstances. Step up Mr Giebner. Munro sent Parkes the wrong way to make it an astonishing Los Angeles Wolves 5 Washington Whips 5 at full time. The organisers were at a loss on what to do next. Replay? Share the trophy? There had to be an overall winner of the Presidents Cup so the game would be decided by 'sudden death'. The next team to score would win.

Six minutes into the overtime period, Wolves scored the winner as a fluke decided the final. A harmless-looking cross was left by McMillan and the ball hit Shewan before deflecting into the net. It was harsh on a brave Aberdeen side who had given everything but being down to ten men for so long took its toll.

Although the final was played in such brutal fashion it almost seemed ironic that both teams shared a lap of honour after the game. After the cup was presented, Ronnie Allen addressed the crowd, 'I think everyone in the stadium has seen one of the most fantastic games of football ever played and I think Aberdeen are as much responsible for this as my team. Aberdeen played hard, and they fought to the end.' The Wolves boss then led applause for the Aberdeen players who looked on at the presentation. Allen later praised the performance of Frank Munro and Jens Petersen and it was no surprise to see Wolves come in for Munro a year later.

The closing comments came from Jack Cook, the sponsor of LA Wolves, 'And when we decided to start soccer here in America, I was warned constantly that this is a dull game. Isn't it one of the most exciting games you've ever seen in your life [the crowd roars in agreement]? There isn't a writer in Hollywood, there never has been one, who could have written a script for the game tonight. Next year, the year after and all the years to come, we're going to be proudly privileged to bring you wonderful fans Major League Soccer here in Los Angeles, and thank you so much.'

Aberdeen played 14 games over two months in what was their close-season. Two weeks after returning from the States, the Dons welcomed Chelsea for a pre-season friendly on 2 August 1967 before the Scottish competitive fixtures commenced a week later. The Dons rounded their season off with a friendly at Nairn County on 29 April. In all they played 63 games in 1967/68.

## Aberdeen in the 1967 Presidents Cup

| Date | Result | Competition | Attendance |
|---|---|---|---|
| 26 May 1967 | Aberdeen 1 Stoke City 2 | ASL East | 9,403 |
| 31 May 1967 | Hibernian 1 Aberdeen 2 | ASL East | 12,000 |
| 4 June 1967 | Aberdeen 1 Cagliari 1 | ASL East | 6,125 |
| 7 June 1967 | Aberdeen 3 Cerro 0 | ASL East | 5,112 |
| 11 June 1967 | Glentoran 2 Aberdeen 2 | ASL East | 5,134 |
| 14 June 1967 | Stoke City 2 Aberdeen 2 | ASL East | 6,162 |
| 20 June 1967 | Aberdeen 1 Wolverhampton 1 | ASL East | 7,487 |
| 25 June 1967 | ADO Den Haag 1 Aberdeen 1 | ASL East | 4,657 |
| 28 June 1967 | Aberdeen 1 Sunderland 1 | ASL East | 8,709 |
| 1 July 1967 | Dundee United 0 Aberdeen 2 | ASL East | 6,839 |
| 4 July 1967 | Bangu 0 Aberdeen 1 | ASL East | 12,380 |
| 8 July 1967 | Aberdeen 1 Shamrock Rovers 2 | ASL East | 9,760 |
| 10 July 1967 | Aberdeen 3 Wolverhampton 0 | ASL East | 7,641 |
| 14 July 1967 | Wolverhampton 6 Aberdeen 5 | Presidents Cup Final | 17,824 |

# Aberdeen 10 KR Reykjavík 0

6 September 1967
European Cup Winners' Cup first round first leg
Pittodrie Park, Aberdeen
Attendance: 14,174

| Aberdeen | | KR Reykjavík |
|---|---|---|
| Bobby Clark | | Gudmundur Petursson |
| Jim Whyte | | Kristinn Jonsson |
| Ally Shewan | | Bjarni Felixson |
| Tom McMillan | | Pordur Jonsson |
| Jens Petersen | | Ellert Schram |
| Martin Buchan | | Ársæll Kjartansson |
| Jimmy Wilson | | Horour Markan |
| Frank Munro | | Gunnar Felixson |
| Jim Storrie | | Baldvin Baldvinsson |
| Jimmy Smith | | Eyleifur Hafsteinsson |
| Ian Taylor | | Sigurthor Jakobsson |
| *Manager:* Eddie Turnbull | | *Manager:* Sveinn Jonsson |

THE OLDEST club in Iceland were the Dons' first opponents in Europe when the sides were drawn in the opening round of the 1967/68 European Cup Winners' Cup. Aberdeen were in Texas of all places when they learned of the opponents on 5 July 1967 after the draw was made in Belgrade.

KR Reykjavík were founded in 1899 and were Icelandic champions on 19 occasions when they travelled to Pittodrie for the Dons' historic debut in the European arena. Reykjavík may have been 'kingpins' in Iceland but they were strictly amateur, captained by Ellert Schram, a 27-year-old Reykjavík lawyer. Their manager Sveinn Jonsson was a player for ten seasons and was in his first coaching job in charge of the side. Bjarni Felixson was the club secretary and doubled up as KR's left-back. To get an idea of how their amateur status worked the Icelandic players had to pay £4 to join the club and purchase their own kits.

KR arrived in Aberdeen for only their fourth appearance in European football. Jonsson declared in the *Press & Journal*, 'If there is one thing our games have taught us, it is how to be good losers. We will take the game seriously and we will do our best.'

Despite their poor record in Europe, KR had an impressive record at home; on top of their 19 league titles they were six-time winners of the national cup. They had also appeared in the European Cup, a feat not achieved at Pittodrie until 1980. The Reykjavík players went sightseeing around Aberdeen before training at the stadium the night before the game. The modern-day tourists, it would seem. For context they were listed in the *Press & Journal* along with their respective trades and professions, their side including a student, an airline pilot, electrician, carpenter, printer and salesman. The Icelandic season was also different to the Scottish league, starting in April and concluding in October with only six teams, three of which were based in the capital Reykjavík.

Aberdeen manager Eddie Turnbull was always careful in the build-up to matches, preparing well and knowing his opposition, but even he predicted his team would score a few goals, 'We know a bit about them and they are an amateur side which means we will be strong favourites. They do possess that unknown quantity so we will, as always, be respectful and get down to building up a lead to take to Iceland.' Turnbull's caution apart, he was certainly proven correct as Aberdeen went on to win the opening tie 10-0, the club's record score in European football. Frank Munro had the distinction of scoring Aberdeen's first goal in Europe and he went on to complete a hat-trick. Since then only Mark McGhee and Adam Rooney have achieved that feat.

The Dons had just come through a controversial League Cup tie on the Saturday beforehand, a heavy defeat at home to Celtic that was ruined by referee J.R.P. Gordon's decision to order the Glasgow team to retake a penalty, which caused mayhem on the field and on the terraces. The national press backed up the Dons' claims against the hapless Gordon. The *Daily Mail* stated, 'Referee Gordon was abysmally wrong and should have been able to realise this from the surprise from the Celtic players and the indignation of the Dons.' The club also had to contend with news from the SFA that both Jimmy Smith and Frank Munro were to be 'carpeted' by the authorities and face sanctions after being ordered off in the Dons' tour of the USA.

Reykjavík held out for 19 minutes but after that Aberdeen imposed themselves on the game and virtually scored at will in what was a one-sided encounter. Bobby Clark had one save to make in the whole 90 minutes, from Hafsteinsson in 82 minutes. Clark was entirely idle in a first half that was played entirely in the Reykjavík half. The goal avalanche came from Munro in 19, 53 and 62 minutes, Jimmy Smith in 32 and 78, Jim Storrie in 21 and 56, Tom McMillan in 44, Ian Taylor in 49 and Jens Petersen in 72.

Tom McMillan was certainly the unsung hero of the Aberdeen defence. While young Martin Buchan often attracted the attention of many, McMillan was a steady centre-half who was underrated during his Pittodrie career. It was in 1965 that Turnbull almost missed out on McMillan as he was about to board a plane, bound for a new life in Australia. McMillan immediately scrapped plans to emigrate and travelled north to join Aberdeen on a full-time contract. His form for Aberdeen saw him capped for Scotland at under-23 level on two occasions in 1966/67, both against Wales. In 1972 he was transferred to Falkirk in a £10,000 deal and spent 15 months at Brockville before moving to Inverness Thistle in 1973.

The *Press & Journal* reported, 'As a football contest last night's game bordered on the farcical. From the start it was a battle between the Aberdeen forwards and all-defensive Icelandic side. Aberdeen's ten-goal victory may well represent a record score.'

On that same evening a certain Alex Ferguson scored for the Scottish League against Ireland in Belfast in a 2-0 win that also came in for criticism despite the scoreline, while at Pittodrie, the 14,000 crowd were surprised to see Aberdeen reserve keeper Ernie McGarr listed as substitute against Reykjavík. Harry Melrose had originally been listed but European rules at that time meant that only a substitute keeper was allowed and not outfield players as had been the way in the Scottish League.

While the Icelandic players treated their trip to Scotland as a holiday there was no such luxury for the Aberdeen squad for the return and a first away leg in European football. Aberdeen prepared for their European away debut with an excellent 4-2 win over Dundee at Pittodrie as the league season opened, giving Dundee their first defeat in 25 games. Turnbull was professional in his approach as he spoke to the *Press & Journal* ahead of the return tie, 'We are not on holiday or going sightseeing. We are here to play football, and this is a game we want to win. My players have been told to score goals. It is important for us as we are now representing Scotland and we want this club to do well in Europe.'

There seemed to be little interest from the locals as it was announced entry to the ground was £1 for seating. Reykjavík coach Jonsson did not have his troubles to seek, 'Don't mention our arrival back in Reykjavík. We received a lot of criticism. Icelandic football in general is being heavily criticised because we lost 10-0 in Aberdeen and the Icelandic team lost 14-2 in Denmark. People are saying that the whole setup is wrong. There will never be professional football here, but our clubs must develop a more professional approach to the game. The whole question of our participating in European competitions will have to be considered by the club.'

The Municipal Stadium in Reykjavík belonged to the city and was shared by three clubs. The attendance record was 14,000 but it was reported that most Icelanders didn't finish work until 7pm and they were only expecting a small crowd for the Aberdeen game. The early kick-off was due to there being no floodlights at the ground.

Aberdeen completed the job in the Icelandic capital a week later with a 4-1 win that also brought them a rebuke from Turnbull, who was annoyed at the concession of an Hafsteinsson volley in the 74th minute after his team had built up a four-goal lead. Ever the perfectionist, Turnbull was frustrated as it had taken Aberdeen more than 40 minutes to open the scoring. It was difficult for the players to remain motivated, such was the low-key nature of the game. Turnbull handed a debut to youngster Jim Kirkland as he rested the experienced Dane Jens Petersen.

With the Icelandic season drawing to a close, it was very different to the setup in Scotland whereby winter football was an accepted period of the domestic game. Incredibly, when, it was considered that Aberdeen had played in the United States in the summer, the visit of Reykjavík was game 22 of the season for the Dons, still only in September.

That same day it was announced that Chris Anderson would be joining the board as a director. Anderson would go on to play a vital role off the field until his untimely passing in 1986. The club was putting the former Aberdeen and Arbroath player forward for election to the board ahead of the club AGM on 5 October. Anderson was to replace the late John Duncan, who passed away two months after resigning from the board in November 1966. Anderson previously joined the Dons from Mugiemoss in 1944 and was a first-team regular in the late 1940s and early '50s. Anderson was also selected for the Scottish League on one occasion. It was after a spell with Arbroath that Anderson retired to look after his business interests. He went on to become a finance director with the Robert Gordon Institute of Technology.

Anderson went on to become one of the best football administrators in the country. He was a great supporter of the new Premier League that came into being in 1975 and was also responsible for taking Alex Ferguson to Pittodrie in 1978. He was behind the development of Pittodrie to become the first all-seated stadium in Britain. He was awarded an OBE in 1981 and was inducted into the Aberdeen FC Hall of Fame as a founding member in 2003.

# Aberdeen 3 Celtic 1

11 April 1970
Scottish Cup Final
Hampden Park, Glasgow
Attendance: 108,464

| Aberdeen | Celtic |
|---|---|
| Bobby Clark | Evan Williams |
| Henning Boel | Dave Hay |
| George Murray | Tommy Gemmell |
| Jim Hermiston | Bobby Murdoch |
| Tom McMillan | Billy McNeill |
| Martin Buchan | Jim Brogan |
| Derek McKay | Jimmy Johnstone |
| Dave Robb | Willie Wallace |
| Jim Forrest | George Connelly |
| Joe Harper | Bobby Lennox |
| Arthur Graham | John Hughes |
| *Sub:* George Buchan | *Sub:* Bertie Auld |
| *Manager:* Eddie Turnbull | *Manager:* Jock Stein |

'A LOT of teams feared them, but we certainly didn't,' record goalscorer Joe Harper claimed some years later after Aberdeen had won the Scottish Cup in 1970. It was a triumph that rocked Scottish football to the core. The Dons were to finish a modest eighth in the league, a massive 22 points behind champions Celtic. It was a mismatch of huge proportions. Outside of Pittodrie they were given little hope. However, manager Eddie Turnbull had a tactical awareness that was not lost on Joe, 'Eddie made sure we had pace on the flanks with Derek McKay, Jim Forrest and Arthur Graham all in the starting line-up. He told me that we had to get in behind them to exploit their defence. Just sit in, he told me, and draw them out. It worked a treat. I remember the second goal when I turned Billy McNeill and sent a diagonal ball to Jim Forrest, who cut in and set up McKay. The third one was the same as I did Tommy Gemmell. As a young player it was the first time that I had been involved in anything tactical and it worked a treat.'

There was little indication leading up to the Dons' opening tie against Clyde that Hampden was on the horizon. Aberdeen had lost 3-2 to Morton at Greenock the week before and there was little sign that Turnbull had decided on his best 11; the defence was still unsettled with Ernie McGarr keeping Bobby Clark out of the side. Jim Kirkland and Jens Petersen were still in his plans although young Martin Buchan had emerged as a real find alongside centre-half Tom McMillan. The only constant in the team was up front where Harper, Forrest and Davie Robb were forming a lethal combination. It was that strength in attack that carried Aberdeen past Clyde with a convincing 4-0 victory, but whereas they had been slick in that match they looked sluggish in the next round against Clydebank. It was an almost surreal atmosphere as the tie was eventually played in midweek after an initial postponement. Strange too that Aberdeen turned out in a blue-and-white-striped kit, after a last-minute demand from the referee so that their red shirts would not clash with those of their visitors, with a diagonal red stripe on their shirts. It was also the first occasion that Buchan captained the side as he took over from Petersen; a clear indication that Turnbull had still not settled on his best starting 11. The Dons even had to endure incurring the wrath of the home support as they struggled to overcome part-time Clydebank in a narrow 2-1 win. There was little room for error and the supporters vented their fury at full time, while it was the part-time visitors who received all the plaudits.

By the time the next round came up it was a different set of circumstances for Aberdeen. While they received no credit for their performance against Clydebank, it was the exact opposite when they travelled to Falkirk for the quarter-final. Their ground at Brockville was at best described as 'spartan', a traditional old Scottish venue with an aged grandstand and open terraces. The build-up to the tie was thrown into chaos as a flu virus swept through the club, decimating players and staff. As matchday rapidly approached the situation did not improve, hastening Turnbull to request a postponement from the SFA. Joe Harper recalled the events, 'Most of the squad was hit by flu and I remember Eddie trying to get the game against Falkirk postponed. But to be honest Eddie was also chancing his luck as we had a few injuries as well. We just had to get on with it.' It was against that adversity that the Dons showed a tough side to their nature as they battled their way through to the last four with a 1-0 triumph.

Conditions were dreadful; the Brockville pitch resembled a mud heap. While the SFA did the club few favours by insisting that the game proceed, it opened the door for the unknown Derek McKay to come into the side.

McKay had been snapped up by Turnbull in 1969 on a free transfer from Dundee, where he only managed 12 first-team appearances in three years. It was a risk from Turnbull but given his acumen in the transfer market, few would have argued against his judgement. It took a bout of illness but the legend that was to become 'Cup-tie McKay' was born. McKay only played in 13 league games without scoring but in three Scottish Cup ties he netted four of the most important goals in club history.

It was McKay who scrambled a second-half winner to send Aberdeen through to a semi-final with Kilmarnock. Muirton Park was the home of St Johnstone and the choice of venue delighted Aberdeen. For once it was a neutral ground in the true sense and the indications were that Aberdeen would be backed in huge numbers. The decision to stage the game in Perth was clearly a fair one but there were still complaints from the Kilmarnock club and west coast observers. There were almost 18,000 Aberdeen supporters at the old ground, and it was McKay who once again popped up with the only goal of the game to send Aberdeen through to the final. This was no stylish performance from the Dons; far from it, as they had to withstand a second-half barrage from Kilmarnock, who peppered their defence at every opportunity. That experience would surely have benefited the Dons as they would expect more of the same in the final. As expected, Celtic eased past Dundee in the other semi-final.

McKay was looking forward to the big day, 'We have improved with each game and I have a feeling we will hit peak form on Saturday. After our win at Parkhead a couple of weeks ago Celtic will be worried.' Jim Forrest had plenty of big-game experience with Rangers and he already had a Scottish Cup winners' medal, 'We are one of the best teams in Scotland, but there have been occasions this season when the breaks have gone against us. We have no cause to worry about Celtic. We showed that we can beat them in Glasgow, and I am sure we will do it again at Hampden.'

Aberdeen also had the one foreign import on show. Henning Boel, the Danish defender who was looking forward to his first appearance at Hampden, said: 'It will be a great day for me. Hampden is well known throughout the football world and I hope I am on the winning side.'

Elsewhere on the day of the final a new mission to the moon was launched. Apollo 13 lifted off for what was expected to be another routine trip, but an explosion in the service module crippled the spacecraft and left the crew's lives hanging by a thread as the world looked on in horror. The moon landing had to be abandoned and after 90 hours of uncertainty the astronauts, packed into the cramped space of the undamaged lunar module for most of that time, successfully returned to Earth and only returned to the main spacecraft for the final re-entry.

James Forbes, the erstwhile reporter for the *Evening Express*, claimed ahead of the final, 'Celtic's great form over the past means they are entitled to be favourites. That was until 8.29pm on the evening of 25 March 1970. That was the moment 17-year-old Arthur Graham, playing in his first full First Division match, cut inside full-back Jim Craig and laid the ball on for George Murray to send a fierce shot past Evan Williams. Another 16 minutes had gone when Graham made his own scoring contribution to a result that put Celtic league celebrations on hold.'

It was a clever move by Turnbull as he played record signing Steve Murray, who was ineligible for the final due to being cup-tied having appeared for Dundee, and the line-up that night suggested the cup final team would be different. Celtic, on the other hand, put out the side that would certainly play at Hampden. Forbes concluded, 'It would be foolish to pretend it will be easy but I think Aberdeen can gain a long-overdue cup success. Their supporters have had to wait long enough and there is no pleasure in being runners-up.'

The Dons were no strangers to Hampden having been there three years earlier, losing to Celtic. The circumstances were similar with the Parkhead side blazing a trail in the European Cup. In 1967 Aberdeen had to play Celtic without Eddie Turnbull as he was confined to his sick bed. It was a more confident Dons side that was to face Celtic on 11 April 1970 as Bobby Clark recalled, 'There was no question we thought we could win. It was a strange run, but we were confident and had great spirit. We had beaten Celtic a couple of weeks before at Celtic Park in the league. They were too arrogant for their own good. We saw crates of champagne outside their changing room. If they defeated us, they would wrap up the league; we took exception to that, obviously. George Murray told the boss, who was livid; no need for a team talk before either. That victory gave us real belief. As for the final itself, Eddie put Joe Harper into the midfield along with Jim Hermiston and Dave Robb. That gave us three against their two: Bertie Auld and Bobby Murdoch.'

Joe Harper opened the scoring through a penalty disputed by half of the Celtic team, who surrounded referee Davidson. Joe recalled the long delay as the Celtic players hounded the official, 'I remember the Celtic players tried to keep the ball while all the arguments went on but I managed to get it back after Tommy Gemmell had kicked it off the spot and I started to play keepy-up with it. It might have looked arrogant, but I was just trying to compose myself really. Even Evan Williams walked off his line to try and unsettle me. The delay went on for almost eight minutes. When I eventually got down to taking the penalty, I always believed in placing the ball. It all worked out perfectly. When the moment came I took my normal run-up, feigned to play it one way then hit the ball to Williams's right. It was the best penalty I had ever taken. Even if Evan had gone the right way he was never stopping it as it went right at the post.'

Aberdeen went on to win 3-1 with 'Cup-tie McKay' scoring the two late goals that brought the silverware back to Pittodrie. Celtic did put the Aberdeen defence under a lot of pressure in the second half as expected. Bobby Lennox missed their best opportunity and when McKay raced upfield to score the first of his two goals the cup was going north. Lennox did eventually pull one back with minutes left but McKay went up the park again to score a sensational third. Aberdeen were the only side to score three goals against Celtic that season. Celtic may have been invincible in Europe, but they were out-thought and out-fought by an Aberdeen side who had a great confidence and belief in themselves. It was a tactical masterclass from

Turnbull who recalled, 'I decided I would trust our defence and hit them on the break. I told Joe [Harper] to move around and try to draw Billy McNeill out of defence to make room for Jim Forrest and our wingers. It was also important to keep the ball on the deck as Celtic had the advantage in the air. Sure enough, Celtic started fast and furious as I predicted, but our defence held out well.'

McKay's first goal in the final was a club landmark as it was the Dons' 500th in the Scottish Cup.

The victorious Aberdeen party retired to their usual Gleneagles Hotel which the club used prior to and after big cup finals. It was a memorable day for young Arthur Graham. 'Bumper', as he became known, was only 17 and had signed for Aberdeen six weeks before the final. His inclusion in the starting 11 proved inspired by Turnbull. The boss recalled a marvellous gesture by young Graham, 'During the evening young Arthur Graham went over to our scout Bobby Calder and handed over his winners' medal, "I want you to have this Mr Calder." Bobby was deeply moved by the gesture as was I. But he insisted that Arthur keep his medal, though he was sure that it would not be the last won by this remarkable lad.'

The welcome home for the players was one of the most passionate ever seen in the city as a reported 100,000 lined the route home. Harper remembered, 'We had all heard about the stories from 1947. We got a taster in Stonehaven; it took us half an hour to get through there. The place was mobbed. It started at Holburn Street as we came down and the crowds increased. Eventually as we got to the top of Union Street the bus was swaying. It was quite amazing. It was a great day and I consider it as one of the best moments in my life.'

Aberdeen director Charles Forbes was ecstatic, 'In 1937 I was with the Dons when they fought their way to the Scottish Cup final against Celtic. Since then I have witnessed many sporting encounters with the result in doubt until the final whistle. Never have I experienced anything like that storybook ending to the 1970 final. I am sure my fellow directors will echo my sentiments when I say well done to the Dons and manager Eddie Turnbull, the thousands of Dons supporters who shared in this magnificent victory. Hopefully there are many more to come.'

Turnbull remembered, 'As we made our way down Union Street the scenes were incredible. The Lord Provost of the city was Robert Lennox, the uncle of the famous singer Annie Lennox. He greeted us at the Town House on the balcony. It was 12 April, my 47th birthday, as announced by the Provost. To have thousands wish you "Happy Birthday" was quite special.'

# Celtic 0 Aberdeen 1

12 December 1970
Scottish League Division One
Celtic Park, Glasgow
Attendance: 63,000

| Aberdeen | Celtic |
|---|---|
| Bobby Clark | John Fallon |
| Jim Hermiston | Jim Craig |
| George Murray | Tommy Gemmell |
| Steve Murray | Bobby Murdoch |
| Tom McMillan | Billy McNeill |
| Martin Buchan | Jim Brogan |
| Ian Taylor | Jimmy Johnstone |
| Dave Robb | George Connelly |
| Jim Forrest | Lou Macari |
| Joe Harper | Davie Hay |
| Arthur Graham | John Hughes |
| *Sub:* Alec Willoughby | *Sub:* Harry Hood |
| *Manager:* Eddie Turnbull | *Manager:* Jock Stein |

THE DECISION to appoint Eddie Turnbull as Aberdeen manager in March 1965 proved to be an astute move from the board. A rookie with Queen's Park, many observers thought it was a huge risk. Five years on and Turnbull had proved to be one of the most promising coaches in the game. His transformation of Aberdeen was complete in 1970 as the Scottish Cup was won and subsequent league challenge in 1970/71 saw the club back at the summit of Scottish football. It was in stark contrast to the sides that were being knocked out of the domestic cups by lower-league opponents in the early 1960s which did for former manager Tommy Pearson.

By 1970 the Dons added some consistency to what was one of the best defensive combinations in the country. A genuine challenge for the league emerged for the first time in 15 years and the visit to Celtic in December was already being billed as 'the game of the season' at Parkhead. Aberdeen went to Glasgow one point behind Celtic at the top of the league. Both sides had played 15 matches and lost only once.

With the form Aberdeen were in, this match could not come quickly enough and the game of the day in Britain attracted a massive 63,000 crowd to Celtic Park. This would be a true test for Aberdeen, who had shown great defensive resilience. They went into the Parkhead clash after winning nine in a row and not conceding in six. Turnbull remained confident, 'Our form has been as good as I could have expected. We sorted out some defensive issues from the start of the season and are looking more like the side I want. Organisation in defence is key to what we hope to achieve. I have asked a lot from Martin [Buchan] who is a young skipper with a huge responsibility in the side. I gave him the captaincy because I believe he has all the attributes to become a great international of the future.'

The league table ahead of the clash at Parkhead confirmed it was a battle between Aberdeen and Celtic for the championship:

|          | P  | W  | D | L | F  | A  | Pts |
|----------|----|----|---|---|----|----|-----|
| Celtic   | 15 | 13 | 1 | 1 | 37 | 6  | 27  |
| Aberdeen | 15 | 12 | 2 | 1 | 36 | 7  | 26  |
| Rangers  | 15 | 8  | 3 | 4 | 29 | 12 | 19  |

The build-up in the press suggested that Aberdeen were not well enough equipped to withstand a Celtic onslaught on their home ground, but such was the dogged determination of the Dons back then they were unfazed; after all, their recent record against Celtic was impeccable. They were the only side to have the 'Indian sign' over Celtic back then and the ring of confidence that the Dons showed in the white-hot atmosphere was inspiring. Aberdeen were also going for a third win in a row against that year's European Cup finalists and reigning league champions.

The *Press & Journal* set the scene, 'The Pittodrie side have registered nine successive wins. Since the Scottish Cup success, they have grown in confidence, and every player has slotted into a pattern. The moment now appears opportune for the Dons to challenge the champions. There is a feeling in some Celtic quarters that they are not as strong as they were 18 months ago.'

Aberdeen keeper Bobby Clark was enjoying his run of not conceding and he was relishing the trip to Glasgow, 'This is a game we would love to win, but we are not treating it differently from any other game. We may have harder games to come after this. I can't really take much credit for keeping my goal intact for so long. The defence are playing well, and we also rely on our front players coming back to help, yet when we break everyone attacks apart from Martin Buchan. This game means a lot but to win the league we must be consistent. At the moment this Aberdeen team are the best in Scotland and among the best in Britain.'

That confidence was backed up by young captain Martin Buchan who spoke to the *Press & Journal* ahead of the game, 'We have played seven matches against top-class continental opposition since the pre-season tour. It was then that we worked on our defensive system and our confidence has grown since then.' That system was based on Buchan being utilised in a sweeper role, first seen in Europe and taken on by Aberdeen. It was a setup that infuriated opposing fans, more so when the Dons were away from home. While the great Arsenal side of the 1990s lay claim to their famed back line, it was perfected by that Aberdeen defence of 1970. The offside trap as so commonly referred to in the press may have upset opposing fans but it worked well for the Dons.

Celtic manager Jock Stein was impressed by the Aberdeen efforts, 'We welcome the challenge from the north-east. Aberdeen have been the one side that has caused us problems over the last year or so. The fact that they are right there beside us in the table is no fluke. We know we will have to be at our best against the Dons. This game will not decide the title, but it will be vital for both sides. We are defending our title and will battle to the end.'

In a first half of few chances as both sides cancelled each other out, Aberdeen were content in sitting in deep as they had full confidence in their ability to keep the Celtic forwards at bay. Led by Buchan, the defence was closing the space for the eager Celtic forwards, much to the frustration of the home support. With Aberdeen keeping Celtic out, the one question that remained was whether they were good enough to snatch a goal and put down a real marker for the season. They answered that in style after 53 minutes as the winner came right from the training ground. Jim Hermiston took a long throw on the left and Davie Robb headed the ball on for

Joe Harper to ghost past a static Billy McNeill to head past Celtic keeper Fallon. You could hear a pin drop in the huge crowd as the Dons shocked their hosts.

The final 30 minutes saw the home side lay siege to the Dons' goal but they were met by a resilient defence with Clark and Buchan outstanding. Full time was met with silence from the big crowd and no real over-the-top celebrations from the Aberdeen players, just a satisfaction of job done as they were now clear of Celtic at the top of the league. Stein was dignified in defeat, 'We knew that the challenge from Aberdeen this season was a real one and they showed that today. It will make for a tremendous battle between us for the rest of the season. Aberdeen have the character required to go the distance, so we know we have a real fight on our hands this season.'

Turnbull told the *Press & Journal*, 'We are probably the only team in Scotland that could have beaten Celtic today. I thought we were tremendous, and we were the better team. There is a long way to go. Now that we are top every game becomes that bit more difficult. I am happy with the way the team is playing. There is an abundance of confidence and courage in the ranks.'

Harper's goal put him top of the scoring charts with 20 goals from 16 games – 'Goal a game Joey' was surpassing his lofty expectations.

The Parkhead victory was not the only Aberdeen success over Celtic that day. Back in the 1970s when matches were almost always played on a Saturday with a 3pm kick-off, it was normal for the respective 'A' or reserve teams to play an alternate fixture. At Pittodrie it was the turn of Aberdeen 'A' to defeat Celtic 1-0, which took the Young Dons to the top of the Reserve League. A crowd of 3,000 were delighted to see Willie Young score the winner in 26 minutes. George Buchan and Derek McKay showed up well for the Dons as did new signing Sandy Clelland, who did well to stop Celtic's Paul Wilson. There was as much interest in the stands as there was watching the reserves in action. Transistor radios were a must back then and as news came through that Aberdeen had taken the lead in Glasgow there were loud cheers in the Main Stand.

Such was the gulf between Aberdeen, Celtic and the rest, the two-horse race for the championship was going the distance. Most observers had pencilled in 17 April 1971, when the Dons would welcome Celtic in the penultimate game of the season, as the decider for the title. By that time there had been a disaster at Pittodrie Stadium. On the morning of 6 February 1971, it was discovered that the Main Stand was on fire. The damage was total. When chairman Dick Donald surveyed the scene in the early hours of the morning he was visibly upset, 'We will get engineers to survey the damage but we shall get this sorted and get the club back to some kind of normality.'

Easier said than done. The damage was far worse than first thought. Gone were the administration areas, offices, gymnasium and dressing rooms. Priceless club memorabilia was also destroyed. As the players gathered at the ground ahead of their trip to Dunfermline that day the kits and equipment for the game had been destroyed. During the height of the fire, the Scottish Cup had to be rescued by the firemen, being passed out of a broken window as flames were being kept under control.

There was little doubt the fire ripped the heart out of the club. The week before the disaster Aberdeen were sitting proudly at the top of the league but a sad weekend was compounded when they went down 1-0 at Dunfermline, a team at the bottom of the table. Subsequent home games were played with the sight of an open corner to the north-east and twisted girders. The players had to get changed in the police waiting area with a makeshift curtain separating the teams as they prepared for matches. Joe Harper recalled the surreal surroundings, 'There was no doubt the damage caused to the ground influenced the team. Everything seemed to be on hold. With no facilities, training was impossible and the preparation for games was nothing like we were used to. When we played Celtic in that deciding game, we could hear everything that Celtic boss Jock Stein was saying. It was a strange experience. Before we went out all I could hear was the police commander telling his men about information on a group of Glasgow pickpockets in the area.'

It is impossible to determine that had the fire been avoided (it was later confirmed a discarded cigarette caused the blaze), would the Dons have gone on to win the title? The league records before and after make interesting reading. Prior to the fire, Aberdeen had won

19 of their 23 matches with two draws and two defeats, scoring 53 goals and conceding ten. After the fire they won five and drew four of 11, losing two, with 15 goals scored and eight conceded.

*Joe Harper*

# Aberdeen 1 Juventus 1

17 November 1971
UEFA Cup second round second leg
Pittodrie Stadium, Aberdeen
Attendance: 29,500

| **Aberdeen** | **Juventus** |
|---|---|
| Bobby Clark | Pietro Carmignani |
| Jim Hermiston | Luciano Spinosi |
| George Murray | Giampietro Marchetti |
| Steve Murray | Giuseppe Furino |
| Willie Young | Francesco Morini |
| Martin Buchan | Sandro Salvadore |
| Jim Forrest | Helmut Haller |
| Dave Robb | Franco Causio |
| Joe Harper | Pietro Anastasi |
| Alec Willoughby | Fabio Capello |
| Arthur Graham | Roberto Bettega |
| *Sub:* Ian Taylor | *Manager:* Čestmír Vycpálek |
| *Manager:* Jim Bonthrone | |

IT IS not often that the most expensively assembled team in the world comes calling to play in competitive action but back in 1971, Aberdeen drew a plum tie when they came out of the hat against Italian giants Juventus in the new UEFA Cup, which replaced the Inter-Cities Fairs Cup.

Aberdeen had defeated European debutants Celta Vigo in the first round. The 2-0 success in Vigo remains one the club's most outstanding victories on foreign soil. Aberdeen had defended well and hit the Spaniards with two second-half goals from Joe Harper and Jim Forrest, the latter direct from a corner kick. A tough return at Pittodrie was decided by a sensational goal from Harper in what was a bruising tie.

The second round was the first time Aberdeen came up against Italian opponents in Europe. The draw was made in Belgrade and Aberdeen were happy to learn they would play the first leg in Turin. However, there was an issue when the draw also paired Turin side Torino with Austria Vienna at home in the European Cup Winners' Cup on the same evening. UEFA stepped in and ordered the first leg of Aberdeen's tie to be switched to Pittodrie. The Dons lodged a protest, and everything seemed to be heading for a resolution when UEFA ruled that the first game would be played in Italy if the clubs could agree on a new date for the fixture. Aberdeen gave Juventus three different options, but they were all turned down by the Italians as unsuitable. It was clear that they were hoping UEFA would go back to their original ruling to switch the first game to Scotland. Aberdeen then approached the SFA and with their help UEFA finally ruled the tie would be played in Turin on 27 October. The arguments over the venue dates strained relations between the clubs and when Aberdeen arrived in Turn and found no Juventus officials there to greet them, things were difficult to say the least. It was not until the day of the game that Juventus began to warm to their Scottish visitors with an arranged luncheon for the club's officials.

The Stadio Communale was a huge, imposing arena and for Aberdeen this was as tough as it got. Juventus were the most expensive side in world football following a year in which they had to settle for a UEFA Cup place. In their ranks was Pietro Anastasi, the world's most expensive player, who had been signed in a £440,000 deal from Varese. The Italian international was a proven scorer and regularly on the mark in the tough domestic league.

Juventus signalled their intent by taking the lead after only five minutes with a superb goal from Anastasi that set Aberdeen back on their heels. The forward ghosted past Willie Young before sending a fierce shot that swerved past Bobby Clark. The goalkeeper recalled, 'The ball swerved fantastically in mid-flight and ended up in the right-hand side corner. I think the Italian footballs were much lighter than what we were used to. Such deviations of the ball when struck were more common over there.'

Aberdeen were under constant pressure throughout a first half that was arguably their toughest on foreign soil, and they were relieved to go in at the break only one goal down. Inexperienced centre-half Young was given a torrid time by Bettega and Anastasi. Aberdeen began the second half more composed and when George Murray brought out a great save from Carmignani, they remained in the tie. However, after 55 minutes good fortune allowed a Capello free kick to deflect off Murray to give Clark no chance and made

Aberdeen's task an almost impossible one. Young was then spared further punishment as he was losing his temper and to save him being sent off he was withdrawn to be replaced by Ian Taylor. Anastasi had the ball in the net again late on, but his effort was ruled offside. On reflection Aberdeen were fortunate to escape with just the two-goal deficit and it was a harsh lesson for the Dons and manager Jim Bonthrone. Juventus at that time were one of the best sides on the planet, on their way to another Italian league title.

The Scottish press gave their view. The *Evening Express* declared, 'Aberdeen lost two bad goals but to their credit they never gave up. There is no doubt Aberdeen have a huge task. Juventus can really play.' *The Scotsman* lavished praise on the Italians, 'Individually I would rate Juventus as skilful a team as I have seen anywhere in the world, but Italian footballers are the world's worst travellers and Aberdeen still have a chance at Pittodrie.'

There was great excitement ahead of the return leg, although any expectations of Aberdeen getting back into the tie were low. Bonthrone was still optimistic, 'We face a huge task but it's not an impossible one. We know how good the Italians are but our record at Pittodrie stands up against any side so we will see how it goes. We know that they are dangerous in forward areas so we will need to be at our best to have any chance. Whatever happens Juventus will know they have been in a game.'

The Juventus squad settled into their stay at the Commodore Hotel in Stonehaven and their Czechoslovakian coach Čestmír Vycpálek told the *Press & Journal*, 'We will not defend what we have. I feel we will need to score at least once. Aberdeen will be a different team on their own pitch. We have negotiated plenty of games like this before, so we know what to expect. Aberdeen are a very good side and we know how formidable they are in Scotland.' The Commodore Hotel was a popular venue for visiting European sides as it was away from the city and only 15 miles south on the east coast at Stonehaven, a well-known holiday spot in the north-east. The hotel was later demolished and is now residential property.

Pittodrie was covered with light snowfall before kick-off. As anticipated by the Aberdeen management team the Italians sat in and defended deep in their own half. With almost 30,000 in Pittodrie giving the Dons superb backing they attacked Juventus at every opportunity. This was a classic, traditional European fixture with the home side throwing everything at the visitors.

Aberdeen were effectively out of the tie when Anastasi scored after a break caught them out in 50 minutes; that goal stunned Pittodrie but the Dons remained focused on getting something from the night. That eventually arrived in 77 minutes when Harper at last escaped his markers to head past Carmignani. It was no more than Aberdeen deserved. They had stuck to their task and were at last rewarded with a 1-1 draw that made sure they remained undefeated at home in European competition. Juventus's defending was almost all in their own third of the pitch. Italian football was renowned for resolute defending and tendency for dirty tricks.

Harper had taken the 'treatment' for 90 minutes and despite being battered and bruised he gave the Juventus defenders a tough evening, 'Their defenders got up to all kind of stuff; kicking, nipping and all that. They were a tough lot and very experienced, but we got through them eventually. We gave them a real fright and we played as well as we could have that night. They were a class side with a nasty streak in them and it was not something we were used to. Looking back, they were a typical Italian side of the time, renowned for their off-the-ball tricks.'

New Scotland manager Tommy Docherty was very impressed with Aberdeen as he told the *Press & Journal*, 'This was the first time I had seen Aberdeen play as a team since I was here with Chelsea in 1967. I have seen Juventus twice recently and they are the best side in Europe now. It was no shame on Aberdeen to go out to such a great team. I thought the crowd were terrific.' Bonthrone was proud of his players, 'I thought they were magnificent. To keep a side as good as Juventus under pressure like that was tremendous. We were unlucky not to score in the first half. Our equalising goal did not come quick enough. I thought we were unlucky not to at least win tonight.'

Vycpálek was delighted to take his side through, 'It was a very good and even match. We expected the Scots to come at us, so we had to be clever in defence. When we scored, I knew we had enough to see us through. Aberdeen played well, better than I expected. We were very good in the first game in Turin in what was one of our best games of the season. We did not expect Aberdeen to be so positive in Scotland. They are a better side than most in Italy thought.'

Aberdeen's European adventure was over for another season, but they would not often come up against such tough opposition. Among the Pittodrie crowd was former Dunfermline keeper Bent Martin, who was then with Rapid Vienna – due to meet the winners of this tie. He was not optimistic of his team's chances against Juventus in the third round. Aberdeen were disappointed that they had not progressed past the second round in Europe at the fourth time of asking, while Juventus joined Standard Liege, Real Zaragoza and Honvéd as the strong sides the Dons had failed to get the better of.

Dave Robb told the *Evening Express* in 2002 as he recalled the Juventus clash, 'It was one of the highlights of my career. Our manager Jim Bonthrone did not have much by way of tactics that night. How often was I going to come up against a world-class player like Anastasi? Juventus were the best side around at that time, but they did like to nip, bite, pull, push and shove you. But I gave as good as I got. After Anastasi scored to make it 3-0 [on aggregate], we were facing an impossible task, so I made the most of it. Looking back, Anastasi was a great player. We could not get near him; he was a special player. For Aberdeen to come back and get a draw against them was a fantastic result. It was a great learning experience for us to come up against Juventus. I enjoyed all the European games I played in. Those games were special.'

Aberdeen had the habit of coming up against tournament favourites in the early rounds of Europe. In 1967 Standard Liege were knocked out by Milan in the quarter-finals after a third game. The Italians went on to win the trophy that season. A year later Zaragoza were knocked out by eventual winners Newcastle United. Manchester City eliminated Hungarians Honvéd, who had beaten Aberdeen on penalties in 1970.

# Aberdeen 3 Hibernian 0

24 April 1976
Scottish Premier Division
Pittodrie Stadium, Aberdeen
Attendance: 11,234

| Aberdeen | Hibernian |
|---|---|
| Bobby Clark | Mike McDonald |
| Ian Hair | Bobby Smith |
| Chic McLelland | Eric Schaedler |
| Joe Smith | Pat Stanton |
| Willie Garner | Derek Spalding |
| Willie Miller | Jim Blackley |
| Dave Robb | Willie Murray |
| Billy Williamson | Lindsay Muir |
| Drew Jarvie | Alex McGhee |
| Ian Fleming | Ally McLeod |
| Walker McCall | Arthur Duncan |
| *Sub:* Jocky Scott | *Sub:* Willie Paterson |
| *Manager:* Ally MacLeod | *Manager:* Eddie Turnbull |

SEASON 1974/75 was a watershed moment in Scottish football history. After years of discussion and debate the member clubs finally agreed to dispense with the two-league setup which had been in place since the war and form three new divisions, with the 'elite' top ten clubs forming the Premier League. It was a bold move coming on the back of apathy prevailing in the accepted 18-team top division that had become outdated. The main argument was that far too many sides were simply existing and the general belief that they were relying on revenue from playing against the bigger-city clubs. There was a trend in attendance figures, in that if a side was knocked out of the Scottish Cup in the early rounds and were outside of European qualification and free from relegation, their crowds dipped at an alarming rate.

It was decided that the final league placings in 1974/75 would shape the new three divisions. From an Aberdeen perspective finishing in the top ten was a straightforward task given that they had not finished below there since 1968/69.

For those in favour of change, the Dons' penultimate home game of 1974/75 provided a compelling case. With Aberdeen settled in fifth and outside of European qualification, visitors Clyde were well away from a top-ten finish and were looking at a position in the new First Division. A meagre crowd of only 3,300 turned out at Pittodrie in wretched conditions in what was the classic meaningless game that those supporting change wanted to see the back of.

What the authorities did not get right was the high casualty rate from the new top division. With two sides being automatically relegated it was like the old setup. What was to follow was cut-throat; clubs were mindful of the financial implications of being demoted and survival was the key. Managers and coaches were clear that it was unlikely younger players would be thrown into the first team under such circumstances. It all made for a chaotic first season of the Premier League.

For Aberdeen it was certainly a memorable time, but not for all the right reasons. Manager Jim Bonthrone left in September after a series of poor results. Bonthrone was 'too nice' for management; a harsh assessment on the former East Fife player who thrived as a coach under Eddie Turnbull. Nevertheless, discipline within the squad was an issue. One on-field incident suggested all was not well at Pittodrie. In a Premier League game against Dundee United on 13 September, centre-half Willie Young was substituted as the Dons were struggling after going behind. He took off his shirt and threw it towards the dugout before walking off towards the dressing room. Young would never play for the first team again and joined Tottenham some weeks later.

Aberdeen turned to Ally MacLeod, the Ayr United manager who was never shy at coming forward, and his enthusiasm was exactly what they required at the time. There had been a malaise around Pittodrie for the past couple of seasons but it was soon to be challenged by the new boss. By his own admission MacLeod made an error after taking over in November 1975. In his first few matches he saw his new charges beat Rangers and Celtic in the same week and he began to look forward to rebuilding the side with a view to making an impact the following season. MacLeod, clearly exuberant at those results, boldly claimed that his team were now looking at winning the league. Even the most optimistic of Aberdeen fans was not buying into that, but such was MacLeod's way.

What MacLeod did not allow for was an alarming dip in form that saw Aberdeen slip down the league. In the new setup a brief loss of form could bring panic, and as the winter months passed the Dons found themselves in a three-way battle for survival. St Johnstone were rooted at the foot of the table and were consigned to certain relegation by February. It was the Dons' Tayside rivals who were in the mix; both Dundee and Dundee United would battle it out with Aberdeen to stay in the new Premier League, although Hearts and Ayr United were still not clear of trouble.

MacLeod was told when he was appointed by chairman Dick Donald that he had more than £100,000 to spend on strengthening the team. MacLeod told Donald to hold on to that cash while he assessed the squad. By his own admission that was a mistake. As Aberdeen were due to face Hibernian at Pittodrie for the final game of the season, MacLeod looked up in the stands and there was Joe Harper, the club's record scorer, who had been brought back to Pittodrie from Hibernian in a £50,000 transfer but was signed too late to play in the final games of that season. Harper had previously been sold to Everton in a record £172,000 deal in December 1972. His arrival delighted the Aberdeen support but signing after 31 March meant he was ineligible to play in competitive games until the following season.

One win in 11 games meant that the Dons were perilously close to a first relegation. Their task was clear: beat Hibernian and their status would be secured, regardless of what Dundee and Dundee United achieved in their final games. The *Press & Journal* summed up a frantic last-day win, 'Tantalising to the last, the Dons waited until the second half of their final Premier Division fixture to produce their best form for many weeks and banish their relegation blues with a buccaneering three-goal victory over Hibernian. There had been many better displays at Pittodrie, but few games in Aberdeen where players and supporters shared an "experience" as totally as they did on Saturday.

'On this occasion the empathy between footballer and fan was almost tangible as together they ran through the gamut of emotions: nervous tension in the opening exchanges; relief at the opening goal; apprehension when that single-goal lead looked vulnerable under Hibernian pressure … and finally the joyous release of two spectacular clinching goals within a minute midway through the second half. For many Aberdeen followers the highlight was Joe Smith's goal in 67 minutes which put his team two up and sparked a spell of inspired football. Smith had been a vital part of MacLeod's early tenure at Pittodrie. The younger brother of Jimmy, who had been sold to Newcastle United for £80,000 in 1968, Joe was a player of real quality.

'Dave Robb scored the Dons' third a minute later with a goal that was scarcely less memorable. After breaking on the left Robb found the net with a left-footed shot which swerved in from a tight angle. These two goals arrived at the right time as Aberdeen had been under pressure from Hibernian for the first time in the game in that second half.'

Aberdeen put their supporters through all sorts of emotions in the first half. Dave Robb saw his penalty saved by Hibernian keeper Mike McDonald before the pressure eased when Drew Jarvie put the Dons ahead soon after. The *Press & Journal* concluded, 'It was perhaps appropriate that the goals were scored by Jarvie, Smith and Robb, players who have so often been cast as "villains" by the terracing critics, and who deserve to be congratulated for their efforts. Robb shrugged off his penalty miss to turn in a display of passion that typified his Aberdeen career.'

Walker McCall was a surprise inclusion in what was his only competitive game of the season and his efforts proved invaluable as he provided the perfect foil for Jarvie and Robb.

The relief around Pittodrie at full time was evident. A mix of delight and frustration that the club should find itself in such a position was a debate for another day.

Who would join St Johnstone for the drop would not be decided until the following week as Dundee United had to take at least three points from their remaining games, at home to Hibernian and against Rangers at Ibrox to consign Dundee, who had lost at Motherwell, to relegation. The Dens Park side eventually went down after their Tannadice rivals pulled off an unlikely win at Rangers.

For Ally MacLeod, it was a learning process, 'The decision to delay new signings was a gamble. I took the view that there was better value signing players after the March deadline. I had learned that frugal approach at Ayr United. Only Ian Fleming, a forward I bought from Kilmarnock in December, was eligible to play that season. I had then brought in Joe [Harper] from Hibernian and Dom Sullivan from Clyde. In the summer I bought Stuart Kennedy from Falkirk and my £100,000 budget was spent. I also released 13 players in the close-season like Ian Hair, Walker McCall and Billy Williamson.'

The day after the Dons' win over Hibernian, the Scottish clubs met at Annfield, home of Stirling Albion, to discuss a proposal from Morton to change the setup to three divisions of 12, 14 and 12. The proposal was rejected by member clubs, so the ten-team top league was to continue. There would be no reprieve for the two relegated clubs. The four-hour meeting eventually decided on no major changes; the only difference was in the First Division, where the much-maligned Spring Cup was scrapped and from the following season, the imbalance came when it was agreed that clubs would play each other three times across the campaign.

That first season of the Premier League was the beginning of a new era in Scottish football. Despite the obvious teething problems and several clubs who had enjoyed the comfort of the old 18-team setup still voicing their concerns, the Premier League was here to stay. Those early days may not have seemed to benefit Aberdeen as such, but in the longer term it was to herald the most successful period in their history. MacLeod made a promise to 'Ally's Red Army' that he would bring a major honour to Aberdeen within 18 months.

## Premier Division 1976

|           | P  | W  | D  | L  | F  | A  | Pts |
|-----------|----|----|----|----|----|----|-----|
| Rangers       | 36 | 23 | 8  | 5  | 59 | 24 | 54 |
| Celtic        | 36 | 21 | 6  | 9  | 71 | 42 | 48 |
| Hibernian     | 36 | 18 | 7  | 11 | 55 | 43 | 43 |
| Motherwell    | 36 | 16 | 8  | 12 | 57 | 49 | 40 |
| Hearts        | 36 | 13 | 9  | 14 | 39 | 44 | 35 |
| Ayr United    | 36 | 14 | 5  | 17 | 46 | 59 | 33 |
| Aberdeen      | 36 | 11 | 10 | 15 | 49 | 50 | 32 |
| Dundee United | 36 | 12 | 8  | 16 | 46 | 48 | 32 |
| Dundee        | 36 | 11 | 10 | 15 | 49 | 62 | 32 |
| St Johnstone  | 36 | 3  | 5  | 28 | 29 | 79 | 11 |

# Aberdeen 2 Celtic 1 (aet)

**20**

6 November 1976
Scottish League Cup Final
Hampden Park, Glasgow
Attendance: 69,679

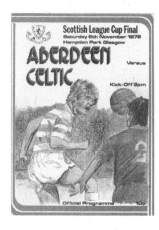

| **Aberdeen** | **Celtic** |
|---|---|
| Bobby Clark | Peter Latchford |
| Stuart Kennedy | Danny McGrain |
| Billy Williamson | Andy Lynch |
| Joe Smith | Jóhannes Edvaldsson |
| Willie Garner | Roddie MacDonald |
| Willie Miller | Roy Aitken |
| Dom Sullivan | Johnny Doyle |
| Jocky Scott | Ronnie Glavin |
| Joe Harper | Kenny Dalglish |
| Drew Jarvie | Tommy Burns |
| Arthur Graham | Pat Wilson |
| *Sub:* Dave Robb | *Sub:* Bobby Lennox |
| *Manager:* Ally MacLeod | *Manager:* Jock Stein |

THE ENTHUSIASM that Ally MacLeod brought to Pittodrie was almost infectious. The man who went on to manage Scotland in their ill-fated World Cup in Argentina in 1978 promised Aberdeen a trophy within 18 months of his arrival from Ayr United. He delivered on that with a League Cup success a year after he joined the Dons.

There was great excitement in Aberdeen leading up to the final. The Dons were in great form and having already beaten Celtic at Pittodrie in the league, hopes were high that they would end their 21-year wait to lift the cup. It had been six years since Aberdeen had reached a major final and there was a strange quirk ahead of the 1976 clash with Celtic. In March 1970 the Dons paid Dundee a record £50,000 for Steve Murray after they had beaten Kilmarnock to reach the cup final. Murray had played in the other semi-final for Dundee against Celtic, so he was cup-tied for the final. In 1976 Aberdeen's Jim Shirra was in a similar position. The Dons paid £25,000 to Falkirk for the midfielder in October 1976 but, having played for his old club in an earlier round, he had to sit out the big day after making a big impression since he came into the side.

The similarities did not stop there. In 1970 Martin Buchan was the 21-year-old captain of the Dons only weeks before the final. In 1976 Willie Miller, also 21, was installed as the skipper. Both were also seen as young prospects in that sweeper role. Miller was desperate to lead the Dons to success but admitted the league title was the one he wanted, 'To win the league means that a team has had to show their mettle over a whole season and win most of their matches. That is what I want for Aberdeen. Celtic and Rangers are not as strong as they were while we have improved a lot. It is important to take each match as it comes and win it. Hopefully that will bring us the rewards we feel we can achieve. I am confident we can beat Celtic, sure it will be tough as they are a great side, but we won't be overawed and will play with no fear. We have a young side but that can work in our favour as they can express themselves in the proper way.' Miller was asked if there were any additional pressures on him, and replied, 'I gave out some complimentary tickets before the game and I pick up the cup after it, that's about it.'

Aberdeen were in great form ahead of the final although they did have to play Motherwell in a league match in midweek four days before the Hampden showdown. Motherwell and Scotland striker Willie Pettigrew thought that the Dons were on course for winning the trophy, 'I thought Aberdeen were brilliant when we played them at Pittodrie. They are a team on form and their confidence must be sky high. I think they will beat Celtic.' Lord Provost Robert Lennox was of the same opinion, 'Aberdeen's last four games have been an inspiration. If they can maintain that standard there should be no doubt about the result.'

The referee for the final was John Paterson, who had taken over from Bobby Davidson as the top whistler in Scotland. He had recently taken charge of AC Milan v Dinamo Bucureşti in the UEFA Cup and was known to let the game flow.

Aberdeen travelled down well in advance of the final to prepare for the big day. With Jim Shirra cup-tied, and Eddie Thomson injured, the side almost picked itself as the Dons were bang in form. An estimated 25,000 of the Red Army would make the trip to Hampden and they turned up in confident mood.

The game kicked off five minutes late. Aberdeen began the stronger and immediately put pressure on Celtic, which seemed to knock them out of their stride. Jocky Scott was first to threaten after being set up by Joe Smith but his early shot went high over the bar. Dom Sullivan was next to try his luck, but his effort was saved by Peter Latchford. Glavin responded with Celtic's first effort but Bobby Clark was untroubled. Arthur Graham was the Dons' most effective player and he was fouled by Glavin as he sped past the Celtic midfielder. Aberdeen then produced a great move and Scott had the ball in the net but their joy was cut short after a linesman flagged for offside. In 11 minutes, against the run of play, Celtic took the lead. The ball was played into the box and Drew Jarvie was behind Celtic pin-up boy Kenny Dalglish. The forward seemed to go down easily and to the disgust of the Aberdeen players John Paterson pointed to the spot. Protests done, Dalglish scored to give Celtic the lead. Joe Harper was involved in a spat with Dalglish following the goal and both were reprimanded by the referee. On reflection it was a scandalous decision but one that seemed to happen so often when Aberdeen sides through the years were up against either of the two Glasgow clubs.

That setback seemed to spur Aberdeen on, and they hit back and went in search of an equaliser. McGrain was booked for a dreadful foul on Scott in 18 minutes, and Arthur Graham then sent in a low cross that Harper just failed to connect with as the Dons kept up the pressure. Aberdeen were on the end of some fierce treatment from Celtic and Sullivan was next to be brought down from behind. Harper retaliated when he went in hard and was also booked, but in 24 minutes the Dons got back on level terms. Graham's cross from the right found Harper at the back post. Harper headed the ball back across goal where Drew Jarvie ghosted in to head home. It was no more than Aberdeen deserved and they gained in confidence after going behind.

Stuart Kennedy had to go off for treatment after a clash with Doyle but Aberdeen continued to press, and their fans were claiming for a penalty after Graham clashed with Glavin in the box. Once again they felt aggrieved as there seemed little difference between

Graham's clash and the penalty that Celtic were awarded. Willie Miller was imperious at the back and he rescued the Dons with a great block after a slip by Willie Garner. As half-time arrived the Dons were more than holding their own although the teams went in level at one goal apiece.

Aberdeen carried on where they left off and took the game to Celtic in the second half. Tommy Burns committed three fouls in as many minutes but went unpunished before Aberdeen squandered a couple of opportunities. Lynch had an effort for Celtic after the ball fell favourably for him, but his shot went wide. In 54 minutes Roy Aitken was cautioned after a dreadful challenge on Graham, and another Dons penalty appeal was turned down when MacDonald clashed with Dom Sullivan. Lynch was then booked for another foul on Sullivan after 57 minutes. Aberdeen were handling the robust tactics from Celtic but in the closing stages it was the Hoops who were pushing for a winner. Miller again came to the rescue when a last-ditch tackle on Bobby Lennox took the final into extra time.

Dave Robb, who had replaced Jarvie late in the game, went on to make an immediate impact in extra time. Graham went on one of his trademark crossfield runs that left four Celtic players trailing. Graham set up Harper, whose low cross fell for Robb to slip the ball under Latchford and put Aberdeen ahead. The closing stages were frantic as Celtic laid siege to the Dons, taking risks by throwing players forward. Clark was the hero as he made some crucial saves, while Harper almost put his side in dreamland when a classic Aberdeen break ended with him hitting the post. In the last moments Clark tipped a Wilson shot over the bar. As the seconds counted down the Dons kept possession, and when the full-time whistle was blown the players danced a jig of joy on the Hampden pitch. MacLeod joined in on the celebrations while the dejected Celtic players were left in dismay; the manager also made sure he went around every one of them to shake their hand. Willie Miller led his team up the stairs to receive the League Cup – the first in a series of successes for the captain. Making Miller skipper was an easy decision for MacLeod, 'Willie had a strong mentality and playing in his role as a sweeper he was ideally suited to be the Dons' skipper. His attitude and desire to win was incredible. He knew what was required for the Dons to succeed and he was a natural for that role.'

The victorious Aberdeen party retired to their familiar Gleneagles Hotel after cup finals where the champagne flowed as the Dons looked forward to a triumphant return to the city the next day. It was something that the Glasgow clubs could never experience. Given the volatile environment with the deep divisions in the west, for clubs like Aberdeen, coming back from cup finals to be welcomed by their citizens was special.

MacLeod recalled the aftermath, 'Exactly one year after I arrived at Pittodrie we had achieved the breakthrough. We had silverware for the boardroom. We had won the League Cup. We paraded through the streets of the Granite City the next day and paid our own special tributes to the wonderful people at the Beach End at Pittodrie. I slipped out of sight; it was an occasion for the players and fans to celebrate.'

In scenes like those of 1970, the sun was out as the squad returned to Aberdeen the next day. They made the traditional open-top bus ride that began in Stonehaven then went through the city and down Union Street to a civic reception at the Town House. With Pittodrie also full it was a historic journey for the players and officials. It was hard to estimate just how man Aberdeen citizens turned out as the crowds lined the streets.

Bobby Clark later revealed that he had dreamed that Robb would score the winner, 'I told Davie and the manager about a dream I had before the final. I imagined Davie coming off the bench and going on to score the winner. It was incredible really, but it seemed so right, after all I had seen it before!'

Ally MacLeod simply said, 'We were magic!'

# Hearts 1 Aberdeen 4

12 August 1978
Scottish Premier Division
Tynecastle Park, Edinburgh
Attendance: 11,500

| Aberdeen | Hearts |
|---|---|
| Jim Leighton | Ray Dunlop |
| Stuart Kennedy | Walter Kidd |
| Chic McLelland | Campy Fraser |
| John McMaster | Dave McNicoll |
| Willie Garner | Jim Jefferies |
| Willie Miller | Frank Liddell |
| Dom Sullivan | Donald Park |
| Steve Archibald | Eamonn Bannon |
| Joe Harper | Willie Gibson |
| Drew Jarvie | George Shaw |
| Duncan Davidson | Malcolm Robertson |
| *Sub:* Ian Scanlon | *Subs:* Lawrie Tierney, Bobby Prentice |
| *Manager:* Alex Ferguson | *Manager:* Willie Ormond |

NOSTALGIA WAS in the air as 1978/79 commenced, with the Dons due to celebrate 75 years since their first game following the amalgamation of the three major clubs in the city. It was also a new era at Pittodrie as the Dons' third new manager in four years would take his place in the Tynecastle dugout: Alex Ferguson, who had been dismissed by St Mirren.

Ferguson had enjoyed a 17-year playing career that saw him turn out for Queen's Park, St Johnstone, Dunfermline, Rangers, Falkirk and Ayr United, although he hadn't won a major honour. His time with Rangers came to a controversial end after he was blamed among others for a humiliating Scottish Cup Final defeat to Celtic in 1969. Ferguson had been at fault for allowing Billy McNeill (his predecessor as manager at Pittodrie) the freedom to score a free header from a corner as Celtic went on to win 4-0.

Other observers were more cynical as to why Fergie was made a scapegoat. He had married Cathy in 1966, a year before he joined Rangers. Ferguson was quizzed about Cathy's religion by a Rangers director and asked to confirm that he did not marry in a chapel. Ferguson informed the Ibrox club that he was married in a registry office, but it was a decision he regretted as his wife was indeed a devout Catholic. In 1969 Ferguson was 'bombed out' by the club, training on his own. It was treatment that he never forgot. During his spell at Aberdeen, Ferguson twice turned down Rangers' approaches for him to take over as manager. For generations Rangers had often plundered their direct opponents for players and coaches, weakening them in the process. Ferguson and latterly Willie Miller bucked that trend, both earning legendary status at Aberdeen as a result.

Ferguson had replaced Billy McNeill at Pittodrie, with Aberdeen turning to him after his controversial exit from St Mirren. The appointment of a young and ambitious coach was the model the Aberdeen board went for. Ferguson recalled the move, 'I had the chance to join Aberdeen when Ally MacLeod left Pittodrie to take over as Scotland coach. Ally approached me after he accepted the Scotland job; however, I felt I had unfinished business at St Mirren, so I declined. Without explaining the insanity of that judgement when the opportunity to join Aberdeen came again a year later there was no way I was turning that job down. After a call with chairman Dick Donald he asked me to become Aberdeen manager and travel north the next day. I accepted both offers. I took the 150-mile journey north thinking about the history of the club and what they were all about – winning the Scottish Cup in 1970 under Eddie Turnbull seemed so long ago. I was determined to bring success to this club.'

Ferguson took charge of Aberdeen in the pre-season with home wins over Middlesbrough and Tottenham as he assessed a squad that was one of the best in the country. He was keen to get down to the serious action ahead of the trip to Tynecastle, and told the *Evening Express*, 'Hearts will no doubt be difficult and starting the campaign away from home will not be easy. They will be keen to make their mark having been promoted to the Premier League. It is never easy for a promoted side coming back into the top league, but we know what to expect and we will be ready. They will have the crowd behind them and will be desperate to do something against us. It will be essential for us to settle early and I will be happy if we come away with both points.'

Jim Leighton was also due to make his senior debut in goal as regular choice Bobby Clark was out with a long-term injury. Clark broke a finger as he punched away a cross in the friendly against Tottenham. That was the first big decision Ferguson had to make, 'We had John Gardiner and Jim Leighton as our young reserve keepers. In training I was more impressed with Leighton, so I decided to play him in the opening game in Edinburgh. It was a wet day with bad conditions for goalkeepers. The ball would be greasy and come shooting off the surface. The boy had an excellent game and gave a superb display of handling. He also proved to be fearless and brave and I was convinced he was going to be a great goalkeeper.'

Aberdeen as a team were very much at a crossroads. They had proved to be worthy challengers to the Glasgow clubs without any prolonged success, and if they were to improve then success in the league and domestic cups was essential. The Dons were the only challengers to Rangers in 1977/78 and with Celtic struggling to make an impact, they looked the best bet to sustain a threat. But with a new manager at Pittodrie there were still questions to be answered.

Ferguson had a message for the Aberdeen support on the eve of the season as he wrote in the *Green Final*, 'My players will be told to adopt an "early door" tactic. That means shooting at the earliest opportunity and I believe that will fire up the players and fans; we want to entertain and win. We must kick on from last season and I will be looking to the Aberdeen support to play their part. We need to get going from the start as any early slip-ups could mean we are playing catch-up. It's vital we start well so we can lay down a marker. One thing I can assure all Aberdeen fans is if I am manager you can take it from me there will not be any non-triers in my squad. I have always demanded a will-to-win attitude and if we work together, we can succeed.'

The new era under Ferguson did not start well as Aberdeen struggled to cope with the conditions and they went behind in four minutes when Bannon swept a Fraser cross past Leighton. As the goal gave promoted Hearts encouragement the Dons gradually worked their way back into the game in what was an early test of their resolve. It took Aberdeen 20 minutes to register their first effort on goal, a

Harper shot that just went wide, but they levelled soon after; a John McMaster free kick found Harper, whose shot was saved by Dunlop only for Duncan Davidson to hammer home the rebound. Then, in 37 minutes, Dunlop blundered when he let a Harper effort slip under his arms after good work by Steve Archibald. Aberdeen were now in control and with the crowd subdued the Dons went on to show their class in the second half. Harper was booked for dissent and he went close again before the Dons added a deserved third in 64 minutes. Archibald had been all over the Hearts defenders all afternoon and he scored after his shot was deflected past Dunlop. The scoring was completed four minutes from time when Archibald added his second after Dunlop failed to hold a Harper shot.

The convincing win away from home put Aberdeen top of the Premier League after the opening day. With Rangers losing at home to St Mirren and Celtic narrowly defeating Morton in Greenock, it was an excellent start for Ferguson.

In the aftermath there was high praise for rookie keeper Jim Leighton as the 20-year-old gave an assured display, in contrast to his opposite number Ray Dunlop, who gifted two of the Dons' four goals. Leighton had appeared for 45 minutes in the friendly against Middlesbrough as Ferguson deliberated on who should get the nod for Edinburgh. He refused to let the loss of an early goal unsettle him.

Clark was still going to be out for some time, so he looked ahead to the new season in his regular *Green Final* column, 'This season we believe we have a great chance for success. Our fans firmly believe that we now have a great team. Last season's great finish was frustrating with two runners-up medals in the league and Scottish Cup. We were disappointed when Billy McNeill went to take over Celtic but when Alex Ferguson arrived, we were impressed by his enthusiasm.

'I think we will see the best of Stuart Kennedy this season. He has proved to be a fantastic signing for the club and with him now being recognised at international level we will see the best of him. I also think winger Ian Scanlon will be a great asset this season. He settled in well after joining Aberdeen last season and looks to be a real find. Our pre-season in the Highlands and against English opposition went well. It is always difficult to predict the outcome, more so in football. Just look at Scotland in the World Cup in Argentina. Who would have thought we would have lost to Peru, drawn with Iran, then beat Holland!'

Scottish football was still coming to terms with their national team failing in Argentina under Ally MacLeod. Aberdeen were well represented with Clark, Kennedy, Miller and Harper all in the 22 players selected for South America. It was to end in agony for Scotland with no little controversy as the squad returned eliminated from the group stages. MacLeod came in for fierce criticism. The exuberance he showed at Aberdeen had disappeared after a disastrous campaign in Argentina.

# Hibernian 0 Aberdeen 5

3 May 1980
Scottish Premier Division
Easter Road, Edinburgh
Attendance: 12,900

**Aberdeen**
Bobby Clark
Stuart Kennedy
Doug Rougvie
Andy Watson
Alex McLeish
Willie Miller
Gordon Strachan
Steve Archibald
Mark McGhee
John McMaster
Ian Scanlon
*Manager:* Alex Ferguson

**Hibernian**
Dave Huggins
Jim Brown
Arthur Duncan
Craig Paterson
George Stewart
Ralph Callachan
Gary Murray
Jackie McNamara
Bobby Torrance
Ally Brazil
Peter Cormack
*Manager:* Willie Ormond

SHAWFIELD, EASTER Road and Tynecastle in Edinburgh may not be the most glamorous of venues, but outside of Pittodrie these three stadiums hold a special place in Aberdeen's history. It was in 1955, 1980 and 1984 that the Dons clinched respective league championships at these grounds.

Without doubt the most celebrated was the Premier Division win at Easter Road in 1980. It brought a tangible reward following a succession of disappointments on the big stage. The Dons had come close under Billy McNeill, being league runners-up and Scottish Cup finalists in his only season in charge. Alex Ferguson had also tasted defeat in the two League Cup finals of 1979. Those bitter memories were swept away in triumphant fashion on 3 May 1980 when Aberdeen defeated Hibernian at Easter Road. 'CHAMPIONS' declared the *Green Final* as news of the success hit the streets. Down at Easter Road more than 8,000 of the Red Army were celebrating on the Easter Road pitch along with a jubilant Ferguson and his players.

Willie Miller said after the championship that many of the younger players in the side did not fully appreciate the magnitude of their achievement, 'I don't think they realise just exactly what they have done. To win a cup is one thing but to become champions is something else and it has not quite sunk in yet.

'Bobby Clark has been here for many years and he epitomised just what an achievement this is for Aberdeen. We think we can improve, and this is only the first real step for us. We have broken the backs of the Glasgow clubs and we have stated our intent.'

That intent was clear as the Dons of course went on to greater success at home and abroad, but there is no doubt that the 1980 league title success provided the platform for those glory days in the decade. For Clark, it was a unique treble as he had now completed a full set of domestic medals with Aberdeen: the Scottish Cup in 1970, the League Cup in 1976 and finally the Premier Division.

On what was the last Saturday of the league season, Aberdeen knew that victory at Easter Road over Hibernian and Celtic failing to beat St Mirren at Paisley would mean that the title was heading north for the first time since 1955. The trip to Edinburgh may not have been as daunting as expected. Hibernian had by their own standards slipped from grace under Willie Ormond and had been marooned at the bottom of the league, already consigned to relegation. However, the Dons had yet to win a Premier Division game at Easter Road so there was no complacency in their ranks.

Aberdeen could do little wrong and had back-to-back wins over Celtic in Glasgow behind them. In hindsight the real hard work had been done; it was just down to the closing matches to see if they could hold their nerve. Aberdeen had the backing of a huge travelling support and with Hibernian having rookie keeper Dave Huggins making his debut the Dons were keen to exploit this at every opportunity. It was a truly nervous occasion for all concerned and it took Aberdeen until the 23rd minute to make the vital breakthrough. John McMaster floated a left-footed cross into the box and Steve Archibald ghosted in between two defenders to glance his header past Huggins. The bulk of the 8,000 Aberdeen support behind the Hibernian goal were ecstatic; the pressure was now on Celtic. Minutes later Andy Watson made it 2-0. From that moment on it was as much as listening for events from Paisley as Aberdeen dominated and went further ahead through Mark McGhee and a brace from Ian

Scanlon. If goals were going to make a difference in the final analysis, then the Dons were leaving nothing to chance.

Bobby Clark was often seen turning around to the massed Red Army behind his goal asking what the score was with Celtic. As the game wore on the nerves were showing in the crowd. Suddenly in the closing minutes a huge roar went up from the Aberdeen support, suggesting a St Mirren goal. It was in fact a Celtic penalty claim that had been turned down by a linesman's flag. It was not quite over yet, but moments later it was. News came through that Celtic had been held in Paisley; Aberdeen were champions. The fans celebrated by invading the pitch as Ferguson rushed on to embrace Clark, the most experienced of his squad. As the Aberdeen players made their way through the thronging crowds the party was only just beginning.

Clark had been at Pittodrie since 1965, the year that a club outside of Glasgow had last won the title. It was the crowning glory on a memorable Aberdeen career. Clark, who remains involved in coaching in the USA, remembered the day clearly, 'It was a nervous time for us all. Even in the first half we knew we were going to win the game against Hibernian, so it was out of our hands. We had to look at what was going on in Paisley. Back then there was no real communication other than the radios that were broadcasting the game. I know there were plenty of them with the Dons fans behind the goal. To be honest I did not have much to do that day, the boys in front of me were terrific and did their job with a professionalism that had been missing in previous Aberdeen sides. Once the third goal went in and the game wore on, I have to say that I really did lose my concentration, as all I could think about was what was happening elsewhere. It would normally be the cardinal sin for a keeper to take his mind off the game, but these were exceptional circumstances. I was not sure of how much time was left in the games and once we hit the fifth goal, we knew then that there was no way we could be caught if Celtic failed to win. What many people don't recall is that St Mirren were a very good side back then and they finished in third place that season behind us and Celtic.

'It was only when I saw the massed Aberdeen fans behind my goal start to jump up and down that I knew that we were champions.

It was a great feeling. To be with such a great club as Aberdeen for so long and to win the championship was a special achievement. We had won cups before, but this was different. So much emphasis had been placed on winning the title that there was always pressure on us to do well. When we won it and gave the Glasgow clubs a real doing in the process, it made it all the sweeter. We had come close before and that day made up for all of the previous disappointments.'

There was no hiding place for the Aberdeen players after the game as the Red Army scaled the high fences around Easter Road to join in the celebrations. Players were carried shoulder-high off the field and the team popped champagne corks inside the dressing room.

There was still one match to play but that was an academic trip to Partick Thistle as the season ended. Aberdeen were held to a 1-1 draw with the Red Army on the triumphant march for the final time that season. Although they had celebrated at Easter Road, the title wasn't quite mathematically wrapped up as, with Celtic having finished their fixtures and the two teams level on points, a ten-goal defeat at Firhill would have sent the championship to Glasgow instead. That was never going to happen.

It was all quite low-key as the Dons brought down the curtain on an incredible season. The supporters were at Firhill in numbers and once again spilled on to the pitch at full time. Ferguson was reflective, 'Tonight was all about us closing down the campaign in the right way. After the celebrations on Saturday we were not expecting too much, but as champions, it was important not to lose. We will be up there next season for teams to knock us over, but we will be back stronger than ever.'

The team returned triumphant and took a special trip down Union Street on an open-top bus all the way to Pittodrie as the trophy was shown to the supporters. The team made their way past the Town House where they were greeted by Provost William Fraser and local dignitaries. From there it was down to a packed Pittodrie where 20,000 fans awaited their heroes. Captain Willie Miller was presented officially with the trophy from Scottish League president Tom Lauchlan. The celebrations continued on the pitch as the squad went on an impromptu kick-about with Gordon Strachan in goal, to the delight of the crowd.

It was Aberdeen's first championship since 1955 and there was no doubt that their away form had made all the difference. The Dons accumulated 24 points on their travels compared to Celtic's 18 and St Mirren's 15. In the goals scored it was the champions who duly delivered with Aberdeen being the only club to show a positive goal difference on the road with 38 scored and 18 conceded, compared to Celtic's -4. Against their Glasgow rivals Aberdeen excelled with three wins and a draw against Rangers with two wins and a draw against Celtic. When you consider the Dons' record against both in all competitive matches that season, it represented the best return recorded by any Scottish club: played 13, won nine, drawn two, lost two, for 24, against 12.

The success was more remarkable when it is considered that Aberdeen had only managed 17 points from their first 15 outings. It was a harsh winter and backlog of fixtures that ultimately helped the Dons hit an unbeaten run of games to claw back Celtic's 'unassailable' 12-point lead. For the record, no Aberdeen player appeared in all 36 league matches that season but Bobby Clark, Stuart Kennedy, Alex McLeish and John McMaster missed only one each.

The classic image of Alex Ferguson on the pitch with arms raised at full time was later immortalised by his statue which was unveiled at Pittodrie in February 2022.

## Scottish Premier Division 1980

|  | P | W | D | L | F | A | Pts |
|---|---|---|---|---|---|---|---|
| Aberdeen | 36 | 19 | 10 | 7 | 68 | 36 | 48 |
| Celtic | 36 | 18 | 11 | 7 | 61 | 38 | 47 |
| St Mirren | 36 | 15 | 12 | 9 | 56 | 49 | 42 |
| Dundee United | 36 | 12 | 13 | 11 | 43 | 30 | 37 |
| Rangers | 36 | 15 | 7 | 14 | 50 | 46 | 37 |
| Morton | 36 | 14 | 8 | 14 | 51 | 46 | 36 |
| Partick Thistle | 36 | 11 | 14 | 11 | 43 | 47 | 36 |
| Kilmarnock | 36 | 11 | 11 | 14 | 36 | 52 | 33 |
| Dundee | 36 | 10 | 6 | 20 | 47 | 73 | 26 |
| Hibernian | 36 | 6 | 6 | 24 | 29 | 67 | 18 |

# Aberdeen 1 Austria Vienna 0

17 September 1980
European Cup first round first leg
Pittodrie Stadium, Aberdeen
Attendance: 20,123

**Aberdeen**
Jim Leighton
Stuart Kennedy
Doug Rougvie
Andy Watson
Alex McLeish
Willie Miller
Gordon Strachan
John McMaster
Mark McGhee
Drew Jarvie
Ian Scanlon
*Subs:* John Hewitt, Doug Bell
*Manager:* Alex Ferguson

EUROPACUP
DER LANDESMEISTER
AUSTRIA MEMPHIS
:
F.C. ABERDEEN
1.Oktober 1980, Wiener Stadion

**Austria Vienna**
Friedrich Koncilla
Robert Sara
Erich Obermayer
Günther Pospisschil
Ernst Baumeister
Josef Sara
Johann Dihanich
Karl Daxbacher
Harald Furst
Felix Gasselich
Walter Schachner
*Subs:* Friedrich Borgan, Franz Zore
*Manager:* Erich Hof

HISTORY WAS made when Austrian champions Austria Vienna came to Pittodrie in 1980 for the Dons' first European Cup tie. For historians the event came 25 years too late after Aberdeen were denied entry to the inaugural competition in 1955.

Alex Ferguson's team had qualified for Europe's premier competition after winning the league in May 1980, the first club outside of Glasgow to win the title for 15 years. The next level for Aberdeen and the ambitious Ferguson was success in Europe. The boss was meticulous in his preparations for European ties. Ferguson hinted at 'special tactics' ahead of the visit of Vienna with Stuart Kennedy likely to be given the role of man-marking Austrian striker Walter Schachner. It was vital that Aberdeen kept the Austrians out in an era when away goals were so vital.

The general feeling was that this tie was too close to call; the Scottish bookmakers could not separate the sides. Vienna boss Erich Hof tried ahead of the first leg at Pittodrie to feign pessimism, which was the usual tone from visiting coaches, 'I have a healthy respect for British football and their style. We know about the Scots' strength and attitude so we will have to be at our best so we are hopeful.'

What the Austrian coach failed to mention was that his side were the seeded team and had far more experience in the European arena than Aberdeen.

Ferguson declared in the *Evening Express* before the match, 'This is definitely the most important game ever played by Aberdeen. If we are to become a real force, then we must do it all at this level. The European platform is where we must be successful. I know I have said this before, but I honestly feel tonight's match is the most vital ever played by the club. We must make our mark in Europe. When you are involved in Europe you can't give guarantees. But I will break from that and give this one to the fans. The players I send out will run themselves into the ground to get the result we all want.'

The preparations included a behind-closed-doors practice session, concentrating on set pieces designed to get at the Austrians' rearguard. Ferguson then gave his players some sleeping time in the afternoon so they would be ready for the challenge.

After a pulsating start as Aberdeen pressed from the off it was the visitors who should have taken the lead in ten minutes. Schachner showed his pace to get away from Alex McLeish and his cross found Gasselich, who should have scored but sent the ball wide to the relief of the home support. That let-off spurred Aberdeen into attack and they forced corners in quick succession in 19 minutes. Schachner was becoming a real threat with his lightning-quick breaks and he came close with a header in 22 minutes, but seconds later Aberdeen took the lead. John McMaster set up Mark McGhee, who ran in an angled low shot past Koncilla. The Austrians were clearly rattled from going behind and they continued to hit Aberdeen with their incisive breaks. Baumeister then had another opportunity but Vienna's poor finishing was letting them down. When half-time came the home side were happy to go in with their narrow lead. It was clear that the visitors were top-quality and streetwise European competitors.

Whatever Ferguson said to his players during the break worked as the Dons came back at Vienna in a torrid second half and created numerous chances, but they could not add to their lead. McLeish came close when his header came back off the underside of the bar, but through bad luck and some inspired saves from

Koncilla the visitors held out to ensure a thrilling return in the Austrian capital.

Ferguson was happy enough at full time, 'I was looking to take any lead to Vienna for the return. The fact we didn't concede was vital; they will need to come at us more over there so that will suit us. We know how difficult it will be over there. We are under no illusions; the job is only half done. To get a second goal would have been great and I thought we did enough in the second half to get that. We will prepare well for the return. I don't think they are as good as Frankfurt, who knocked us out of the UEFA Cup last season.'

Erich Hof was happy enough to be only one goal behind, 'We believe Aberdeen will have a much stronger defence, but they will try to attack us as well. I am happy with the result. I believe we got our system and tactics correct on the night. We looked to contain Aberdeen in midfield and use the long ball to get in behind them. We look forward to the second game, there is a strong chance either side will go through.'

The *Press & Journal* reflected on the Dons' European Cup debut, 'The European Cup is something special. The Pittodrie crowd responded to the occasion as Aberdeen passed their entrance examination against Austria Memphis [as they were also known at the time]. At the end of an engrossing 90 minutes the Dons had rid themselves of their novice label to defeat one of the most seasoned campaigners on the continent. Here we had quality play from two worthy champions, a breathtaking exhibition of goalkeeping from Austrian international Friedrich Koncilla and a Mark McGhee goal which would have graced any European tie.'

Just to keep things ticking over there was a moment of high controversy when McLeish's second-half header appeared to be over the line. For all the visitors' spurned chances in the first half, after half-time Aberdeen dominated and were unlucky not to score a second goal.

Ferguson revealed how he had to deal with Schachner and explained what he told his players at half-time, 'We had no doubt he was the biggest danger to us, but we were guilty of our defenders being tempted to go upfield. We had to shut off the supply to him in the second half and we did that well. We were able to put pressure on them in the second half. They told us all kinds of stories about their keeper being unfit. If he was then I would not like to see him when he is at his best. He saved them tonight.'

With only a one-goal advantage the tie was finely balanced as the Aberdeen charter flight headed towards Vienna. There was good news before that when Doug Rougvie agreed a new four-year contract extension. The Fifer had been on the staff for eight years and had forced his way into the first team in recent months. Rougvie was as tough as they came, a rugged, no-nonsense defender who was never shy in winding up opponents and fans alike. He had the ideal temperament that Ferguson admired.

The Dons had some injury concerns, but Ferguson was hopeful that McLeish, Drew Jarvie and Ian Scanlon would all be available. McLeish was vital in the heart of the defence. Having made his debut in 1978 he had also been included in the Scotland national side and was without doubt the best emerging centre-half in the country.

Vienna prepared with a narrow victory over Eisenstadt in their own Praterstadion before a poor crowd of 7,000. It was expected that the Aberdeen tie would attract a near-capacity attendance which was limited to 48,000 due to stadium improvements.

Aberdeen were dealt a blow ahead of kick-off when McLeish failed a last-minute fitness test and his place was taken by Willie Garner. McLeish was a vital part of the defence although Garner had proved to be an able deputy when called upon. Garner had been with the Dons since 1975 and was vastly experienced although he did lose his place to the emerging McLeish.

The Austrians, backed by their noisy crowd, went at Aberdeen from the outset as expected and Jim Leighton was called into early action as they piled on the pressure. After defending well in those opening exchanges, the Dons found a foothold in the game and began to hit back with some clever breaks upfield. Vienna were starting to show their frustration as the first half ended with Aberdeen foiling everything that the home side could muster. Captain Willie Miller was at the heart of the defence and he was inspired, as was Leighton. This was a classic brave performance from a Scottish club on foreign soil.

Anxiety kicked in during a torrid second half but as Vienna were getting more desperate the Dons showed a class and maturity to hold out and claim a sensational first European Cup victory. The 0-0 draw was a fair reflection on the game, but the Dons could have scored late on when McGhee was foiled after he weaved past four defenders before Koncilla saved at his feet. Aberdeen finished the game in the Austrians' half as they showed an almost arrogant streak in those tense closing stages. It was a masterclass and described at the time as one of the greatest performances from a Scottish side on foreign soil.

At full time there was trouble in the stadium as the home supporters vented their fury at their own side and then turned to the 300-strong Aberdeen faithful, also smashing the windows of a travelling bus. Among those unfortunately caught up was Janette Jarvie, the wife of Drew. It was a frightening experience and there would be sanctions forthcoming for the Vienna club.

On reflection it was very much a night on which Aberdeen had come of age in European football. Ever since they had their first outing in 1967, this was by far their best performance. They had impressive results away from home before, such as a 0-0 draw in Sofia in 1968, but the Vienna tie was another level and one that this Aberdeen side looked very comfortable with.

As an unseeded team the Dons ran the risk of coming up against any of the top sides left in the competition. With only two rounds to negotiate before reaching the last eight, progression in the European Cup was a real possibility. Aberdeen, though, were drawn against English champions Liverpool in the next round. It was going to be the ultimate test for Scotland's title holders.

# Aberdeen 3 Ipswich Town 1

30 September 1981
UEFA Cup first round second leg
Pittodrie Stadium, Aberdeen
Attendance: 24,000

| Aberdeen | Ipswich Town |
|---|---|
| Jim Leighton | Paul Cooper |
| Stuart Kennedy | Mick Mills |
| Doug Rougvie | Steve McCall |
| Andy Watson | Frans Thijssen |
| Alex McLeish | Russell Osman |
| Willie Miller | Terry Butcher |
| Gordon Strachan | John Wark |
| Neale Cooper | Arnold Muhren |
| Mark McGhee | Paul Mariner |
| John Hewitt | Alan Brazil |
| Peter Weir | Eric Gates |
| *Subs:* Neil Simpson, Doug Bell | *Sub:* Kevin O'Callaghan |
| *Manager:* Alex Ferguson | *Manager:* Bobby Robson |

THE ONE black mark on Aberdeen's European report card was that after 15 years of competition they had not managed to get past the second round. When the draws were made in July 1981 for the respective competitions, the prospect of Aberdeen progressing further seemed remote as standing in their way were UEFA Cup holders Ipswich Town. Managed by the astute Bobby Robson, the English league leaders were a potent force with a mix of English, Scottish and European internationals. The immediate reaction in the media was as expected as it was arrogant; the *Daily Express* declared, 'It is a pity two British sides have been paired together in the first round but holders Ipswich will be expected to be far too strong for Aberdeen.' That was reflected in all the English press and it was something that Scottish clubs had got familiar with. The 'siege mentality' that Alex Ferguson honed to an art form at Pittodrie kicked in, 'The draw could have been more kind to us but this is a glamour tie for us and a platform for us to show the nation what we are all about. If Ipswich are happy with the draw, then good on them.'

Ferguson was a master of 'mind games' and he saw that as part of his management style. Getting inside the heads of opponents before games, doubting whether referees would be strong enough; Ferguson would never refrain from stirring it.

Ipswich for their part were a side packed with quality and virtually unbeatable at their Portman Road home. The Suffolk ground was like Pittodrie in many ways with a similar capacity and atmosphere on those European nights. Included in the Ipswich ranks were John Wark and Alan Brazil, two proud Scotland internationals who were desperate to beat Aberdeen.

The expected 'Battle of Britain' headlines were around, and it was a tie that Ferguson relished, 'We allowed the support and media to get caught up in the frenzy ahead of the first leg. I was quietly confident we would do ourselves proud down there and at the very worst still be in the tie for the return. I knew that Bobby Robson had been to watch us at Airdrie in a League Cup tie, but as we had already qualified, I played five reserves that day. He was disappointed and left at half-time. Archie [Knox] saw them at Anfield against Liverpool and at home to Sunderland and we both watched them at Portman Road against Birmingham. We knew it was going to be difficult but the experience against Liverpool [Aberdeen lost out to Liverpool in the 1980 European Cup] had matured us as a team. Our tactics at Ipswich were right. We played a 4-4-2 formation with Strachan and Weir playing deep and wide so they could get at their full-backs and tighten midfield. That meant Muhren and Thijssen would have to move infield where they would come up against the strength of Andy Watson and Neale Cooper. The game went well for us. We had plenty of possession and Strachan and Weir gave them all sorts of problems. We should have won there but settled for a 1-1 draw.'

Ferguson relied heavily on his assistant Archie Knox for spying on opposition ahead of any European tie. The fact that the club had been meticulous and thorough when it came to watching their opponents no doubt helped the management team decide on how they were going to approach any tie. Perhaps Ipswich were confident enough without similar scrutiny of the Dons. It was a huge error on Robson's part. Watching a shadow Aberdeen side for 45 minutes in a game that had no competitive edge was hardly the best preparation.

There was huge anticipation in Aberdeen ahead of the return leg. Alex McLeish was looking forward to 'welcoming' Ipswich to Pittodrie as he wrote in the *Daily Express*, 'It seems the whole city is buzzing now. I have never known so many ticket requests. Many feel the hard work has been done but we know they will come here looking to put one over us. We surprised them down there and caught them out. They will be hurting so we know this will be a tough task.'

The *Evening Express* declared in a headline on the eve of the game that Aberdeen were 'just 90 minutes from immortality'.

The news from the Ipswich camp was that Thijssen, Mills, Brazil and Butcher were all struggling with injuries but Ferguson was having none of it, 'I had a look at them training on our pitch last night and they looked fine to me.'

In what was a classic European night at Pittodrie, the Dons showed a class and guile that was too much for Ipswich who were eventually out-thought, outplayed and outclassed by a slick Aberdeen side. Peter Weir was the hero with two goals in the second half as the supporters in the Beach End behind the goal almost took the roof off the old place. Weir was in direct opposition to England captain and full-back Mick Mills, who was tormented by the winger for long spells. Aberdeen could even afford a missed Gordon Strachan penalty late in the game as the 3-1 second-leg win was one of the finest results that the club had achieved in the European arena.

Ferguson was delighted, 'Peter Weir absolutely destroyed them in the second half. It was a great night for us and after that game it was obvious, we had learned a lot playing in Europe. Our patience was getting better as was our possession and belief in ourselves. Our young midfielders Neale Cooper and Neil Simpson were outstanding.'

Weir had been the final piece put in the Aberdeen 'jigsaw' by Ferguson. Already a Scotland international with St Mirren, the self-confessed Aberdeen fan became a record transfer between two Scottish clubs when he joined for a £440,000 fee with Ian Scanlon going to Love Street as part of the deal.

Defeated Ipswich boss Robson was disappointed as he spoke in the after-match press conference, 'There is a danger of people getting carried away with the result. Aberdeen did well and I hope they will be able to emulate us, but will they be able to do the same job in Poland or Czechoslovakia if the need arises?'

There was no hiding Robson's reference to the cross-border fervour that the Aberdeen tie generated. He was bitter and almost grudging in his praise for an Aberdeen team that deservedly ousted his holders, 'They did play as a team and I don't feel they have any superstars in their side. I would not like to assess how Aberdeen would cope in the English top flight. Could they maintain that standard for 42 matches? On reflection I think they would do OK. We were fine by half-time but when Weir scored the second goal it changed the match. We lost it in between the second and third goals. When Strachan missed that penalty near the end it was fair, I didn't think we deserved to lose by three goals. Really Aberdeen did not win the game until the end.'

To put the Aberdeen result into some perspective, as well as Ipswich having won the previous season's UEFA Cup they were also at the summit of what was seen by some observers as the toughest league in the world. Aberdeen inflicted their first defeat that season, something the likes of Liverpool and Manchester United had failed to achieve.

Ferguson insisted in the *Evening Express* that domestic success was his priority, 'I am looking on the UEFA Cup as a bonus. It is the only way. My priority is to do well on the domestic scene, but if we can keep this team together, we should be looking at doing something special in Europe in a couple of years.' Prophetic words indeed.

Looking ahead to the draw, Ferguson did not have a preference, 'As far as I know we are in with the likes of Spartak Moscow, Feyenoord and Carl Zeiss Jena. We should avoid Southampton and Arsenal. To be honest we will take on any side. Whoever it is, they will not fancy playing us.'

Mick Mills certainly did not take defeat well, 'Aberdeen didn't beat us last night; the real victory came at Portman Road.' The Ipswich skipper was clearly having difficulty coming to terms with defeat, 'We played well, Aberdeen didn't, and we go out. If we had played in the first leg like we did last night, then the match at

Pittodrie would be no more than a formality for us. I did not think we were ever going to lose to Aberdeen, even on penalties. I was not that impressed with Aberdeen and they only played when they went 2-1 up.' Bitter words indeed from an experienced player who was clearly still smarting from being schooled by Weir in what was surely his most uncomfortable 45 minutes of football. It was a reminder and a timely one that the arrogance that came from English opposition would never recede. For Aberdeen it made victory all the sweeter.

Doug Rougvie recalled that night as he spoke to the *Evening Express* in 2003, 'Mick Mills boasted he was going to "sort us out" and that we were "unknown" Scottish opponents. I never forgot that.' Of the two coming face-to-face at Pittodrie in front of the Main Stand, Rougvie recalled, 'It was probably more 70-30 in his favour to get the ball but I decided I wasn't going to hold back after all the things he said. I decided that I was going to get stuck in and charged forward. He surprised me as he backed away and didn't even want to challenge me. We never had any problems from him after that and Peter Weir went on to destroy him. None of us could understand why Bobby Robson had been disrespectful to Peter. He was the most expensive player in Scotland, but Robson said he was our weakest link. Peter certainly proved him and his captain wrong.'

The club announced that their ticket voucher system would return in anticipation of another huge European night in the next round.

# Motherwell 0 Aberdeen 1

23 January 1982
Scottish Cup third round
Fir Park, Motherwell
Attendance: 12,679

| Aberdeen | Motherwell |
| --- | --- |
| Jim Leighton | Hugh Sproat |
| Stuart Kennedy | Ian McLeod |
| Doug Rougvie | John Wark |
| John McMaster | Steve McLelland |
| Alex McLeish | Joe Carson |
| Willie Miller | Graeme Forbes |
| Gordon Strachan | Brian McLaughlin |
| Neil Simpson | Stuart Rafferty |
| Mark McGhee | Willie Irvine |
| John Hewitt | Tom O'Hara |
| Peter Weir | John Gahagan |
| *Sub:* Doug Bell | *Subs:* Brian Coyne, Bruce Cleland |
| *Manager:* Alex Ferguson | *Manager:* Davie Hay |

THE WINTER of 1981 was one of the worst in Scotland for many years. In the days before undersoil heating (only Murrayfield, home of the national rugby union team, was protected), Aberdeen went six weeks without a competitive fixture. After being knocked out of the UEFA Cup in Hamburg on 9 December, they did not play again until they travelled to play Motherwell in the Scottish Cup on 23 January. The only action they found was a couple of hastily arranged friendlies against Hearts at Pittodrie and at Norwich. They also managed a short break in Benidorm where the squad was able to train on grass again. A trip to London to face Queens Park Rangers was postponed due to the adverse weather.

The visit to Motherwell was a tricky one. The Fir Park side were in the First Division that season but were clear at the top and favourites for a return to the Premier League. Aberdeen for their part were desperate to do well in the Scottish Cup after falling behind Celtic in the race for the league championship. The Dons were encouraged after their impressive 4-1 win at Norwich.

The real question for Alex Ferguson was whether his players had recovered from going out of the UEFA Cup. It was a devastating exit as at several stages over the two ties against Hamburg it was the Dons who looked more likely to progress. They had weeks to mull over what might have happened; their real test would come at Fir Park.

Aberdeen were also delighted to learn that Ferguson had turned down a lucrative job offer from Wolverhampton Wanderers. The spirit within the camp was no doubt boosted by the manager's decision to stay loyal to Aberdeen. Such euphoria can have its dangers but in this instance the players would be expected to respond in the proper way and justify the loyalty demonstrated by their manager. It would not be the last occasion that Ferguson would be coveted by other clubs.

The trip to Benidorm and benefits gained were vital for the Dons as they looked ahead to the second half of the season. In the modern era it is common for most clubs to get away to sunny climes in the winter period but back in the 1980s any such trips were reserved for summer holidays. These breaks were treasured by Ferguson as he took the opportunity to help his squad bond and foster team spirit. The management and players took full advantage of the great conditions and even managed a friendly against the local side, winning 3-1 on 12 January.

For the Motherwell tie, Doug Rougvie had recovered from a cartilage operation and would come back into contention. Motherwell were relishing the chance to put Aberdeen out. Manager Davie Hay, the former Celtic midfielder, was keen to play things down although his side were on a long winning run, albeit it in a lower division. Aberdeen for their part were experienced campaigners and they were aware of the perils of playing a confident team away from home in the cup.

Hay was looking forward to the tie, 'Aberdeen are one of the best teams in Scotland and although a big crowd will help us, we must be at our best to have a chance. We will do what has been successful for us so far this season. We know that we have been tested against the best so the Aberdeen tie will give me an idea of where we are as a team.'

John Hewitt, the Dons' 18-year-old forward, wrote his name into Scottish football history when he opened the scoring against

Motherwell. Timed officially at 9.6 seconds, it remains the quickest goal scored in the history of the oldest cup competition in the world. The game began with MacLeod letting a long Stuart Kennedy cross slip to Hewitt and he was quick enough to send a rising shot from 15 yards into the net as keeper Hugh Sproat was left helpless. The earliest of goals gave Aberdeen the confidence to control proceedings and quieten down the stunned home support. There was a large Aberdeen following and there was trouble before and during the game between both sets of fans.

Motherwell captain John Wark headed a Weir effort off his line while a Mark McGhee lob just went past the post. The home side were clearly rattled, and Forbes was spoken to after a nasty challenge on Gordon Strachan. While it was fair to suggest that Motherwell had been doing well in their own division, they had not come up against the quality that was in this Aberdeen side. It was ten minutes before Dons keeper Jim Leighton was first called into action when he punched clear Motherwell's aerial attack. The home side kept battling and they were prone to send in long balls to the Aberdeen defence, adopting a more direct approach. Conditions were far from ideal so the opportunity to make some passes and keep possession was not easy. Motherwell continued to bombard the Dons' defence, which stood up well although Irvine missed a chance for the home side just before the break. Strachan had been taking some rough treatment in a pulsating first half and he was unable to resume, his place being taken by John McMaster. Given the physical nature of the game it was perhaps better suited to McMaster than the mercurial talents of Strachan, who was often the target of brutal attention from the more robust Scottish defenders. Strachan's almost impudent style combined with a natural ability made him a formidable player. His transfer from Dundee to Pittodrie in 1977 for a £40,000 fee with Jim Shirra going in part-exchange remains an outstanding piece of business for Aberdeen.

The Dons could mix it up when they had to, and Doug Bell was booked after he took out Carson, then in 63 minutes Motherwell were reduced to ten men when Brian McLaughlin was sent off after a second booking when he fouled Bell.

The midfielder was never a regular starter for the Dons but his contribution to the team was vital. A surprise free signing from Ferguson's old club St Mirren, Bell was a player of great natural ability and often deployed as a 'secret weapon' in European ties. His contribution in the big domestic matches and in Europe cannot be overstated. Ferguson got the best out of Bell, who will go down as one of the Dons' greatest signings.

For Motherwell it was a hard lesson. They had been riding high at the top of the First Division and set for a return to the Premier Division, but it would take more than blood and guts to challenge the quality that Aberdeen had. Any side coming up against the Dons would be aware they would not be able to bully or intimidate them. This Aberdeen team could handle themselves when they had to. The mix of technical awareness, ability and toughness when needed was to define the Ferguson era at Pittodrie.

Ferguson was relieved as his side went through to a home clash with arch-rivals Celtic, 'This game underlined that the Scottish Cup is a great leveller. I felt that some of my players were affected by nerves. Playing a decent side on their own pitch in difficult circumstances was not easy and we had everything to lose. The players were aware of that. The important thing was that we won the tie. It was not easy after such a long spell away from competitive action. The difference between the ferocity of competitive football and friendlies is stark so we had to be ready for that. We look forward to playing Celtic and getting the opportunity to knock them out at home. It is a hard one, but we fear no side at Pittodrie.'

The Celtic tie was also the Dons' first at home in the Scottish Cup for two years. It was clear that Ferguson would have preferred an easier encounter, but the reality was that Aberdeen's record at Pittodrie was impressive and their chances of putting their great rivals out at home were perhaps higher than a clash at a neutral venue.

The brutal winter had forced the clubs to consider a scheduled shutdown for six weeks from mid-December. The meeting of all clubs in Dunblane seemed to agree that there should be a break. The attendance figures over the winter period suggested an alarming drop in gate receipts. The only issue was that the traditional new year games were always popular at a time when the holiday period did attract local support. The suggested break would have involved an extension to the season well into June. It was some weeks later that most clubs voted against the idea, citing as and when the break should be set. The unpredictable Scottish weather won the day and the traditional Christmas and new year games were set to continue, as they had done since league football was first established in the late 19th century.

The significance of the victory at Fir Park had long-term implications for Aberdeen. It was the start of a historic run by the club in the Scottish Cup as they went 23 consecutive games undefeated in the competition to bring three successive victories in 1982, 1983 and 1984. No club outside of Glasgow has ever achieved that, a record that stands to the present day. This also brought automatic qualification for the European Cup Winners' Cup, leading to the 1983 success in that competition which has endured and defined the club for a generation.

# Aberdeen 4 Rangers 1 (aet)

22 May 1982
Scottish Cup Final
Hampden Park, Glasgow
Attendance: 53,788

| Aberdeen | Rangers |
|---|---|
| Jim Leighton | Jim Stewart |
| Stuart Kennedy | Sandy Jardine |
| Doug Rougvie | Ally Dawson |
| John McMaster | John McClelland |
| Alex McLeish | Colin Jackson |
| Willie Miller | Jim Bett |
| Gordon Strachan | Davie Cooper |
| Neale Cooper | Bobby Russell |
| Mark McGhee | Gordon Dalziel |
| Neil Simpson | Alec Miller |
| John Hewitt | John McDonald |
| *Subs:* Doug Bell, Eric Black | *Subs:* Colin McAdam, Tommy McLean |
| *Manager:* Alex Ferguson | *Manager:* John Greig |

IT HASN'T been a regular occurrence for Aberdeen to go into a major final as firm favourites against one of the Glasgow clubs, but back in 1982 they were odds-on to beat an ageing Rangers. The previous week Aberdeen had finished their league programme with a thumping 4-0 win over the Ibrox side at Pittodrie. The clinical nature of that victory suggested that Aberdeen would simply need to turn up to win the cup at Hampden. It was never going to be that straightforward; Aberdeen had struggled over recent years in major finals with two League Cup final defeats in 1979 and a bitter loss in the 1978 Scottish Cup Final to Rangers. It was time to change that.

Aberdeen had missed out on the Premier Division title to Celtic. They never recovered from a poor spell in winter, but they did take their challenge to that final game against Rangers at Pittodrie. They needed a miracle though; defeat Rangers and hope that Celtic would lose at home to St Mirren and with a five-goal swing in their favour. By half-time on that final day it was still on as the Dons had hit four first-half goals while Celtic were being held. Celtic eventually overcame St Mirren to take the title, so for Aberdeen all attentions turned towards securing a first Scottish Cup success since 1970.

The road to Hampden was a tough one for the Dons. After their narrow win at Motherwell it did not get any easier with a visit from Celtic. Former Aberdeen striker Mark McGhee recalled, 'When you set off on a cup run, you don't think that far ahead, just the next game coming up. We had a tricky draw away to Motherwell but then we got a couple of home ties and that was always a boost as we felt we could beat any side at Pittodrie.'

It took a marvellous John Hewitt scissor kick to defeat Celtic in the fourth round and that was followed up with a comfortable 4-2 win over Kilmarnock. Alex Ferguson had been dismissed by St Mirren before he joined the Dons in 1978 and the Saints were still a decent side when they held the Dons to a 1-1 draw in the semi-final at Celtic Park. Aberdeen won the replay at the more neutral Dens Park in Dundee. The game was played in horrendous conditions and a tough, energy-sapping tie ended with the Dons prevailing 3-2. By contrast, Rangers' route to the final was hardly inspiring. Their semi-final went to a replay against lowly Forfar Athletic.

McGhee remembered the 1982 final fondly, 'When we got to Hampden it was 12 years since Aberdeen had last won the cup and that was something we wanted to put right. For many of us it was a first Scottish Cup Final we had played in so there was a lot of excitement, and apprehension. We were still a very young team, we had the likes of Neale Cooper, Neil Simpson and John Hewitt. In contrast Rangers were ageing in key positions. They were on the verge of breaking up, so there was a big difference between the teams.'

The preparations for the final were overshadowed by political turmoil with the Falklands War, which had threatened Scotland participating in the World Cup in Spain. The Scottish Professional Footballers' Association felt that it would be inappropriate to take part in the competition as Argentina were holders. Ernie Walker of the Scottish Football Association dismissed the PFA claims. The decision to take part was good news for Jim Leighton, Stuart Kennedy, Alex McLeish and Willie Miller, who had been selected in Scotland's final 22-man squad.

Aberdeen prepared for Hampden at Cruden Bay Golf Club in what was a very relaxed approach, but they were dealt a blow when

Peter Weir was unfit to take his place at Hampden. Ferguson was still confident, 'I have absolutely no fears whatsoever about this game. The only thing is that a final is a final and anything can happen on the day.' There was no doubt that Ferguson was relying heavily on his World Cup quartet to get Aberdeen through the early stages so his side could then impose themselves on the game. The Dons started well enough and McLeish came close with a header that just went over the bar from a Strachan free kick. Jim Bett was perhaps the most influential player in the Rangers side (he later joined Aberdeen from Lokeren in 1985) and he was booked for a cynical challenge on Strachan. However, the Dons were stunned in 15 minutes when Rangers took the lead after a Dalziel cross was flicked past Leighton by John McDonald. For many fans it was an undue familiarity that was not part of the script.

Going behind in the Scottish Cup Final to Rangers, who had the bulk of the support, would perhaps have crushed weaker teams. This Aberdeen team though had been evolving ever since Ferguson took over four years earlier and having been hardened on foreign fields in England, Romania and Germany, they were to show a steely resolve reflecting their manager's hunger to succeed. In 33 minutes Aberdeen drew level with a sensational goal from the most unlikely source. A John Hewitt corner found John McMaster, whose shot was blocked. The ball broke to the edge of the box and there was McLeish, who turned and sent a curling shot into the top corner of the net. The centre-half was emerging as one of the best around and having established himself in the national side, he was adding the occasional goal to his skillset. Any doubts as to whether he meant it were dispelled when McLeish later revealed he scored an identical goal at their training camp at Cruden Bay earlier in the week.

Just before half-time Doug Rougvie crunched into Sandy Jardine to earn a booking. Jardine was not to emerge for the second period, his place being taken by Colin McAdam.

The second half was uneventful as Aberdeen dominated possession without creating the chances they craved. Try as they might they could not get past Rangers' resistance, which on reflection was admirable given the superior fitness of their opponents. When extra time did arrive, the Dons had the luxury of putting on Doug Bell and Eric Black, the young striker making his mark in his first season for the club. Rangers, by contrast, could only turn to the out-of-favour winger Tommy McLean.

The additional 30 minutes proved to be one of the greatest victories in club history. Ferguson had been on the pitch after full time, expressing the need for his players to stretch Rangers in wide areas as they were clearly tiring. Within three minutes of the additional period starting Aberdeen went ahead. The influential Bell crossed to the far post where Mark McGhee ghosted in to head past Jim Stewart in front of the bulk of the Red Army. If there was a tendency for Aberdeen to defend their lead those thoughts were swept aside as they continued to go forward, and as the first period ended they scored again. This time Rangers' Alex Miller slipped and injured himself, allowing McGhee a free run near the goal line. The striker looked up and passed to Strachan in splendid isolation to score from all of two yards into the empty net. Strachan ran off and attempted a somersault celebration as the supporters were in raptures, knowing now that the cup was won after all those years of hurt.

Aberdeen completed what turned out to be a convincing win with another goal in the second period of extra time. Rangers were struggling with Miller a passenger due to his injury and their experienced players were virtually on their knees. The Dons were almost imperious, and their final goal perhaps typified the attitude that was around Pittodrie back then. Young Neale Cooper powered his way upfield and after goalkeeper Stewart attempted to clear the ball rebounded back off Cooper and fell kindly in front of him. With an empty goal and no opponent in sight, Cooper waltzed towards goal before slamming the ball into the net from all of a few inches. In front of the Rangers supporters it was a statement from Aberdeen that this team was here to stay and the days of being intimidated by Glasgow's finest were long gone.

Captain Willie Miller lifted the trophy one-handed, a ritual he was to make his own with plenty of practice in the coming years. Miller recalled, 'At the end of 90 minutes the boss and Archie [Knox] came out. At such a time it was not so much a tactical talk but more of a knock-you-down-and-lift-you-up job. Fergie would put you down and Archie would lift you up in a classic good cop, bad cop play that they were brilliant at. Usually Fergie would say one thing that was important. He was very bold making changes and I once saw him make a substitution after ten minutes and it was not through injury. When we went ahead in extra time there was no signal from the bench to sit on our lead. We knew Rangers would have to come out; they did, and we scored two more. After the final Rangers made an approach for me and I had two telephone calls with Rangers manager John Greig. The first was their good offer. The second was to thank him but tell him that I was staying to see my career out at Aberdeen. I firmly believed that Aberdeen had more chance of winning trophies than Rangers did. In the next few seasons, I was proved correct.'

The Aberdeen party went on the Gleneagles Hotel that evening as the celebrations continued before a return to the city street parade on the Sunday. A curious hotel guest was none other than Hollywood legend Burt Lancaster, who met the players and management. Lancaster was in Scotland filming *Local Hero*, a Scottish comedy-drama film directed by Bill Forsyth.

Mark McGhee looked back on that cup success, 'It was a fabulous period for Aberdeen, because we did dominate Scottish football and then after winning the Scottish Cup, we went out and won in Europe as well. It was amazing, for a club like Aberdeen to go out and beat the likes of Bayern Munich and Real Madrid and win the European Cup Winners' Cup. When you look back at what's happened since to the players we had then and to the manager as well, it starts to make more sense, you can see how we were able to do it because clearly we had something remarkable there. Alex Ferguson was an extraordinary manager, he's done everything there is to do in the game, and we had some good players too who also had bags of character to go with it. The guys who scored in the final, Alex McLeish, Gordon Strachan, Neale Cooper, all went into management, Willie Miller was a huge figure, Jim Leighton another, all the guys.

'That team had such personality and character and the truth is you can never get enough of that into a team. Every manager looks for it all the time; personalities, people that can bring something more than just their right foot or their strength in the tackle to games, players who bring something to the dressing room, to the spirit of the team and the club, on and off the pitch. Go through the team, there was nobody that would let you down, everybody in their own way was a character.'

As was the tradition, the players and management would take their bow through the streets of Aberdeen in what was a familiar trodden path for the team that was evolving into the greatest ever to grace Pittodrie.

The success also opened the door for European qualification and further triumphs. Aberdeen were on the threshold of what was to become their golden era in the 1980s.

# Bayern Munich 0 Aberdeen 0

2 March 1983
European Cup Winners' Cup quarter-final first leg
Olympiastadion, Munich
Attendance: 35,000

**Aberdeen**
Jim Leighton
Stuart Kennedy
Doug Rougvie
Neale Cooper
Alex McLeish
Willie Miller
Eric Black
Neil Simpson
Mark McGhee
Doug Bell
Peter Weir
*Sub:* Gordon Strachan
*Manager:* Alex Ferguson

**Bayern Munich**
Manfred Müller
Wolfgang Dremmler
Udo Horsmann
Wolfgang Grobe
Klaus Augenthaler
Wolfgang Kraus
Norbert Nachtweih
Paul Breitner
Dieter Hoeneß
Karl Del'Haye
Karl-Heinz Rummenigge
*Manager:* Pál Csernai

ALEX FERGUSON made no secret of his admiration for German football. After the Dons had gone up against Fortuna Dusseldorf (1978) and Eintracht Frankfurt (1979) he had been determined to take what positives he could from those ties. Ferguson liked the German organisation and discipline. His thinking was to bring some of that to his Aberdeen side. Together with the Scottish appetite for a scrap, it was the perfect combination for success.

As Aberdeen were making progress in the European Cup Winners' Cup in 1982 it was not until they reached the quarter-final that they came up against one of the giants in European football. After the Dons had beaten Sion (Switzerland), Dinamo Tirana (Albania) and Lech Poznań (Poland) it was almost inevitable they would face one of the favourites. The Sion tie was a preliminary round as Aberdeen, as an unseeded side, had to start their campaign early. The Scottish League had to assist with the Dons' opening League Cup ties to accommodate the games against Sion. The first leg at Pittodrie offered a glimpse of what was to come from Aberdeen, a 7-0 hammering leading to Sion coach Jean-Claude Donzé declaring that they would take some stopping and could win the tournament.

The 1-0 aggregate win over Tirana in the first round was a narrow escape as the Dons had to handle the heat of Albania to protect their first-leg lead. The next challenge was against Polish league leaders Lech Poznań, victories home and away suggesting that Aberdeen were worthy of their place in the quarter-finals.

The draw was made in Zurich and news came through that Aberdeen would travel to face German giants Bayern Munich on 2 March 1983. With several months to dwell on that prospect it was a draw that Ferguson had a 'feeling' about, 'A lot will depend on our form at the time. We really need to be at the top of our game, but the experience most of the team have had against top German opposition in the last few years will help us for the challenge.' Ferguson made no secret of his desire to avoid Barcelona at this stage as the full draw for the quarter-finals emerged: Austria Vienna v Barcelona, Inter Milan v Real Madrid, Paris Saint-Germain v Waterschei and Bayern Munich v Aberdeen. The Germans had eliminated Tottenham Hotspur 5-2 on aggregate in the previous round.

In the Bayern ranks was 1974 World Cup winner Paul Breitner, who had notified his manager Uli Hoeneß that he was to retire at the end of the season. Hoeneß said, 'I have spoken to Paul about his decision and he told me he wants to bring further success to the club before he leaves. He has put the Cup Winners' Cup at the top of that list.' Breitner was determined to bow out by lifting the Cup Winners' Cup in the Nya Ullevi in Gothenburg on 11 May. Hoeneß told the *Evening Express*, 'Although Paul would settle for winning one of our domestic tournaments, he has put the European Cup Winners' Cup as top of his list. We know he will give his best if Bayern are playing in Germany and Scotland.' Breitner had scored in that 1974 World Cup Final, and had also won two Spanish titles with Real Madrid, as well as being on target in the 1982 World Cup Final against Italy. Ferguson was drawing up plans to deal with Breitner ahead of the trip to Munich and he had arranged for Archie Knox to have Bayern watched on at least two occasions. Hoeneß also intimated he was going to watch Aberdeen at Celtic Park in February where he took the view that he would see them at their best.

There was still a perception in Germany that Aberdeen were a relatively unknown quantity and that Bayern would be too strong for them. There was enough merit in that belief but ahead of the first leg in Munich, Hoeneß was respectful of how difficult Aberdeen would be. Speaking in the *Green Final*, he declared that he would rather have come up against Barcelona than Aberdeen, 'People may find that strange, but we know what to expect from the Spanish side. They do not have anyone we don't know about. Aberdeen are a totally different prospect as they are an unknown quantity for us and that could be dangerous. We like to know all about our opponents and pick up on their strengths and weaknesses.'

German legend Franz Beckenbauer, who was in the Hamburg side that played Aberdeen in the 1981 UEFA Cup, was not so complimentary towards the Dons' chances, 'Aberdeen gave us a hard time in Scotland, but like most British teams they don't travel well in Europe. I expect Bayern to be far too good for Aberdeen. The Scots will provide a test but technically Munich are better.'

The German media concurred as Aberdeen were not that well known across Europe. *Bild* declared, 'Aberdeen will not present Bayern with any difficulty. It is a good draw for Munich who could have been paired with far more difficult opponents.'

Hoeneß took a more cautious view after watching Aberdeen dismantle Celtic at Parkhead, 'We will need to be at our best to get through this tie. Aberdeen are well organised; technically superior to any British side I have seen in recent years. They present a real test for us, and it is important for us to take a lead to Scotland.'

Bayern warmed up with a 5-0 win over Armenia Bielefeld but they also had an injury scare after Breitner limped off. The bookies offered Aberdeen at a generous 9/2 with 3/1 for the draw and Bayern odds on at 4/9 to win the first leg. The German players were being offered a rich harvest if they defeated Aberdeen – 5,000 marks (£1,357) each and a further 4,000 marks if the attendance topped 40,000.

Tottenham manager Keith Burkinshaw was more optimistic for the Dons against his side's conquerors, 'It is a big stadium over there and it could be frightening for the younger Aberdeen players, but I am sure they have enough experience to overcome that. Make no mistake about it: Bayern are a very good side and they have skill right through their team. Aberdeen must remain compact as a team and not get dragged about. Aberdeen will go there with a lot of confidence and they have a few young players who will run their socks off and get in about them. Bayern will not like that. Rummenigge is the best striker in Europe at the moment and he must be stopped. He is strong and quick and very accurate. He would be a threat against any side in the world just now. You have got to congest the area in front of him to stop him and close him down quickly.'

Hamburg captain Manfred Kaltz, the German international right-back, also voiced his admiration for the Dons, 'Aberdeen were undoubtedly our hardest opponent last year in the UEFA Cup. They could have scored seven goals against us in Scotland.' Breitner was determined to play after picking up a knock. 'Even if I have to play in crutches I will play against Aberdeen,' he said on the eve of the game.

Aberdeen recorded a 3-1 win over Dundee before travelling to Germany. Bayern had not long come through a six-week winter Bundesliga break but they had been busy enough as they took part in a lucrative indoor tournament in Switzerland and spent a week at a training camp in France. A series of friendlies against a Luxembourg XI and two German amateur clubs brought in additional revenue.

Ferguson was looking forward to the tie, 'After watching them defeat Karlsruhe 6-0 I took my usual notes and we had a few things to sort out, namely Rummenigge and Breitner. Archie had also gone to see them, and it was obvious they were a very good side. Although Breitner was reaching the twilight of his career, he had played in World Cup finals and we knew how big a threat he was going to be for us. As for Rummenigge, he was obviously going to be difficult to handle. We decided that if he came into midfield, then our midfielders would take care of him. When he came into forward positions then Willie Miller would pick him up. As for Breitner, Neale Cooper was going to look after him once he approached our half.'

Aberdeen had a big injury doubt over the influential Gordon Strachan and Ferguson didn't want to risk starting the Scotland international, so he was listed among the substitutes.

159

Bayern had been on an impressive run to the quarter-finals, but they found the Dons a different proposition.

The Olympiastadion was a huge arena and had been built in 1972 for the Olympic Games. It was also the venue for the finals of both the 1974 World Cup and the 1988 European Championship.

Aberdeen were backed by around 1,500 supporters who were noisy in their backing throughout. The team began well and had some good early possession. Willie Miller had gained huge experience in Europe and he was immense in the heart of the defence. Bayern launched plenty of attacks, but Aberdeen stood firm and grew in confidence as they frustrated the Germans. Not only did the Dons hold out but they began to control the midfield as the Germans ran out of ideas. The 0-0 draw was described as one of the best displays by a Scottish side on foreign soil. The threat of Rummenigge was constant and it took superb concentration from the Dons to keep him quiet. Breitner also showed his class on occasion with some positive play in the Aberdeen half, but he was superbly marked by young Cooper. The midfielder had once been likened to the great Franz Beckenbauer as a 16-year-old playing for the Scotland youth team. With Alex McLeish and Willie Miller as solid as Aberdeen granite in the centre of the defence it was in midfield where Cooper excelled. As the home support grew in frustration, the Red Army were in full voice at full time.

It was the night Aberdeen came of age in Europe. Previous clashes with German opponents had ended in disappointment but to hold Bayern, the most powerful team in the Bundesliga, and on their own pitch, was a phenomenal achievement.

Uli Hoeneß was complimentary about the Dons' efforts, 'Aberdeen were as good as anyone in Europe tonight. They rank with the best in tactics, skill and stamina. We have a tough task in the second leg.' Bayern were jeered off at full time by their support, frustrated at their team's inability to break down their visitors. Jim Leighton was inspired as he made several superb saves in a tense second half. Hoeneß, to his credit, had been warning his countrymen that Aberdeen were the real deal; maybe now they would listen.

Ferguson was delighted with what was as good a performance as he could have expected, 'We got it tactically spot on. They were dangerous through the middle and we were ready for that. Willie [Miller] was magnificent and the others took their lead from him. The support was tremendous and were convinced we were on our way to the semi-final. Deep down I knew we still had a hard task ahead. Bayern were a class side and clearly underestimated us in Munich. I knew they would not make the same mistake again.'

John Hewitt, who was on the bench that night, recalled, 'The boys stuck to their task. It was a very tough place to go and to get something out of the game. We were virtually playing against a German national team. We did well in Munich. Fergie and Archie had the opposition watched thoroughly. We would sit down with a dossier of the team and each individual player. Archie [Knox] would then focus on their strengths and weaknesses.' Knox was full of praise for the performance, 'That was one of the best shown by the boys in Munich. There was no doubt we gained respect after that game.'

The stage was set for a thrilling second leg at Pittodrie. Could Aberdeen fulfil their potential and knock out the tournament favourites to finish the job?

**Fußballmannschaft F.C. BAYERN MÜNCHEN e.V.**
Welt-Pokal-Sieger: 1976 · Europa-Pokal-Sieger: Cup 1967 · der Landesmeister: 1974-1975-1976
DFB-Meister: 1932-1969-1972-1973-1974-1980-1981     DFB-Cup: 1957-1966-1967-1969-1971-1982

# Aberdeen 3 Bayern Munich 2

28

16 March 1983
European Cup Winners' Cup quarter-final second leg
Pittodrie Stadium, Aberdeen
Attendance: 24,000

**Aberdeen**
Jim Leighton
Stuart Kennedy
Doug Rougvie
Neale Cooper
Alex McLeish
Willie Miller
Gordon Strachan
Neil Simpson
Mark McGhee
Eric Black
Peter Weir
*Subs:* John McMaster, John Hewitt
*Manager:* Alex Ferguson

**Bayern Munich**
Manfred Müller
Wolfgang Dremmler
Udo Horsmann
Wolfgang Grobe
Klaus Augenthaler
Wolfgang Kraus
Hans Pflügler
Paul Breitner
Dieter Hoeneß
Karl Del'Haye
Karl-Heinz Rummenigge
*Sub:* Reinhold Mathy
*Manager:* Pál Csernai

SUCCESSIVE ABERDEEN managers have spoken about those special European nights at Pittodrie. Ever since the Dons first entered European football in 1967 they have always placed a huge emphasis on competing favourably on the continent. It is difficult to pinpoint exactly when those 'special' nights came to the fore but the meetings against Honvéd, Celta Vigo and Juventus in the early 1970s were as good an indication as any other period.

The quarter-final second leg against Bayern has been accepted as 'Pittodrie's greatest night', revered in memory and club video. It was the night when Aberdeen defied the odds and claimed the scalp of one of the top clubs in world football. The Dons were dining at the top table in the European arena and Alex Ferguson's side were revelling jousting with the elite.

It was certainly the best of times at Pittodrie and a full house gathered for the return leg on 16 March 1983. Aberdeen made only one change from the team that started in Munich with Strachan fully fit to replace Doug Bell. Bayern also made one change with Pflügler coming in to take over from Nachtweih. The general belief was that the first goal would be all important, and Ferguson was concerned as to how his players would react if they went behind. That realisation came in ten minutes when Augenthaler fired a fierce shot past Jim Leighton from the edge of the box. Breitner played a short free kick before the German side-stepped McLeish and hit a screamer past the goalkeeper. It was a hammer blow to the Dons' hopes and they would now have to find at least two goals to rescue the tie.

For the next 20 minutes Aberdeen laid siege on the Germans who defended as impressively as the Dons had done in Munich. They almost levelled when Weir's corner was turned in by Kennedy and Black's header rattled the bar, but their resolve was strong, and they kept at their task before finally being rewarded with an equaliser in 38 minutes. McGhee crossed for Eric Black at the far post and the young forward headed the ball back across goal. Kraus seemed in control as he tried to take the ball away from danger, but Neil Simpson swept him aside to score. It was all Aberdeen from that point as they peppered the Bayern goal, which at times was leading a charmed life. Black went past three defenders before setting up Strachan who shot wide, then Bayern defender Grobe hit his own bar when attempting a clearance. Just before the break a Weir corner was headed narrowly wide by McLeish.

The second half began in the same manner, but it was Bayern who shocked the Dons in 61 minutes as Del'Haye's cross was cleared by McLeish only for Pflügler to volley past Leighton from the edge of the box. It was a hammer blow for the Dons and one that suggested their European dream was all but over. The relief on the Bayern bench was obvious as they danced with delight after they had taken the lead. Ferguson then made changes when he took off Kennedy for John McMaster with Cooper moving to left-back and Rougvie to the right. Black was clattered by Horsmann in the box, but no penalty was awarded. Then Ferguson played his last card when he brought on John Hewitt for Simpson. In 77 minutes the game turned on its head as Aberdeen hit two sensational goals to take the lead. First McLeish headed past Müller after a superbly worked free kick from McMaster and Strachan had fooled just about everyone apart from the players themselves. With the Germans caught off their guard McLeish powered his header home to make it 2-2. Aberdeen still required another goal and within seconds it arrived. A Black header was only palmed out by Manfred Müller and John Hewitt squeezed the ball through Müller's legs to send Pittodrie into ecstasy.

There was an air of disbelief among the Germans, who had 14 minutes to rescue the tie. For many home fans it was perhaps the longest 14-minute spell imaginable, but Aberdeen reverted to their 'Munich mode' and effectively closed out the tie. It had been an astonishing end to the night and the scenes of jubilation among the players and supporters at the end of the game were unprecedented. It was without doubt the greatest ever night at Pittodrie. Some supporters spilled on to the trackside as the celebrations began.

In the city that night, many local pubs had applied for late licences as the fans partied into the early hours of the morning.

The belief that was in the Aberdeen squad was now apparent in the Scottish media as expectations grew on the back of the Dons' stirring performances in Europe. That additional pressure was well managed by Ferguson. He knew his side were well equipped to meet such high demands and he was keen to temper the growing expectancy, 'We have won nothing yet. The team have done well to get us into a position where we could make history. We have to keep our focus on the next challenge.'

As the results came through from around Europe there was further encouragement for the Dons as Belgian club Waterschei had turned around a 2-0 deficit at home to Paris Saint-Germain while Austria Vienna had knocked out favourites Barcelona on away goals. Real Madrid eased past Inter Milan to complete the semi-final line-up. With PSG and Barcelona out, the optimism around the support was off the scale.

It was the Dons' greatest victory in Europe to that point and set the club up for an amazing finish to a season that still had so much to offer. Aberdeen were still going for a unique treble of European Cup Winners' Cup, Premier Division and Scottish Cup, but with so many huge games coming in a short space of time it was going to be a big ask.

Ferguson made no secret of his desire to avoid Real Madrid in the semi-final and his preference was the relative unknown quantity that was Waterschei Thor from Genk in Belgium. 'Not that I would care who we get now but coming up against Madrid so soon after the Bayern game may be that bit too much for our younger players,' he added.

The turning point in the win over Bayern was that audacious free-kick routine involving John McMaster, Gordon Strachan and Alex McLeish. It was the supreme irony that such an experienced side like Bayern, renowned for their organisational and technical skills, would be caught out with what was an outrageous set piece. McMaster was arguably the unsung hero of that side. Having been at Pittodrie as a youngster he eventually settled in the first team in 1981. A cultured player with a sweet left foot, his ability at set pieces for the Dons should never be underestimated. Greenock-born McMaster looked back on the Bayern game in the *Evening Express* on its 20th anniversary. 'I remember thinking what has he [Alex Ferguson] come up with now?' McMaster admitted as he looked back on how Ferguson went over his free-kick plans. 'Gordon and I just thought it was plain silly and would never work, but Fergie was always looking for ways to keep us one step ahead of opponents. It's amazing such a simple idea went on to play such a significant part in Aberdeen FC history. We were a bit shell-shocked when the Germans made it 2-1, but big Alex's header got us going again and those last 15 minutes were the most memorable of my career. The noise inside Pittodrie was incredible. I don't think there has ever been a repeat of the atmosphere generated by the Aberdeen fans that night.'

Neil Simpson, the powerhouse of the midfield, recalled his goal that levelled the tie at 1-1 just before the interval, 'It wasn't the prettiest of goals, but it was one of the most valuable I ever scored. I just remember seeing the ball bobble in front of me inside the six-yard box and decided I had better get there and put the ball into the net. I ended up putting one of the Germans in with it because there was no way any of them was going to stop me scoring.'

Ferguson had to make changes after the Dons went behind and needed to find two goals in 30 minutes. His alterations swung the tie in Aberdeen's favour, 'Doug Rougvie was having a bit of a nightmare and Stuart Kennedy had his hands full dealing with

Pflüger, so I decided to take John McMaster on into the midfield and put Neale Cooper back to left-back and switch Rougvie to the right. Taking Kennedy off was an unpopular move with the crowd, but it was necessary on the night. John McMaster came on and made an immediate impact with his variety and range of passing. Things started to improve but we still needed to make the breakthrough. I then had to use my second substitute and I decided to put John Hewitt on. I took a gamble by taking Neil Simpson off. Neil had run himself into the ground and had been marvellous. We pulled Peter Weir back to midfield, so we had a front three of Eric Black, Mark McGhee and Hewitt. Scoring two goals in as many minutes changed everything. We had 13 minutes to hold on. They would throw everything at us, but they were on their knees. Augenthaler was injured and Breitner was hobbling about. The wee winger was also getting the treatment from Cooper, so his threat disappeared. Their only threat was Rummenigge. I was left with McMaster, Strachan and Weir in midfield and none of them were that strong in the tackle. Eric Black was tired up front, so I had to rely on my defence to get us through. Thankfully they only had one chance with an overhead kick from Rummenigge that Jim Leighton saved. It was only in the dressing room afterwards that we realised how close we were getting to the final.'

A few days after the game, at the Skean Dhu Hotel in Altens Ferguson told me that the Bayern players who were staying at the hotel sat in the lounge and could not believe that we had planned that particular free kick. It was obviously a tremendous disappointment for them.

There was now a firm belief that Aberdeen could go all the way. Up until the Bayern ties there was more hope than expectation; after all, this was new territory for the Dons, who were in the mix with some of the best football sides in Europe. Publicly Ferguson showed cautious optimism but privately he was convinced Aberdeen had a great opportunity to create history.

# Aberdeen 5 Waterschei 1

6 April 1983
European Cup Winners' Cup semi-final first leg
Pittodrie Stadium, Aberdeen
Attendance: 24,000

| **Aberdeen** | **Waterschei** |
|---|---|
| Jim Leighton | Klaus Pudelko |
| Stuart Kennedy | Győző Martos |
| Doug Rougvie | Tony Bialousz |
| Doug Bell | Danny David |
| Alex McLeish | Adrie van Kraay |
| Willie Miller | Aime Coenen |
| Gordon Strachan | Pier Janssen |
| Neil Simpson | Lei Clijsters |
| Mark McGhee | Eddy Voordeckers |
| Eric Black | Lárus Guðmundsson |
| Peter Weir | Roland Janssen |
| *Subs:* Neale Cooper, John Hewitt | *Subs:* Johan Connix, Ivo Plessrs |
| *Manager:* Alex Ferguson | *Manager:* Ernst-August Künnecke |

THE DRAW that manager Alex Ferguson wanted was realised when news came through that the Dons were to face Belgian side Waterschei in the semi-final of the European Cup Winners' Cup. Plans were immediately made to have them watched, although the management team had already had their quarter-final with Paris Saint-Germain monitored.

Archie Knox went over to Belgium to see Waterschei beat Tongren 2-0. Both goals were scored by former Belgian international Eddy Voordeckers. Waterschei were sitting in fourth place in their league behind Anderlecht, Antwerp and Standard Liege and Knox was wary, as he told the *Press & Journal*, 'They are a very experienced side and are very organised. They don't give much away and look very good in possession. It would be a mistake for us to treat them lightly even though they do not have the big names or glamour of Bayern Munich. I still think we have enough to beat them, but we will need to be at our best. The one man who stands out in their side as an individual is captain Pier Janssen, a Dane. He plays in left midfield and contributes a lot to their play. They build up from the back with possession the key.'

Meanwhile, there was no rest for some of the Aberdeen players. Their 'Famous Five' of Jim Leighton, Alex McLeish, Willie Miller, Gordon Strachan and Peter Weir were all in the Scotland side that played Switzerland at Hampden. It was the first occasion Aberdeen had five players in the national team, which was an indication of how strong the Dons were at that time. McLeish replacing Liverpool's Alan Hansen brought about the discussion that Hansen's days were numbered in the Scotland squad.

Waterschei announced that the return in Belgium was a 23,000 sell-out even ahead of the first leg. They were backed by a local industrialist with Hermans sponsoring their kits. They were bankrolled in the transfer market and they had a real cosmopolitan look with players from Germany, Hungary, Belgium, Italy and Iceland.

Ferguson was wary not so much of the players but the 'wily, shrewd coach Ernst Künnecke'. The boss was aware that Künnecke had changed Waterschei's fortunes within the last couple of years, 'They had been in the lower divisions, gained promotion and here they were in a European semi-final. They had beaten some very good sides and we could not underestimate them. As for my team I decided to leave Neale Cooper out and bring in Doug Bell along with Neil Simpson. We thought that was our best pairing for that night.'

Ferguson called it right again as Aberdeen hit the Belgians hard from the kick-off. Within four minutes the Dons were two goals up in a whirlwind opening. The blitz began in the second minute when Doug Bell's mazy run ended with Eric Black scoring from close range. Then Neil Simpson slalomed his way through the Belgian defence and his shot went in off Waterschei keeper Pudelko. After the break Bell was again in the thick of it as he set up McGhee to make it 3-0 and in 69 minutes Peter Weir scored with a header, before Iceland international Lárus Guðmundsson pulled one back for the visitors. In 84 minutes Aberdeen scored a fifth after some confusion in the Waterschei area, leading to a couple of deflections and a grounded McGhee scoring from two yards. The Dons were on their way to Gothenburg. Winning in such an emphatic way was an incredible achievement in what was the club's first European semi-final.

Black recalled that first leg, 'We had become favourites to get past Waterschei which was something we were not used to. To win a semi-final 5-1 in Europe is almost ridiculous. We had put ourselves in such a strong position and it was a phenomenal achievement. Even though we overran Waterschei that night, it wasn't something I got carried away with. I was always of the opinion that we played; we won a cup. I would go on holiday, come back and start all over again. I thought that was how it worked up until when I left Aberdeen!'

Waterschei had requested that the second leg be advanced 24 hours to Tuesday, 19 April and Aberdeen agreed, which would allow them the opportunity to see the conclusion of the other semi-final in Madrid. After a 2-2 draw away to Austria Vienna, Real Madrid looked favourites to progress to the final.

Although the Belgian officials had conceded that there was no way they could get back into the tie, Ferguson was reluctant to call it but he did say that he could not visualise Aberdeen losing four goals in any game to any opposition. He did, however, refer back to the previous season when Aberdeen went to Romania to face Argeş Piteşti with a 3-0 lead and were pegged back quickly, trailing 2-0 at half-time on the night: 'We have to go to Belgium to play with the same discipline we showed in Munich, defending early and keeping the play away from our box. Making allowances for our two early goals, Waterschei impressed me as a competent outfit. Certainly, Hamburg who we played last season did not give us as much trouble as Voordeckers and Guðmundsson did on Wednesday night. However, we were clinical in front of goal. Even going back to my own playing days, I cannot recall a performance by a Scottish team comparable to winning 5-1 in a European semi-final.'

Eddy Voordeckers left Scotland bemused at why the Scotland national team was struggling in the European Championship, 'When you see Aberdeen doing so well in Europe, it beats me why your national team does not do better.' The forward exited Pittodrie with his head bowed less than an hour after his side's defeat. However, he did have more to say after enduring manager Künnecke's 'pennance' session. Speaking to the Belgian press in broken English, Voordeckers readily conceded that there would be no Waterschei interest in the final, 'We are certainly out of it now for no team can pull back four goals at this stage of a European competition. Our form was not really puzzling against Aberdeen. We were almost out of this one before the game had started. We were supposed to keep it tight until half-time and then try and grab a goal in the second half. But all that changed when we were two down after some of our players were still waiting to touch the ball. We then had to scrap our prepared pattern, and that was difficult. We must improve now and show the Scottish fans that we are a good team.'

There were also some doubts cast as to the sanity of former England manager Sir Alf Ramsey as he picked out Voordeckers and Guðmundsson as the semi-final's best players. Ramsey's comments were dismissed by most observers. The general feeling was that top players do not end up in a side hammered by five goals. Even before the second leg Waterschei looked like they were breaking up. The tough-tackling Lei Clijsters (father of tennis star Kim Clijsters) was attracting interest from Anderlecht, who had a £400,000 bid rejected.

Tickets for the game in Belgium went on sale ranging from £7.50 to £17. It was expected that around 1,000 Aberdeen supporters would make the trip.

Künnecke was clearly hurting from his Pittodrie experience and looked for his side to get some pride back, 'We must beat Aberdeen at least and show we are a good team. Aberdeen have yet to lose a game in Europe this season, but we are a very good side at home.'

Ferguson of course was respectful to Waterschei and he insisted that they were a far better side than many would believe, 'I watched a video of their last round tie against PSG. They came back from being two goals down to win the return 3-0. It should have been a lot more. They are a better side than Hamburg and their two strikers would cause problems for any side. Possession is always an important factor in European football but never more so than in this game. Our aim must be to have as much of the ball as possible and defend high.'

The Belgians did manage to get some pride back with a 1-0 win that did inflict a first European defeat of the season on the Dons, but it was a reserved performance from Ferguson's men as they rarely went through the gears at any time in what was a relatively quiet evening.

They were still going for the league and Scottish Cup and had just come through a brutal semi-final win over Celtic at Hampden before travelling to Belgium.

It was also the final game for Aberdeen full-back Stuart Kennedy whose injury late on in Belgium was more serious than first thought. Kennedy had been one of the best full-backs at Pittodrie. The ultimate professional and often used as an example for the younger players by Ferguson, Kennedy was signed in 1976 and went on to make over 300 appearances, also playing for Scotland on eight occasions. Ferguson admired the legend, who he had played alongside at Falkirk in 1973, 'Stuart caught his studs at the edge of the pitch and suffered a knee injury. No one realised at the time, but that was to be his last game as an active player for the club.' Ferguson paid Kennedy a tremendous tribute when he listed the still-unfit defender as a substitute for the final in Sweden, such was his respect.

Meanwhile, European fever had swept through the city with the realisation the Dons would be playing in a major final. Archie Knox went over to Madrid and watched Real beat Austria Vienna 3-1 in monsoon conditions in Spain. It was confirmed; the European Cup Winners' Cup Final of 1983 would be Aberdeen taking on Real Madrid in the Nya Ullevi in Gothenburg on 11 May.

# Aberdeen 2 Real Madrid 1 (aet)

**30**

11 May 1983
European Cup Winners' Cup Final
Nya Ullevi, Gothenburg
Attendance: 17,800

**Aberdeen**
Jim Leighton
Doug Rougvie
John McMaster
Neale Cooper
Alex McLeish
Willie Miller
Gordon Strachan
Neil Simpson
Mark McGhee
Eric Black
Peter Weir
*Sub:* John Hewitt
*Manager:* Alex Ferguson

**Real Madrid**
Agustín
Juan José
José Antonio Camacho
Johnny Metgod
Paco Bonet
Ricardo Gallego
Juanito
Ángel
Santillana
Uli Stielike
Isidro
*Subs:* Isidoro San José, José Antonio Salguero
*Manager:* Alfredo Di Stéfano

'ABERDEEN ARE a team that money can't buy; they have a soul, and a family spirit,' said the great Alfredo Di Stéfano, the crestfallen Real Madrid manager who paid tribute to Aberdeen after the 1983 European Cup Winners' Cup Final in Gothenburg. There is no doubt the Dons' memorable win over the Spanish giants in that final remains their finest hour.

Di Stéfano had been one of the greatest players of his generation. Born in Argentina, it was while he was with Real Madrid between 1953 and 1964 that he graced European football and was one of *Los Blancos'* first superstars. Aberdeen could have crossed paths sooner with Di Stéfano had the Dons been put forward for the first European Cup in 1955. As it turned out, a Di Stéfano-inspired Madrid stamped their class all over Europe with five consecutive European Cup wins for the rest of the decade. The former Argentine and Spanish international scored in each of those finals.

While Aberdeen may have struggled to cope with Di Stéfano as a player, they had no such problems coming up against him as the manager of Real Madrid in 1983. Alex Ferguson was unsure how to approach Di Stéfano ahead of travelling to Sweden. For support he asked Jock Stein to accompany the party for the final. Stein had been the manager of Celtic when they became the first British team to lift the European Cup in 1967. Stein had a wealth of experience at home and abroad and Ferguson believed his presence would be of great benefit. He asked Stein how he should deal with his Madrid counterpart. 'Bring him a bottle of Scotch whisky, a nice malt perhaps,' was Stein's advice. Ferguson recalled the build-up prior to departing for Sweden, 'Although we were offered the training camp used by visiting international teams we decided to stay in a place called Farsaat, which seemed to have been named especially for someone with a Doric dialect, "Where is that?" It was in a small hamlet called Kungalv outside Gothenburg and we had access to a beautiful training ground at an amateur club there.

'We flew from Aberdeen on the Monday as we wanted to get there early and get the squad settled. There was more media attention than usual which was understandable. Before our flight from Dyce [Aberdeen airport] we were given rosettes and the players received a singing telegram which was arranged by their wives. It was a carnival of excitement. I was keen to keep the preparations as low-key as possible. I made sure Archie and the staff showed no nerves as that might get to the players.'

As the team settled into their camp, the Red Army was mobilising; an estimated 15,000 would make their way to Sweden by road, rail, air and sea. Stories emerged about how some fans would be getting there, from the weird to the wonderful. The excitement in the city was unprecedented; here was Aberdeen going to Sweden to face the legendary Real Madrid in a European final. Attention on the club was nationwide.

Tickets for the final went on sale at Pittodrie with undercover seats at £9.50, while open seating came in at £7.70 with terracing tickets at £5. Archie Knox had been across to Madrid to watch their second leg against Austria Vienna and came back with some real optimism of the Dons' chances. Those thoughts though were kept in house. Ferguson was happy to allow Madrid to take all the attention. Given their marvellous history in Europe it was almost a mark of respect from the manager. The more informed would argue that it was Ferguson engaging in his mind games.

Meanwhile, European fever swept through the city as everyone looked forward to what was the biggest game in the club's history. Pubs were given special licences to open late as thousands across Britain would watch the final on television. Even in the far-off fields of Sedgefield in north-east England a certain Labour Party candidate was made to wait to confirm his nomination. A young Tony Blair ended up watching the final with five Sunderland fans as the beers flowed before Blair was eventually endorsed as the Labour Party candidate for Sedgefield. Blair went on to become MP for Sedgefield on 9 June 1983, a post he held until 2007. He swept to power as prime minister in May 1997.

There was one group of supporters who made their way to Gothenburg before the team flew out. The 'Red Armada' as it became known were on board the *St Clair* ferry, all 500 of them. The ship had been the link between Aberdeen and Shetland for many years. Operators P&O Ferries commissioned it to take supporters to the final for what was a 'once-in-a-lifetime' event.

P&O, mindful of their links with the Shetlands, offered 30 per cent of the ship's accommodation for supporters in Shetland. Many of the islanders were to join the rest of the fans for the trip. Details of the Cup Winners' Cup cruise were released by P&O manager Eric Turner; the *St Clair* would leave Aberdeen at 1pm on the Monday and return to Aberdeen Harbour on Friday morning. Turner announced in the *Press & Journal*, 'This is something we have been planning for some time, though we could not announce anything until after the semi-final. We will have all-inclusive packages and the trip should be treated like a cruise.' It was just as well the ferry had on board accommodation as reports came in that travel agents warned that supporters may be accommodated up to 100 miles outside of Gothenburg due to the interest in attending the final.

The *St Clair* was sold out in rapid time as every cabin, room and seat was snapped up. It was bedecked with red and white streamers on the morning of Monday, 9 May. Hundreds of well-wishers lined the harbour to see the ferry safely on its way. Alex Ferguson was on hand to personally see them off. The 32-hour journey would get the seafarers to the port of Gothenburg early on Tuesday evening.

Meanwhile, more than 20 aircraft were booked to fly supporters to Gothenburg. On the morning of the final the city was engulfed in football fever. Aberdeen airport was awash with supporters and even the airport staff joined in by wearing red rosettes and wishing the Dons good luck. Schoolchildren were turning up for class in Aberdeen colours. Many of the city shops were showing their support with an array of window displays. In Gothenburg, thousands of fans were already in the Swedish port enjoying the local pubs, despite the high prices. There was plenty of praise from the British Consul, 'There has been a great atmosphere. The Aberdeen support are a credit to their team and city.'

The *St Clair* arrived in marked contrast to the departure late on Tuesday afternoon as she slipped into dock three miles from the city centre, docking behind three trawlers from the north-east who had made the 560-mile journey.

Gothenburg police were also in praise of the Red Army, their press spokesman declaring, 'Extra police have been drafted in but that was no slur on the Aberdeen support. We are expecting 40,000 to attend the game so the extra help is necessary. The Aberdeen fans are boisterous but full of good humour.'

Thames Television revealed that the final was the biggest event it had covered since the royal wedding of Prince Charles and Lady Diana. More than 150 million viewers throughout the world were due to tune in. In Sweden, the banner headlines in the Gothenburg press screamed, 'Invasion!' as the city's newspapers welcomed 15,000 Scots fans for the final. The *Gothenburg Post* had a photo and feature with Gordon Strachan and two unemployed Dons supporters who hitch-hiked their way to Gothenburg.

By that time the Aberdeen players had their first training session at the Nya Ullevi. Ferguson was happy with the relaxed approach, 'We trained at the stadium and all the press were there. Real Madrid were due to train after us. We did a thorough and varied session whereas when Madrid came in, they just practised penalty kicks. That gave us a sign of their intentions. On the day of the game we had our usual practice session before an evening game before packing the players off to bed in the afternoon.'

In the *Evening Express*, the stage was set for the Dons' finest hour. Eight months and ten gruelling ties had passed since Aberdeen embarked on their assault on Europe and now they were one game away from European glory. Ferguson made his last pre-match press briefing a rallying cry, 'Yes, we have a marvellous chance to do it and I know each player will give his last ounce of energy to win the cup. We intend to play our normal game, and that is to attack. It would be foolish if we were to change that now. I don't believe the fact we are playing a big name like Real Madrid is anything to do with it. We have beaten Bayern Munich, so if we go into the final like underdogs, we will end up with memories but no medals. We are not in Gothenburg to finish as losers.'

The Cup Winners' Cup trophy itself had been taking pride of place in a huge department store within the city centre and Ferguson wanted nothing more than his captain Willie Miller accepting it from UEFA president Artemio Franchi after the game. Miller started his European career on a winning note nine years earlier in Gothenburg in an under-23 tie played only 100 yards from the Nya Ullevi. It would be a fitting moment if he were to crown the club's greatest achievement in the Swedish seaport in his 55th successive game for the Dons of 1982/83. Aberdeen were also looking to create European football history by becoming the first team to win the trophy after playing in a preliminary round.

Aberdeen's public relations efforts were praised by the 200 reporters attending the final. Ferguson was given a civil passage through a crowded conference of foreign writers. However, Alfredo Di Stéfano was not so lucky. Looking rather shell-shocked, the Real boss was asked by a Swede, 'What will happen to you if Real lose?' Without flinching, he declared he would return to his hotel and have a meal like he always did.

In the warm-ups, the Spanish players looked confident, but Di Stéfano looked boorish and concerned in stark contrast to Ferguson, who was in jovial mood. Di Stéfano was asked to retract a statement he made on Aberdeen who he described as rough, 'No, the Aberdeen side I watched against Celtic was tough and worrying.' One rule that may sound hard to believe today was that back then only two foreign players could play at any one time. It was not an issue for Aberdeen in a team full of homegrown Scots. For Madrid, though, it was very different. Included in their side were Jonny Metgod (Netherlands) and Uli Stielike (Germany), both vital to Di Stéfano. The odd one out was Laurie Cunningham, who was then on loan to Manchester United from Madrid until the end of the season. Cunningham expected his team-mates to win, 'Madrid deserve to win it. There is not much between the teams but I believe Real's experience will see them through. Aberdeen have never got to this level before and are a young side. The Madrid fans are desperate for a return to the glory days and there is a lot of pressure on them to win this trophy.'

The Spanish giants had cost a mint to assemble, whereas the total cost of Fergie's Furies was just over £400,000. Surely this was a mismatch, but conditions favoured the Dons when torrential and persistent rain doused the pitch on matchday.

From the outset the Dons were positive, and early pressure almost brought a reward. Gordon Strachan crossed from the right and Eric Black's athletic volley crashed against the bar. Aberdeen continued to press, and a textbook corner brought them the first goal. It was Strachan whose deep kick found Alex McLeish on the edge of the box. His downward header allowed Black to clip the ball past Agustín in the Madrid goal.

Real had not expected Aberdeen to come at them so early and it was 15 minutes before they mustered their first attack – but it brought an equaliser. McLeish's back-pass slowed in the wet and gave Santillana the opportunity to tumble over Jim Leighton, and Juanito scored from the penalty. McLeish later revealed how he was told not to tempt fate with passing back to Leighton in such conditions. Real seemed content to hold the Dons and it was not until the second half that Aberdeen regained their earlier initiative. The heavy conditions had been energy-sapping but wave upon wave of red attacks might have been better rewarded. Strachan's volley was saved by Agustín's legs, then the goalkeeper kept out Black's header. Neale Cooper came close with a searing drive.

It appeared that Real were content to take the tie into extra time and, if necessary, to penalties. John Hewitt had replaced Black late in normal time and, 12 minutes into the additional 30, Peter Weir fed Mark McGhee down the left. McGhee's perfect cross was missed by Agustín and dropped for Hewitt to head home.

Hewitt turned to salute the Aberdeen support, famously wiping his hands on his shirt as bedlam broke out in the stands. The expected riposte from Real only materialised in the dying minutes. A twice-taken free kick from Salguero whizzed past the post and it was all over. Amid scenes of unbridled joy, the Dons had done it. When Willie Miller was presented with the trophy on the Nya Ullevi pitch, it sparked wild scenes of celebration in the stands as the Red Army lapped up the moment. This was Aberdeen's night and the celebrations went long into the Swedish evening.

The team returned to a heroes welcome in the city the next day. Pubs were open and shops were closed. Schools gave up on taking registers and factories and industry ground to a halt as the team made their way through the city on the now familiar open-top bus.

In the cold light of day Aberdeen had achieved what only Celtic and Rangers in Scotland had done before them. For the Dons it was remarkable. They were welcomed back by the now-traditional open-top bus ride down Union Street. The only stragglers were the 500 or so supporters still on board the *St Clair*. The 'boat people', your author included, were not to arrive home until Friday.

Such was the impact of the result, there were repercussions all through the Spanish club with supporter revolt and the infamous 'white flags' being raised.

Real Madrid were on a real downer as a testimonial match scheduled against Aston Villa for their talisman Goyo Benito was sensationally cancelled as fans turned their back on their side.

Ferguson looked back at the victory with pride, 'At the end of the first half I felt that Stielike was getting far too much room. He was a great influence on their team and on the night he was magnificent. He was the one player we could not get the better of on the night. To combat him we told our strikers to work back more and squeeze the area that Stielike was playing in. The second half was different. Peter

Weir tore them apart more as a winger than a midfielder. We were well on top, but we could not get that decisive goal. The game went into extra time. That period worried me. I remembered the reports of the Madrid players practising penalties and I dreaded the thought of the match being decided like that. I put John Hewitt on for Eric Black, who was injured. Then Weir beat two men down the line and set Mark McGhee away on the left. I can still see McGhee taking on their substitute and then crossing for Hewitt to beat Stielike to the ball and head into the net. A wonderful moment!

'The rest of the game could not go quick enough. A retaken free kick from the edge of the box had Bryan Gunn, our reserve keeper, down on his knees praying they would miss. The ball flew just past the post and that was it. When we got back to the dressing rooms there was an air of unreality. There were two rooms; one for the players and the other for the directors and backroom staff. The players were singing and dancing which was understandable. The directors' area was surprisingly quiet, as if we could not believe it. It is a strange feeling, but you feel quite humble at moments of such triumph. You also feel sympathy for the losing team on such a big occasion. That was the way with Aberdeen Football Club in general. Chairman Dick Donald was not one for getting carried away and he generated a sense of humility throughout the club.'

# Aberdeen 2 Rangers 1 (aet)

31

21 May 1983
Scottish Cup Final
Hampden Park, Glasgow
Attendance: 62,970

| Aberdeen | Rangers |
|---|---|
| Jim Leighton | Peter McCloy |
| Doug Rougvie | Ally Dawson |
| John McMaster | John McClelland |
| Neale Cooper | Dave McPherson |
| Alex McLeish | Craig Paterson |
| Willie Miller | Jim Bett |
| Gordon Strachan | Davie Cooper |
| Neil Simpson | Dave McKinnon |
| Mark McGhee | Sandy Clark |
| Eric Black | Bobby Russell |
| Peter Weir | John McDonald |
| *Subs:* John Hewitt, Andy Watson | *Subs:* Gordon Dalziel, Billy Davies |
| *Manager:* Alex Ferguson | *Manager:* John Greig |

IT IS not very often that a manager who has just led his team to a national cup success would launch fierce criticism of his players immediately after the final whistle. Such were the high standards set by Alex Ferguson back during his Aberdeen career that was exactly what happened after the Dons had completed a marvellous European Cup Winners' Cup and Scottish Cup double in 1983.

After what was their 60th and final competitive game of the 1982/83 season, it was an astonishing outburst by Fergie as he watched his players take the all-too-familiar lap of honour around Hampden Park. Ferguson lambasted his players except for Willie Miller and Alex McLeish, stating of the pair, 'They won the cup for Aberdeen, no one else. The players were a disgrace. It is not an acceptable performance from Aberdeen. We set high standards and we fell well below them today.' Alex later retracted his statements made immediately after the final whistle in front of the watching millions on live television. He gathered his squad around the breakfast table the day after at the team hotel and apologised to his players. McLeish recalled that Ferguson went up in his estimation as a manager and a person after that moment as he believed that it must have been a difficult thing to do. McLeish claimed, 'We didn't know how to take it. We had just won the Scottish Cup but the mood in the dressing room was subdued. Alex had high standards and after winning in Europe I am sure he wanted us not just to win the cup but to do so with style and flair. It does not always work out that way.'

No doubt Fergie learned a lot about himself as much as his players that weekend. Aberdeen went into the 1983 Scottish Cup Final as hot favourites to make it a memorable trophy double. The euphoria that surrounded the club and the city was centred around what Aberdeen had been doing in Europe; all new territory for the Dons as they beat the famous Real Madrid to win the Cup Winners' Cup on a memorable night in Sweden. The squad had been stretched to the limit as the Dons retained an interest in both cups and the Premier League right up until the final kick of the season. There was no doubt that despite the outstanding success the strain of achieving their targets had taken its toll. It may be an astonishing fact for younger Aberdeen supporters to believe these days but after the Dons had won the European Cup Winners' Cup in Gothenburg on 11 May that year, there was nothing that could have compared with that and the Scottish Cup Final was merely looked upon as just another day at the office. While that approach may have been over-confidence on the Dons' part, there was no doubt that back then they believed they could take on any side in world football and rarely lose. It was such a steely belief and ring of confidence among the players that helped them achieve so much.

The more cynical have always claimed that any domestic success is not worthy of merit unless it is achieved against either of the Old Firm in their own backyard, and Aberdeen were on course for a second Scottish Cup in a row after outclassing Rangers in the 1982 final. With Rangers still struggling to catch up with Aberdeen on the field the pressure was on the Ibrox club to end the Dons' domination. Under John Greig, Rangers had improved but were still seen as rank outsiders against an Aberdeen side that looked unbeatable that year. Ferguson's team had been battling on three fronts and only fell at the final hurdle in the league race with Celtic and Dundee United going for the title. The later rounds of the Scottish Cup were also played at the same time as Aberdeen were battling their way through to the Cup Winners' Cup Final as Bayern Munich and Waterschei were defeated along the way. There was no easy road to Hampden for the Dons as they beat Hibernian 4-1 at Easter Road in the third round, Dundee 1-0 at Pittodrie, then Partick Thistle 2-1 at Firhill in the quarter-final. The semi-final brought Aberdeen and Celtic together at Hampden and with the Waterschei tie in Belgium coming up in midweek, it was a critical point in the season. A Peter Weir header was enough to take Aberdeen through to the final and keep the Dons on course for a dream cup double.

In contrast Rangers made heavy weather of a kind route to the final with wins over Falkirk, Forfar, Queen's Park and then St Mirren in the semi-final. It took a late goal from future Aberdeen coach Sandy Clark to send Rangers through in their replayed semi against the Paisley side. Willie Miller was wary of his team being tagged as hot favourites to lift the trophy, 'Rangers have a great record in the cup, and they have beaten us this season so it might be difficult for us to be seen as overwhelming favourites. We have to prove we are a better team than Rangers at Hampden on Saturday.'

Aberdeen had a couple of injury doubts before Ferguson could name his line-up, but he was keeping that under wraps. Ferguson was confident his side would prevail, 'Rangers' best chance might be the fact that they are underdogs for the final. Their supporters will expect a lot from their team, and this will make them a dangerous opponent. However, if we show anything like our Gothenburg form, we will do all right.' The Dons prepared for the final with a relaxed attitude and combined a stay on the Aberdeenshire coast at their usual Cruden Bay base with a round of golf to relax the players, who had achieved so much in a hard season. McLeish, Eric Black and Mark McGhee were all nursing knocks but all three would make it into the starting 11, which showed only two changes from the side that demolished Rangers the year before. Andy Watson and Peter Weir came in to the 13 for the injured Stuart Kennedy and Doug Bell. Ferguson dismissed claims that Aberdeen winning the Cup Winners' Cup would make his side less interested in lifting the Scottish Cup, 'That is ridiculous. I can assure you that the players' appetite for honours is just as sharp as it was in Gothenburg. There is no lack of incentive. We could become the first team outside of the Old Firm to win the Scottish Cup two years in a row and this could be the first time that Aberdeen have won two major trophies in the same season; the players will be prepared.'

Rangers' confidence took a hammering after they lost their last game to Celtic 4-2 after being two goals ahead at the interval. John Greig admitted that he would have to raise his players' morale, 'If the match had finished at half-time last week we would be bubbling, but I will have to lift our spirits after what happened in the second half. This is the last week of the season though and what better way than to finish with a cup final?'

Rangers showed no fewer than six changes to their side that had been beaten by Aberdeen 12 months previously and included Scotland international Jim Bett.

The final itself was a disappointment for the 62,979 attendance as the Dons struggled to show their European form at Hampden. In a tense match bereft of any clear-cut chances the best opportunity in the 90 minutes fell to Bett, who brought out a great save from Jim Leighton in the second half. Bett's fierce drive from the edge of the box looked goalbound until Leighton threw himself to tip the ball over the bar. While Aberdeen controlled the match for long spells, they barely mustered any real scoring opportunities and the inevitable extra time loomed with both teams showing signs of a long, hard season. Cup finals back then would go to a second game if they ended in a draw, which would have been the last thing Aberdeen wanted at the end of such a long season.

With just four minutes left of extra time, Aberdeen conjured up the winning goal to the delight and relief of the 25,000 travelling Red Army. McGhee set off down the right and his cross spun wickedly off Rangers defender Craig Paterson high up into the penalty area. Big-game specialist Eric Black reacted first, and he rose to head past a despairing Peter McCloy in the Rangers goal to give Aberdeen a victory and round off a memorable season. For Rangers it was a bitter blow against their big rivals and another victory that confirmed Aberdeen as the best team in the country. Rangers drew comfort from the fact that Aberdeen, as holders, would be defending their European Cup Winners' Cup crown the following season which allowed the Ibrox club entry into the competition on the back of the Dons' success.

IT'S OVER ... Dons skipper Willie Miller with the Scottish Cup, supported by team-mate Doug Rougvie.

## Fergie blasts happy heroes

**F**URIOUS Dons boss Alex Ferguson blasted his players just minutes after they had beaten Rangers for a second successive season in the Scottish Cup Final.

And thousands of TV viewers watched in amazement as Fergie raved: "They were a disgrace."

Asked why he thought his team had played so badly, he said:

"You'd need to open up their heads and look into their minds to find out."

Tight-lipped, he said: "We didn't win the Cup today. We had it tough all the way through, while Rangers really didn't play anyone until they met us.

"WE LOOKED A KNACKERED TEAM.

"If Aberdeen players think I will accept that standard of performance, I will be looking for new players next season.

There was obviously little pleasure for Ferguson in the Dons becoming the first British team to win the European Cup-Winners' Cup and their national Cup in the one season.

He was in no mood to be humoured.

He admitted: "You don't judge players on one game and it has been a marvelous season for us. But looking at them today they looked as if they needed a holiday."

Rangers manager John Greig, who came so close to grabbing something from a miserable season, said: "I think we were unlucky to lose.

"I thought young Billy Davies had written his name in the history book when he headed that extra time goal.

" I am not arguing with the decision, but I think if the goal had stood we would have won the cup."

### SUNDAY MAIL COMMENT

## What's the point?

**I** AM astounded that Fergie should blast his players publicly after winning the Scottish Cup at Hampden Park.

What does it achieve?

Surely the sign of a good side is when they win a game they might have lost, because they played beneath their normal standards.

The Dons have had a long, hard season. Sixty games in all.

AND SIGNIFICANTLY, THE BEST SEASON IN THEIR HISTORY.

Fergie has a lot of young players in his squad. They are bound to be showing signs of wear and tear.

But they won the European Cup-Winners Cup and they won the Scottish Cup.

THEY ARE GOOD PLAYERS.

Fergie should have praised them publicly, not bruised them.

# Aberdeen 2 SV Hamburg 0

20 December 1983
European Super Cup Final second leg
Pittodrie Stadium, Aberdeen
Attendance: 24,000

| **Aberdeen** | **SV Hamburg** |
|---|---|
| Jim Leighton | Uli Stein |
| Stewart McKimmie | Manfred Kaltz |
| John McMaster | Bernd Wehymer |
| Neil Simpson | Ditmar Jakobs |
| Alex McLeish | Holger Hieronymus |
| Willie Miller | Jimmy Hartwig |
| Gordon Strachan | Michael Schröder |
| John Hewitt | Jürgen Groh |
| Mark McGhee | Dieter Schatzschneider |
| Doug Bell | Felix Magath |
| Peter Weir | Wolfgang Rolff |
| *Sub:* Eric Black | *Subs:* Wolfram Wuttke, Allan Hansen |
| *Manager:* Alex Ferguson | *Manager:* Ernst Happel |

THE HISTORY books will tell you that Aberdeen remain the only Scottish team to have won two titles in European football. That success is reflected with the two stars in the club logo. And when Aberdeen defeated Hamburg at Pittodrie on 20 December 1983, UEFA presented the Dons with a special plaque which adorns the Pittodrie trophy cabinet to this day. That was later rectified as a replica of the Super Cup was sourced and remains part of the Pittodrie boardroom.

There was no doubt that the eyes of the world were focused on Pittodrie for the second leg of the European Super Cup Final. It was being beamed live to more than 100 countries worldwide and the stadium's press facilities were at bursting point with 40 different nations sending reporters to the game. Never before or since had the club's profile been so distinguished and on the back of that stunning success the Dons completed a memorable year when they edged out European Cup winners SV Hamburg.

The European Super Cup was created in 1972 on the back of the successful Ajax side that brought the 'total football' concept to the game. They were keen to be tested by the best and to determine the best side in Europe. The proposal to UEFA was that the European

Cup winners would play the Cup Winners' Cup winners on an annual basis, and this was met with widespread approval. The UEFA Super Cup as it is now known has gone through many changes. The first trophy was in fact a plaque which Aberdeen won along with the likes of Aston Villa, Nottingham Forest and Liverpool. The present trophy is relatively new and stands at an imposing 58cm, designed in Milan and is as impressive a piece of silverware as you will see in modern-day football.

The competition had its problems in its first year when the inaugural final was between Ajax and Rangers. With Rangers banned for a year due to the trouble their supporters caused in the 1972 Cup Winners' Cup Final in Barcelona, it went ahead in an 'unofficial' capacity with the Dutch side winning.

The format of two-leg finals was kept until 1997, although the Super Cup was decided in one single match in 1984, 1986 and 1991 due to political or scheduling issues. In 1992/93 the European Cup was rebranded and parcelled up as the UEFA Champions League. The Super Cup was subsequently renamed as the UEFA Super Cup. Since 2000 the Super Cup has been contested by the winners of the Champions League and the UEFA Cup and latterly the Europa League.

Aberdeen remain the only Scottish club that has won the European Super Cup. Beaten Cup Winners' Cup finalists Real Madrid share the most wins with arch-rivals Barcelona on five wins each. Aberdeen currently sit in 18th place in the all-time table. The Dons share their one win with Sevilla, Porto, Manchester United, Dynamo Kyiv, Nottingham Forest and Aston Villa.

Spanish clubs have dominated the competition with five clubs in the top 12 previous winners. Four English clubs are in the top 20 but with only nine wins against 16 shared between the Spanish clubs. In the overall table by country Scotland, by virtue of the Aberdeen success, are in 11th place from a total of 15 successful nations. Former Aberdeen manager Alex Ferguson has overseen both Aberdeen and Manchester United in four Super Cup finals.

Mark McGhee and Neil Simpson scored the goals that won the Super Cup for the Dons. Other Scottish-born players who have scored in Super Cup finals are: Ken McNaught (Aston Villa), Kenny Dalglish (Liverpool), Brian McClair (Manchester United) and Kenny Burns (Nottingham Forest).

When Aberdeen came up against Hamburg in 1983 it provided them with an ideal opportunity to avenge their UEFA Cup defeat in 1981. That result rankled with Alex Ferguson as he felt that they should have eliminated the Germans at that time, and it was a great opportunity missed. Hamburg had progressed to become worthy European champions in 1983 after defeating Juventus to lift the trophy while Aberdeen beat Real Madrid to win the Cup Winners' Cup. Both sides agreed to play the ties in December after the Dons had safely secured their passage to the last eight of the Cup Winners' Cup in defence of their trophy, while also having enough points for a substantial lead at the top of the league.

Ferguson provided the club with a massive boost when he announced that he had turned down the opportunity to manage Rangers. Fergie declared, 'I have unfinished business with Aberdeen. This is a great club and I firmly believe that there is much more that can be achieved here. This side is a great one and I want them to impose themselves on Scottish football and really make their mark. If I did not believe that, then we would all be wasting our time here.'

The first leg of the final was played in the Volksparkstadion in Hamburg on 22 November. Ferguson had always admired the German approach to the game, and he had learned much from the Dons' battles against German opposition on four occasions in Europe. Aberdeen went into the game looking to at least keep their goal intact, which was a measure of their confidence back then. The general belief was that they could beat anyone at Pittodrie, although challenges did not come much bigger than the European Cup holders. In freezing conditions, the Dons once again deployed their 'early defence' approach which had upset German opponents in previous ties. The tactic was simple enough in that Hamburg would not be allowed the time or space to play in their own half as they had been used to. It meant that the Dons' work rate would have to be exceptional and that chances would have to be taken. It worked a treat for the visitors, who dominated the game for long spells. The

0-0 draw was about right as Hamburg did create some chances of their own but came up against what was arguably the best defence in European football at the time.

On another night it could have been better for Aberdeen as they spurned several chances to take an away goal with them, but with the tie finely balanced it set up the decider at Pittodrie. It was a busy time for all concerned at Aberdeen and there was a blow for the Dons after Donald Mackay resigned as Dundee manager and Archie Knox left Pittodrie to take over as boss at Dens Park in his own right before the return match against Hamburg. At the same time the club snapped up 21-year-old full-back Stewart McKimmie in a £90,000 deal from Dundee. In the international arena, Aberdeen had a record six players in the Scotland side that played Northern Ireland; it would have been a magnificent seven had it not been for a rare injury to Willie Miller. The captain, however, was back in his usual place for the Super Cup Final and it was also a first European appearance for McKimmie.

The all-ticket sell-out crowd was joined by millions all over the world who were watching on television – some 80 countries worldwide were taking the game live. Conditions were far from perfect but that did not stop the slick Germans from looking lively in the opening stages with some good early possession. Uli Stein was the first goalkeeper called into action though when he had to be alert to smother a low Gordon Strachan cross. Captain Felix Magath was the major influence in the German side, and he was well policed by Neil Simpson who was given the task to shadow the playmaker. Magath did get free of Simpson's shackles to send a shot just past the post as Hamburg went in search of an away goal that would have made the Dons' task more difficult. Aberdeen responded in style and they should have taken the lead when a McKimmie cross was headed on by Hewitt to McGhee, whose overhead kick was turned away for a corner. Stein then saved from John Hewitt and McMaster in quick succession as Aberdeen began to turn the screw on the Germans. Hamburg retaliated with some fine moves in the Dons' half and they looked a real threat going forward. Just before half-time a Doug Bell header narrowly went over the bar as a tense half finished without a goal.

The second half got off to a great start as Aberdeen broke the deadlock with a goal in the opening minute. Weir created the opening with a typical 60-yard run down the left. Hewitt latched on to Weir's cross and he set up Simpson to score from close range. That goal almost brought the roof down at the old stadium as the Dons drew confidence and went on to dominate. There was no let-up as McGhee then Hewitt both came close to extending the lead, and in 64 minutes Aberdeen struck again. Weir had been inspired in the second half and it was from his corner that McGhee scored from close range after Miller had cut the ball back from the touchline. That second goal secured the victory and they played the game out with a ring of confidence that was a joy to behold. The Dons should have scored more but they came up against Stein, who made some sensational saves as the pressure increased. Hamburg were a well beaten side long before referee Horst Brummeier blew for full time. The whole ground rose to acclaim the Dons as they were presented with their prize and went on a deserved lap of honour. Aberdeen had conquered Europe that year and they were now 'Kings of Europe' as the local *Press & Journal* claimed in the first match reports to emerge. It completed a remarkable year of success and there was no sign of any let-up.

Jim Leighton went on to become the most-capped keeper for Scotland with 91 appearances. He moved to Manchester United in 1988 after a memorable Aberdeen career, and later returned to Pittodrie in 1997 from Hibernian. McKimmie amassed 40 caps for Scotland, the last of which came in Euro '96 as he flourished at his hometown club in the aftermath of Gothenburg, receiving a testimonial from the Dons in August 1994. John McMaster returned to his native Morton in 1987 and went on to scout for the Dons. Neil Simpson was another local boy made good and another Scotland international. 'Simmy' returned to Pittodrie after his playing career and is currently involved in the award-winning community department at Pittodrie. McLeish was the last of the Gothenburg side to leave the Dons in 1994. Miller remains the club's greatest servant and captain and an iconic figure for everything the Dons achieved during the 1980s. Gordon Strachan returned to Scotland after spells in English football as a player, coach and manager. John

Hewitt remains the local lad who scored THAT goal in Gothenburg in 1983 and thus earned his place in Pittodrie folklore. McGhee moved to Hamburg in 1984 after his performances against them in the red of Aberdeen. Doug Bell missed the date with Real Madrid through injury but he was a potent weapon in the European arena. Weir also had a double celebration on the night against Hamburg as his wife gave birth during the game and Peter was told immediately after the final whistle.

As for Weir's greatest game, the consensus would be that the Cup Winners' Cup win in Gothenburg would come out on top, but it was the Super Cup triumph at Pittodrie that remains his abiding memory. He recalled, 'Gothenburg is a fantastic memory. But nothing has ever come as close to the emotions I felt against Hamburg at Pittodrie. Not only did I lift the trophy in front of 22,000 ecstatic Aberdeen fans, but within seconds of the final whistle I discovered that my wife had gave birth to another son!

'On the day of the game I left our home in the Bridge of Don to join up with the lads for a pre-match meal. It was not until later that I realised my wife had been taken into hospital less than half an hour after I had left her. She knew I couldn't be told. It would have put me right off my game. Fortunately, my parents were on hand and everything was fine.

'In those days Alex Ferguson had us totally focused on matches. It was yet another huge game for Aberdeen in Europe. We had won the Cup Winners' Cup while Hamburg were European Cup holders. To me it was the match that would decide the best team in Europe. Hamburg had the likes of Felix Magath and Manny Kaltz in their team; they were a formidable outfit. But we were flying, and I played well. Kaltz was directly up against me. He wasn't the quickest and I took advantage of that. Joe Harper later made me man of the match on TV. It was a magical night as once again we had rose to the occasion. Having beaten the likes of Bayern Munich and Real Madrid, nobody was going to tell us we were not Europe's best.

'I remember lifting the shield and the club secretary Ian Taggart came down to tell me that my wife had given birth to a boy at 7pm. I was totally stunned. Fergie came up to me and produced one of his famous bruising pats on the back. Then the rest of the lads joined in. For about an hour in the dressing room I was in a daze, I could not believe it. Ninety minutes after the game I was able to see my son. I had a party back at my house and I recall sitting in a quiet moment reflecting; does it get any better than this? Not many people can say they have lifted the Super Cup and then celebrated the birth of your son the same night. I have still got a video in the house of that Super Cup night. I never get tired of watching it; my greatest game.'

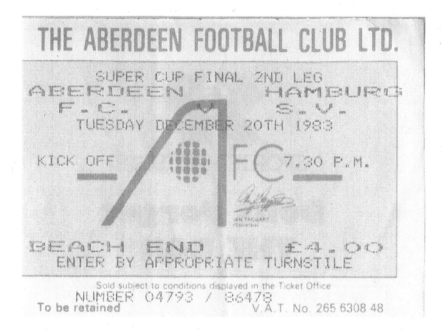

# Hearts 0 Aberdeen 1

2 May 1984
Scottish Premier Division
Tynecastle Park, Edinburgh
Attendance: 12,000

| **Aberdeen** | **Hearts** |
| --- | --- |
| Jim Leighton | Henry Smith |
| Stewart McKimmie | Walter Kidd |
| Doug Rougvie | George Cowie |
| Neale Cooper | Sandy Jardine |
| Alex McLeish | Roddie MacDonald |
| Willie Miller | Craig Levein |
| Gordon Strachan | Dave Bowman |
| Neil Simpson | Gary Mackay |
| Mark McGhee | Jimmy Bone |
| John Hewitt | John Robertson |
| Peter Weir | Donald Park |
| *Sub:* Eric Black | *Sub:* Willie Johnston |
| *Manager:* Alex Ferguson | *Manager:* Alex MacDonald |

THE EARLY 1980s will always be remembered for Aberdeen's double success in Europe and three Scottish Cups won in a row. What was missing since 1980 was the one that Alex Ferguson demanded – the Premier Division title, 'It is the mark of consistency and when you are league champions there is no doubt as to which side are the best. It is important that we maintain that level to remain at the top.'

From the outset of season 1983/84 the boss made the Premier Division his prime target and his players were left under no illusions as to what Ferguson was after. Trying to balance that with the three cup competitions was always going to difficult. Progress was made in the League Cup and Scottish Cups as well as the defence of their European Cup Winners' Cup crown. Aberdeen came back from a tough clash at Porto in the first leg of their Cup Winners' Cup semi-final to face a rejuvenated Dundee in the semi-final of the Scottish Cup at Tynecastle. Aberdeen came through 2-0 in what was a bruising tie. The squad was stretched as Mark McGhee, Stewart McKimmie and Peter Weir were all missing through injury. Ferguson recalled, 'Although we were never in danger, it was a real battle and it was obvious that Archie Knox had already improved the Dundee team considerably.' Knox had been Ferguson's assistant through their successful European campaigns but was persuaded to take over at Dundee as manager in 1983 between the two legs of the European Super Cup Final.

Aberdeen had stretched their lead at the top of the Premier Division by the end of April and the impossible dream of a grand slam of four trophies had been trimmed down to a league and Scottish Cup double. With five league games left, the Dons travelled to face Hearts at Tynecastle knowing that one point would take the title north. Nearest challengers Celtic had virtually given up as Aberdeen were unstoppable in the league, but as preparations for the celebrations continued there was also disappointment as the defence of the European Cup Winners' Cup ended with a defeat at home to an emerging Porto side. It was a bitter blow as Aberdeen were favourites to make the final in Switzerland but it just never happened on a night that saw Pittodrie shrouded in the famed north-east sea 'haar' as it's called locally, and an uncharacteristic performance ended with the Dons bowing out.

As Aberdeen were preparing to head south to Tynecastle for the midweek clash, their most prized possession, the European Cup Winners' Cup trophy, was on its way back to UEFA headquarters in Switzerland. It was packed up in a specially built, velvet-lined case bound for Berne.

One point at Hearts would have been enough but Ferguson wanted to clinch the title with a win. With Aberdeen due to face Hibernian at Pittodrie on the Saturday it was certain to be a sell-out to hopefully welcome the new Scottish champions. The supporters though would still travel to Edinburgh in big numbers. The league and cup double were very much on.

With the championship all but secured the Dons had plenty of time to prepare for the Scottish Cup Final against Celtic. Ahead of the visit to Hearts it was well known that Gordon Strachan was leaving at the end of the season. Italian side Verona were among a raft of interested clubs, but it was reported that the playmaker had turned down the offer from Italy. That left Cologne as favourites to sign Strachan and end his seven-year spell in red.

As Strachan was considering pastures new, for another Aberdeen player it was smiles all around at a Pittodrie photocall. On the day of the Hearts game, it was Willie Miller's 29th birthday and as he was ready to lead the team to more success, he received more good news as he was named as the Scottish Football Writers' Association Footballer of the Year for 1984. Miller was the unanimous choice with the biggest winning margin since Billy McNeill took the first award in 1965. What was unique about the results was that there was no runner-up to Miller as he polled 60 out of 63 votes. Miller became the third Aberdeen player to win the award, following on from Martin Buchan in 1971 and Strachan in 1980. Miller had been the runner-up to Charlie Nicholas in the previous season and was on hand at Pittodrie before the team left for Edinburgh to accept the congratulations of the staff and his team-mates. Miller was delighted when speaking to the *Evening Express*, 'I must admit I was a bit disappointed when I didn't win it last season but that made winning it this year all the better. Some great Scottish players have their names on this award and it certainly is an honour.' The award was to be presented at a gala dinner in Glasgow the following week, where Alex Ferguson was the guest speaker.

It was back then that Ferguson paid tribute to his captain in a statement that has endured to this day, 'Willie is the best penalty box defender in Europe, if not the world.' High praise indeed.

Hearts were determined to spoil the party; the last thing they wanted was to see more Aberdeen success in their own backyard. The Edinburgh side by tradition have long been vying with Aberdeen in terms of stature in the Scottish game, although during that period the team from the Granite City eclipsed anything that the capital club could muster. Indeed, Hearts had gained a reputation of being a 'yo-yo' club having been relegated and promoted on more than one occasion. In contrast Aberdeen were not only dominating in Scotland but their European Cup Winners' Cup and Super Cup double success was something the Edinburgh club could only dream of.

The formality of clinching the Premier Division title was completed with a hard-fought win over Hearts, who had been looking for the two points that would have assured them of a UEFA Cup place. Aberdeen were aiming considerably higher with another tilt at the European Cup to follow. The winner came from full-back Stewart McKimmie's first goal for Aberdeen. Hearts, to their credit, did make a real game of it but the Dons' class ultimately made the difference. Jim Leighton was called into action on several occasions. Hearts were first to show aggression, winning an early corner, but the first opportunity fell to the Dons when a cross from McGhee was almost turned into his own net by Walter Kidd. Shortly after that, Hewitt controlled a long ball from Rougvie and set up Peter Weir, whose shot went just wide. Hearts were keen to attack but they rarely troubled the Aberdeen defence. McKimmie and Rougvie switched flanks before Craig Levein had the first real chance for the home side when he headed over. John Robertson then saw his effort go over the bar, and Aberdeen should have taken the lead just before the break when Neil Simpson just missed the target after being set up by Cooper.

Aberdeen were under more pressure in the second half, but the champions-elect opened the scoring in 61 minutes. A long throw-in by Rougvie was headed on by McGhee and McKimmie, making a diagonal run from the right, dragged the ball into space before wheeling to flick it into the opposite corner. It was a superb goal, one that was worthy of winning any championship.

Aberdeen went on to win the title with 57 points, a new Premier Division record. In what was an exhausting season the Dons played 63 competitive matches, 27 of which were cup ties.

Ferguson had achieved his prime target, 'It was important that we won the championship in style. Also, with four games to spare it was a tremendous achievement. I was confident throughout the season that we would win the league. We had grown as a team and our continued success was down to several of the team gaining so much big-game experience.'

In the aftermath of the league success, it was no surprise that the Dons were targeting the European Cup which was immediately placed at the top of the wanted list. There was no arrogance in these claims. At that time the Dons were a household name in European football and had gained respect that their domestic rivals could only dream of. Ferguson was in a bullish mood when he spoke to the *Evening Express*, 'The European Cup is undoubtedly the big one, and that is the one we are going for now. Next season we will be making a serious assault on the European Cup. We hope and believe we can go all the way. We have already brought the European Cup Winners' Cup and Super Cup to Pittodrie, so we have the experience to handle a run in the European Cup. We would like to succeed again in Europe but there is already another target to aim for. Only one team outside of Glasgow has retained the championship and that was Hibernian back in 1950. Naturally we want to keep the championship here next season.'

Ferguson summed up the difference between his side and their opponents. 'Class,' was his claim, and he added, 'We have a new points record and won the league with games to spare.'

Aberdeen director Chris Anderson was quick to point out that the title was wrapped up after only 32 games, 'It has been a creditable performance, considering we have been so heavily involved with European games and the Scottish Cup at the same time.'

McKimmie also revealed his winning goal was not as clinical as first thought, 'It was a real scalff of an effort. For a start I don't know why I was even in the penalty box. Mark [McGhee] headed on a long throw and I just happened to be handy. But to tell the truth I didn't hit the ball properly at all with my left foot. The ball still found its way into the net and that will do me fine.'

McKimmie had been a surprise signing in December 1983 from Dundee. The Aberdeen-born defender cost £90,000 in a transfer that was kept under wraps. He would go on to establish himself in the side for the next 14 seasons. He also went on to play for Scotland on 40 occasions and led Aberdeen to League Cup success as captain in 1995.

Jim Leighton was nominated as the man of the match at Tynecastle and the Scotland keeper was his usual calm self at full time, 'We won the league because we are a team in the true sense, all playing for each other. Before the game we didn't feel any extra pressure as we knew it would happen and we are all happy that it is over and done with.' Leighton had 19 shut-outs from 32 league games and had only conceded 16 goals. Ferguson was full of praise,

'Jim was unbelievable, and he showed great composure. Some of his saves were first class, even when the shots were getting past Willie Miller!'

## Scottish Premier Division 1984

|  | P | W | D | L | F | A | Pts |
|---|---|---|---|---|---|---|---|
| Aberdeen | 36 | 25 | 7 | 4 | 78 | 21 | 57 |
| Celtic | 36 | 21 | 8 | 7 | 80 | 41 | 50 |
| Dundee United | 36 | 18 | 11 | 7 | 67 | 39 | 47 |
| Rangers | 36 | 15 | 12 | 9 | 53 | 41 | 42 |
| Hearts | 36 | 10 | 16 | 10 | 38 | 47 | 36 |
| St Mirren | 36 | 9 | 14 | 13 | 55 | 59 | 32 |
| Hibernian | 36 | 12 | 7 | 17 | 45 | 55 | 31 |
| Dundee | 36 | 11 | 5 | 20 | 50 | 74 | 27 |
| St Johnstone | 36 | 10 | 3 | 23 | 36 | 81 | 23 |
| Motherwell | 36 | 4 | 7 | 25 | 31 | 75 | 15 |

# ABERDEEN PUT ON A CHAMPION SHOW

### Willie Miller in runaway success

CHAMPAGNE DONS. The Aberdeen players are the picture of happiness as the celebrations start in the dressing room after the game.

WHAM! Defender Stewart McKimmie (right) hits home the Dons title winner at Tynecastle last night.

# Aberdeen 2 Celtic 1 (aet)

34

19 May 1984
Scottish Cup Final
Hampden Park, Glasgow
Attendance: 58,900

| Aberdeen | | Celtic |
|---|---|---|
| Jim Leighton | | Pat Bonner |
| Stewart McKimmie | | Danny McGrain |
| Doug Rougvie | | Mark Reid |
| Neale Cooper | | Roy Aitken |
| Alex McLeish | | Willie McStay |
| Willie Miller | | Murdo McLeod |
| Gordon Strachan | | Davie Provan |
| Neil Simpson | | Paul McStay |
| Mark McGhee | | Frank McGarvey |
| Eric Black | | Tommy Burns |
| Peter Weir | | Brian McClair |
| *Subs:* Doug Bell, Billy Stark | | *Sub:* Jim Melrose |
| *Manager:* Alex Ferguson | | *Manager:* Davie Hay |

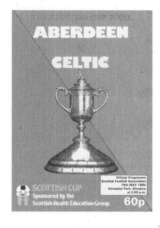

ABERDEEN CREATED history in 1984 when they won their third Scottish Cup in a row. It was perhaps a defining moment as after the 2-1 victory over Celtic the great Gothenburg team was heading towards its inevitable break-up. Once the euphoria of a third glittering success had sunk in, the final was to be the last appearances for three Aberdeen legends. Gordon Strachan had already intimated that he wished to move on, and he eventually joined Manchester United after initial reports claimed he was going to Cologne in Germany. Strachan had been at Pittodrie since 1977 and remains one of the most talented midfielders to ever play for the Dons. He first came to the attention of then United boss Ron Atkinson in Martin Buchan's testimonial at Old Trafford against Aberdeen in 1983. His good friend Mark McGhee was also on his way and he did go to Germany, signing for Aberdeen's old European Super Cup foes SV Hamburg. McGhee's goal in extra time was his final act as a Don and created an historic treble cup success. The departing striker was to return to Hampden a week later as a Hamburg player and he scored Scotland's goal in the 1-1 draw with England in the British Home Championship. The last player who was to leave was a bit more of a surprise. The long-serving Doug Rougvie had been at Pittodrie since 1972 but he refused new terms with the club and signed for Chelsea in a £150,000 deal. Rougvie was a regular in the Chelsea side along with the likes of Kerry Dixon and Pat Nevin but his robust style eventually proved his undoing. Following a raft of on-field indiscretions Rougvie was sold to Brighton in 1987 after he was sent off ten minutes into a game against Wimbledon for punching Dave Beasant and head-butting Carlton Fairweather. Rougvie made Micky Droy, his Stamford Bridge team-mate, look like a lightweight in comparison.

Aberdeen's preparations for their final game of the season were along regular lines. Their usual stay at Cruden Bay involved some light training, relaxation and the occasional round of golf. The Dons were now frequent visitors to the national stadium and had amassed a wealth of experience at home, in Europe and in the international team. The side that started against Celtic that day boasted ten Scotland internationals, with young Neale Cooper the only player who never did gain a full cap for Scotland although he had 13 under-21 appearances to his credit.

The Dons had clinched the Premier Division title in style with four games to spare, and a first Premier Division and Scottish Cup double would make up for their disappointing semi-final exit in their defence of the European Cup Winners' Cup to Porto. It was hard to imagine that the last four left in that season's Cup Winners' Cup was made up of holders Aberdeen, Porto, Juventus and Manchester United. Such was the Dons' stature back then they were installed as the bookmakers' favourites to become the first side to retain the trophy. Aberdeen were now an established seeded club in European competition.

Aberdeen reached their third Scottish Cup Final in a row and their 63rd competitive game of the season after a comfortable 2-0 win over Dundee in their semi-final at Tynecastle. Celtic eased past St Mirren to reach what was the competition's 109th final, and their fifth final meeting with the Dons. While Aberdeen had lost the first three in 1937, 1954 and 1967, they had begun to change that trend with a famous 3-1 win in 1970. Incredible as it may seem and unheard of in the modern era, Celtic's Irish goalkeeper Paddy Bonner was the only foreign player involved in the two matchday squads – the rest were all born in Scotland.

Celtic were facing a barren season without a trophy unless they could stop the Aberdeen juggernaut, although they would qualify for the European Cup Winners' Cup regardless of the result at Hampden.

Roy Aitken will never look back on the 1984 final with any fond memories. The future Aberdeen manager was Celtic's captain at that time but he was not to make it all the way through the match.

It is not very often that a provincial side would go into a final against either of the Glasgow clubs as the favourites but that was accepted back then as Aberdeen had not only crushed the Celtic and Rangers dominance in Scotland, but had cut their teeth in the European arena with outstanding success in 1983.

From the moment that Aitken clattered Mark McGhee with the Dons leading following an early Eric Black goal, Celtic were up against it. Referee Bob Valentine sent Aitken off; the first player to be dismissed in a Scottish Cup Final since Jock Buchanan in 1929.

Aberdeen had opened the scoring when Black pounced on an Alex McLeish knock-down from a corner. Celtic claimed that the striker was offside, but Black's hooked finish past Bonner stood. While Celtic were incensed, the match was no place for the faint of heart and the tackles and yellow cards were prominent. It all came to a head with Aitken's chest-high challenge on McGhee that brought remonstrations from Gordon Strachan. When it all calmed down, ten-man Celtic to their credit fought back and when Paul McStay levelled with four minutes left, alarm bells were ringing in the Aberdeen camp. Aberdeen were no strangers to extra time in cup finals and their experience and fitness told in that energy-sapping period. The outcome was decided on 98 minutes when McGhee scored the winner. Aberdeen had dominated extra time and after Doug Bell's shot from 25 yards came back off the bar, the alert Strachan set up McGhee who scored from a tight angle.

For Aberdeen it was a first league and cup double in their history, while Celtic licked their wounds as runners-up in all three domestic competitions.

Alex Ferguson recalled the day, 'We started the game exceptionally well and gave notice when Eric Black scored early on. With half an hour gone Roy Aitken was rightly sent off but I wished the incident had never happened. Playing against ten men sometimes is the worst thing that can happen to a team and that proved to be the case for Aberdeen on the day. In the second half we seemed to go into a lower gear and found it difficult to keep going. It was a nightmare. Celtic fought so hard and deserved their late equaliser to take the game into extra time.

'I was desperate to get on to the players at full time and get them playing like the Aberdeen we knew. It was different in that extra-time period. Celtic had their chance, now it was down to us to go on and win the cup. Billy Stark and Doug Bell coming on brought a freshness to the team and Celtic were drained. I switched Neale Cooper to look after Davie Provan, who was giving Rougvie a hard time. From that point on there was no way back for Celtic. Doug Bell had a marvellous shot come back off the post and Mark McGhee scored from a tight angle. The Scottish Cup was ours for the third year in a row.'

The summer of 1984 may have been a time of celebration for Aberdeen but politically all was not well. The miners' strike was at its height and there was a special point to one banner that greeted the team on their return to the city, 'Willie Miller stops more strikers than the police.' Another banner had a pop at their opponents, 'Another poor harvest for Hay [Celtic manager] and McGrain [Celtic defender].'

Aberdeen were now at their peak, a real power in Scotland and were entitled to consider themselves superior to both Celtic and Rangers. Such was the confidence and expectations at Pittodrie that there was a wonderful quote in the *Press & Journal*, 'If there are any more triumphs the open-top bus will have to be put on the regular city bus timetable.'

Willie Miller recalled the cup win, 'When you play Celtic or Rangers in Glasgow you always have the crowd to contend with, yet the two sides give you a different game. Rangers are strong physically while Celtic are more improvised. I preferred the Rangers games.

Challenge strongly, win the ball, deny possession. Celtic on the other hand would keep attacking you so they had a different approach.

'There was some doubt over Eric Black's opening goal. You can never judge offside from 30 yards out. I remember we had been on the end of some ridiculous decisions in big finals before. Decisions that cost us winners' medals so, I would never make any apology for getting a break.

'My immediate reaction to the Roy Aitken tackle was that it was a red card. It was clumsy. It was a surprising challenge for such an experienced player to make and he was an enormous loss to Celtic.

'We had a poor second half and I don't think we consciously decided to hold our one-goal lead. Fergie had been quite kind to us at half-time and I had noticed before on occasion such praise saw us take our foot off the accelerator and allow the likes of Celtic to come back at us. We eventually wore them down and they were caught off guard when Doug Bell's shot came back off the woodwork. Mark followed up to score the winner. We had won the Scottish Cup three times on the trot and that was something even Celtic had never achieved.'

# Aberdeen 1 Celtic 1

27 April 1985
Scottish Premier Division
Pittodrie Stadium, Aberdeen
Attendance: 23,000

| Aberdeen | Celtic |
|---|---|
| Jim Leighton | Pat Bonner |
| Stewart McKimmie | Willie McStay |
| Tom McQueen | Danny McGrain |
| Billy Stark | Roy Aitken |
| Alex McLeish | Tom McAdam |
| Willie Miller | Murdo McLeod |
| Ian Porteous | Peter Grant |
| Neil Simpson | Paul McStay |
| Frank McDougall | Maurice Johnston |
| Doug Bell | Tommy Burns |
| John Hewitt | Frank McGarvey |
| *Subs:* Steven Cowan, Neale Cooper | *Sub:* Davie Provan |
| *Manager:* Alex Ferguson | *Manager:* Davie Hay |

ABERDEEN HAVE won the Scottish league title four times, in 1955, 1980, 1984 and 1985. On each occasion Celtic were the runners-up. In 1985 the Dons retained the Premier Division and it was also the first time they had clinched the championship on home soil. It was a sweet moment for all concerned. This clash with Celtic, however, was never a league decider unlike the meeting with the Parkhead side at Pittodrie in 1971.

It was an indication of how successful Aberdeen were at the time that the league championship, the Dons' only success that season, brought a tinge of disappointment. Despite being held to a 1-1 draw the players celebrated in style and the game will always be remembered for the goal scored by captain Willie Miller and subsequent celebration in front of the South Terrace.

Aberdeen, as reigning champions, showed their intent from the outset, reeling off five straight wins to put them top of the league early in the season. It was a position they were to hold for the next nine months. Once again they clinched the title with games to spare and created a new points record after winning their final two matches, at Hearts and Morton. Celtic were their only serious challengers all season and the Dons could not defeat the Glasgow club in both their meetings at Parkhead.

When Celtic came north for Aberdeen's final home game of the season, they were only delaying the inevitable title success. For the Dons it was their desire to clinch the championship in front of their own fans that was paramount. Alex Ferguson was keen to get the job done, 'Celtic have been chasing us all season in the league and it is appropriate that the rivalry between us should climax in tomorrow's game. Although we will welcome the title whenever it comes, the players would love to make sure of it in front of our own supporters.' Celtic manager Davie Hay was accepting of the Dons' ultimate success, 'We know it is our last chance, except that, unlike a cup final, even if we win, the odds are still against us. We do intend to push Aberdeen all the way and keep the league alive for as long as possible.'

Aberdeen had beaten Celtic on their last four visits to the Granite City, scoring nine goals and conceding three.

The game itself, not unlike others, was full of controversy. Celtic were getting used to playing second fiddle to an Aberdeen side that was imperious and virtually unbeatable at what had become known as 'Fortress Pittodrie'. The conditions were not great with a swirling wind and occasional showers and the match was never going to be a classic with so much at stake.

Aberdeen began well but missed early chances with Stewart McKimmie, Billy Stark and Frank McDougall all passing up good opportunities. That gave Celtic encouragement to get into the game. To be fair on the visitors they did claw their way back and went ahead through a controversial penalty in 38 minutes. As Stark climbed to head the ball clear, Celtic forward Maurice Johnston fell to the ground. Even the Celtic players did not appeal but referee Smith pointed to the spot. Bedlam ensued after Roy Aitken scored from the penalty and promptly celebrated in front of the home support behind the goal. That prompted angry scenes both on and off the field as Paul McStay seemed to be struck by an object thrown from the stands. It was an unsavoury moment but typical of the time. Alastair MacDonald, the renowned journalist for the *Press & Journal*, commented, 'Without condoning in any way the loutish behaviour of the spectators who pelted the Celtic players, I feel that the incident underlines the folly of players deliberately provoking opposing supporters in this way. Aitken may not have left the pitch after his penalty, but the attitude adopted was inflammatory, particularly as the Aberdeen supporters were already incensed at the unjust penalty award. There is little point in the authorities curbing crowd violence if players do not act responsibly.'

Aberdeen came out in the second half with renewed vigour, still harbouring anger at the penalty decision. The champions-elect eventually got the goal that secured the title and it came from Miller. An Ian Porteous free kick found Miller in the box and his header back across goal was no more than Aberdeen deserved. The goal itself was memorable but the celebration afterwards remains part of Pittodrie folklore. Miller turned to the South Terrace after scoring and raced along the pitch, shaking his arm in jubilation as the home support were ecstatic. It took Miller's team-mates all of 40 yards before he was caught and eventually swamped in celebration.

Miller looked back on another fantastic day, 'I can't really remember what I did. I was just overcome with emotion after I scored. It was sheer emotion that drove me up towards the fans and towards the halfway line. There is nothing like winning a trophy in front of your own fans.' It was Miller's 24th goal for the club and the most important. He looked ahead, 'I have got three years of my contract left and I will be playing here for that time at least; if the manager thinks I'm fit enough of course. There is so much to look forward to here, more so now we are back in the European Cup. The supporters here love the European atmosphere, as do the players. There are youngsters at this club who have never experienced what I have in the past. And I certainly want to taste that again before I finish playing.'

There was late drama as a Celtic goal was disallowed after a clear infringement on Jim Leighton. In the closing seconds John Hewitt missed a glorious opportunity to give Aberdeen the victory but the game ended all square, which was enough for the Dons as although Celtic could mathematically catch them the 13-goal swing in two games was never realistic. Celtic manager Hay admitted, 'All credit to Aberdeen for their achievement, they deserved the title. The championship was not lost today. While Aberdeen were going about their business in the correct fashion we were going to places like Dundee and Dumbarton and struggling. Aberdeen were consistent.'

As the celebrations continued with the players taking their bow, Ferguson was already looking ahead, knocking back any speculation as to his own future, 'As far as I am concerned, I see myself as part of this club for a while yet. There is still scope for this present Aberdeen team to progress and develop, so I would like to think we can grow together.'

It was great news for Aberdeen as rumours persisted with the likes of Real Madrid, Arsenal and Benfica all being interested in speaking to the boss. Not for the first time Ferguson had his sights on the European Cup, 'Our European challenge suffered this season from the inexperience of some players who came into the squad in the summer. We also had to do without Weir, Bell and McDougall which would have made a difference in the game in Berlin [Aberdeen had been beaten on penalties by Dinamo Berlin in the first round of the European Cup]. In hindsight we benefited in the league being out of Europe as we could focus entirely on retaining the title. I am not interested in speculation. I have a contract at Aberdeen and my main priority is to try and win the European Cup for Aberdeen.'

It was an impressive championship success. Following on from their league and cup double from the previous season, the loss of three of their Gothenburg side was hard to take. With Gordon Strachan, Doug Rougvie and Mark McGhee all moving on, two direct replacements were brought in – Tom McQueen, a full-back from Clyde, and Frank McDougall, a £100,000 buy from St Mirren. Billy Stark had already been at the club for a year as Ferguson prepared for the departure of Strachan in advance.

Critics were quick to suggest that Aberdeen were on the decline. Ferguson used that to great effect. All through his seven-year spell at Pittodrie he used his famed mind games to upset, annoy and irritate anyone who stood in Aberdeen's way. It made for some heated exchanges and frayed tempers, but it worked a treat. The adopted siege mentality that Ferguson created formed a ring of steel around his players. The west coast media lapped it up, even though some of the more astute journalists knew exactly what Ferguson was up to: whipping them into a frenzy and letting the chaos unfold. It was with almost monotonous regularity on the eve of a big game, usually in Glasgow, that Ferguson would cast doubts on referees, players and supporters. By the time the Dons reached the 'killing fields' of Parkhead and Ibrox, it was all set up perfectly for them to prove themselves time and again against the powerful Glasgow clubs. Between 1979 and 1986 until Ferguson left for Manchester United, the Dons dominated Scottish football on a scale they have not done before or since.

## Scottish Premier Division 1985

|  | P | W | D | L | F | A | Pts |
|---|---|---|---|---|---|---|---|
| Aberdeen | 36 | 27 | 5 | 4 | 89 | 26 | 59 |
| Celtic | 36 | 22 | 8 | 6 | 77 | 30 | 52 |
| Dundee United | 36 | 20 | 7 | 9 | 67 | 33 | 47 |
| Rangers | 36 | 13 | 12 | 11 | 47 | 38 | 38 |
| St Mirren | 36 | 17 | 4 | 15 | 51 | 56 | 38 |
| Dundee | 36 | 15 | 7 | 14 | 48 | 50 | 37 |
| Hearts | 36 | 13 | 5 | 18 | 47 | 64 | 31 |
| Hibernian | 36 | 10 | 7 | 19 | 38 | 61 | 27 |
| Dumbarton | 36 | 6 | 7 | 23 | 29 | 64 | 19 |
| Morton | 36 | 5 | 2 | 29 | 29 | 100 | 12 |

# Rangers 0 Aberdeen 3

29 September 1985
Scottish Premier Division
Ibrox Stadium, Glasgow
Attendance: 37,600

| Aberdeen | Rangers |
|---|---|
| Jim Leighton | Nicky Walker |
| Stewart McKimmie | Hugh Burns |
| Brian Mitchell | Stewart Munro |
| Billy Stark | Dave McPherson |
| Alex McLeish | Craig Paterson |
| Willie Miller | Ian Durrant |
| Eric Black | Ally McCoist |
| Neil Simpson | Bobby Russell |
| Frank McDougall | Bobby Williamson |
| Neale Cooper | Doug Bell |
| John Hewitt | Davie Cooper |
| *Subs:* Steve Gray, Willie Falconer | *Subs:* Ted McMinn, Dave McKinnon |
| *Manager:* Alex Ferguson | *Manager:* Jock Wallace |

IT SHOULD never be underestimated just how the Aberdeen side of the 1980s had such an effect not only at Pittodrie, but on the whole of the Scottish game. In the 1950s and early '60s the league championship had been shared between seven different clubs: Aberdeen, Celtic, Rangers, Hearts, Hibernian, Dundee and Kilmarnock. That was to change in 1965 after Kilmarnock pipped Hearts to the title on the last day of the season. It took another 15 years for a side outside Glasgow to win what was now the Premier Division, and that Aberdeen triumph was the beginning of a decade of success. To put it into context, their title of 1985 remains the last time a side other than Celtic or Rangers have won the Premier League.

Aberdeen's success may have been condensed into a glorious ten-year period but three Premier Division titles, four Scottish Cups, one League Cup and of course their two European trophies surpassed anything that any Scottish club had achieved in such a period.

In the modern era such a feat is unthinkable as so much has changed in Scottish football. It was the Dons' success back then that prompted drastic action by Rangers. The Ibrox club may have been embarking on a huge upgrade of their stadium, but on the park they were simply miles behind Aberdeen. It was intolerable for the Rangers support who had watched on for years as first Aberdeen had taken over at the top of Scottish football, then they saw their former player Alex Ferguson turn down the opportunity to manage the Glasgow club. Aberdeen captain Willie Miller had also turned Rangers down as the Dons continued to rule.

The 'Aberdeen way' as it was back then was to bring through their younger players and give them the chance when merited so they could develop in the first team. Buying some of the best players in the Scottish leagues was not monopolised by the Glasgow clubs; Aberdeen were very adept at picking up some of the best around. Gordon Strachan, Peter Weir, Stuart Kennedy, Stewart McKimmie, Doug Bell, Billy Stark and Frank McDougall were all prised away from Scottish opponents in the late 1970s and early '80s. With the marvellous defensive trio of Leighton, McLeish and Miller all scouted from the west and developed at Pittodrie, it was little wonder Aberdeen were the envy of all Scotland.

That envy spilled over in an explosive encounter at Ibrox in September 1985. At that time the Dons were reigning league champions and looking at going far in the European Cup. With a League Cup Final on the horizon, those were heady days down Pittodrie way. The critics who suggested that Aberdeen would never be the same as their 1983 side began to break up were misguided. Under Ferguson this was like a dynasty at Pittodrie as the silverware continued to flow north.

By contrast Rangers were struggling. They may have been gradually redeveloping their Ibrox ground, but they were struggling to fill it. Aberdeen and to a lesser degree Celtic and even Dundee United were all ahead of them back then.

In 1983 they returned to their former manager Jock Wallace to lead them after Ferguson had turned them down. Wallace was the third choice as Dundee United boss Jim McLean, a close friend of Ferguson, also rejected the Ibrox job. Wallace had a fearsome reputation, but fury would never win over tactical nous. His return was met messiah like by the Rangers support, but the problem was his first game was at Pittodrie. A 3-0 win for the Dons was a chastening experience for Wallace, who insisted on his players reverting to their old black and red socks for some reason. Two years on and not much had changed.

Wallace was in a typical bullish mood as he looked ahead to the Aberdeen game, 'I reckon that if both teams play to their potential, we will come out on top.' Such a statement was intended to perhaps boost his own players' confidence as opposed to a genuine opinion. Wallace did not find many who supported his view, but it did offer defiance, a trait that he was renowned for.

Aberdeen travelled to Ibrox protecting an impressive record there; in their last 15 league games they had won seven and drawn five. The expectation was that Rangers would try to assert themselves physically to stifle what had become a fluent Aberdeen team. What Rangers and many other opponents back then attempted to do was to mix it up. The problem for them was that this Aberdeen group could more than handle themselves when it came to it. Being able to adapt to different game situations was something that Ferguson prided himself on. Aberdeen announced a 16-strong squad to travel to Glasgow on the Friday. Included were recent injury absentees Peter Weir and Jim Bett, neither of whom were expected to start in such a potentially explosive fixture. In normal circumstances Bett would certainly be starting against his old club, but with so many big games coming up Ferguson had to use his squad to the full. Going the other way was Doug Bell, who had signed for Rangers after leaving the Dons some months earlier. One Aberdeen player looking forward to the game was Billy Stark, who would make his 100th appearance for the Dons after his move from St Mirren in 1983.

The fixture would be remembered more for the chaos on the park than the Dons' comprehensive win. The atmosphere at Ibrox was toxic as Rangers lost their heads and were reduced to nine men in a frantic first half. The SFA would certainly be investigating as play was suspended for four minutes to allow spectators to be cleared from the pitch during the second half after they had spilled on to the field from the main stand enclosure. Referee George Smith had sent off Hugh Burns and Craig Paterson in addition to booking two other Rangers players, and two Dons also were carded. Although at one point the official took the players off the pitch, it was not certain if the Disciplinary Committee would regard the intrusion as crowd disorder. The source of the trouble came from those in that area who were throwing objects, mostly coins, on to the pitch. During the first half one Rangers player was struck and laid low; the referee and linesman were the target for a hail of missiles as they left the field at half-time. It was the dismissal of Burns that incurred the wrath of the home support. His 29th-minute red card for his lunge at Hewitt was merited and it could be argued he was paying the price for earlier indiscretions. McCoist, Paterson and Bell had already been booked along with Neale Cooper in a crazy 16-minute period. The experienced Edinburgh referee took further action four minutes after Aberdeen took the lead. Paterson had been given a torrid time of it and after his first booking he clattered into Cooper with a violent body charge. Rangers were down to nine men after only 34 minutes.

In between times some football did break out and it all came from Aberdeen. With Weir still struggling for fitness it was John Hewitt who stepped in and was the architect of the convincing victory. More than a third of his 240 appearances had been as a substitute. However, the striker was at last showing the consistency that the management were looking for. Hewitt was played in a free role up front, switching wings and causing Rangers' defence all sorts of bother. After providing the free kick from which Alex McLeish headed the opening goal on the half-hour mark, Hewitt was deprived of a goal just before the break when he was denied by a save from Nicky Walker.

The second goal came in 38 minutes and reflected what was by then the Dons' two-man numerical superiority. An Eric Black cross was headed against the bar by Frank McDougall and Stark pounced on the rebound to score. It was Stark's 45th goal in his 100th appearance, an incredible return for a midfielder.

The second half was not as frantic as Aberdeen, masters of game management, went about retaining possession and avoiding further trouble or injury. Had the Dons really gone for it then the final score could have been a lot worse for a Rangers side that had been taught a football lesson by their slick opponents.

Walker saved the home side again in 59 minutes when he kept out a close-range header from Willie Falconer, but in 80 minutes, Hewitt capped a fine performance with a delightful goal, his clever lob from 25 yards consigning Rangers to another humiliation on their own patch. The creation of the three goals was the highlight of a game that ceased to be a contest when the home side were reduced to nine men. It was Aberdeen who produced the football in between the bedlam where 26 free kicks were awarded in the first half alone. Rangers boss Wallace commended his 'survivors', stating that it had been the best his team had played for weeks. The Aberdeen domination of the Glasgow clubs was not done yet.

# Aberdeen 3 Hibernian 0

27 October 1985
Scottish League Cup Final
Hampden Park, Glasgow
Attendance: 40,061

**Aberdeen**
Jim Leighton
Stewart McKimmie
Brian Mitchell
Billy Stark
Alex McLeish
Willie Miller
Eric Black
Neil Simpson
Frank McDougall
Neale Cooper
John Hewitt
*Sub:* Steve Gray
*Manager:* Alex Ferguson

**Hibernian**
Alan Rough
Alan Sneddon
Ian Munro
Ally Brazil
Mark Fulton
Gordon Hunter
Paul Kane
Gordon Chisholm
Steve Cowan
Gordon Durie
Joe McBride
*Subs:* John Collins, Colin Harris
*Manager:* John Blackley

THE LEAGUE Cup was the one trophy that had eluded Alex Ferguson since he joined Aberdeen in 1978. It could be argued that was down to bad luck but on closer scrutiny it can perhaps be down to his priorities. There is no doubt that in his later managerial career, Ferguson never looked upon League Cup success as a target. During his seven years at Aberdeen there was enough to suggest he had already made up his mind on the competition. That was to change in 1985, 'It was the one trophy that I had never won, and I was keen to set the record straight.'

In the 1985 competition, Aberdeen had progressed to the last four without conceding a single goal. They would come up against a Dundee United side that had on occasion caused some difficulties for the Dons in recent years. At that time the League Cup semi-finals were played on a home and away basis. The first leg would be at Tannadice; both teams usually fared well away from home against each other. On 25 September Aberdeen gained a valuable lead by winning in Dundee through another Eric Black goal. The young striker had the knack of popping up with some vital goals and against United he was a constant threat. The game was never allowed to flow freely with a succession of fouls and personal battles on the field. Neale Cooper was brought into the starting line-up to replace the injured Jim Bett and he was involved in several physical challenges. Black's priceless goal came in 63 minutes when he headed past McAlpine after a superb John Hewitt cross. Shortly afterwards Richard Gough was sent off after a succession of fouls as he had been given a torrid time of it by Black and Hewitt. His scything lunge at Hewitt as the striker swept past him was worthy of a red card alone. There was a total of nine bookings in a match that threatened to get out of hand on more than one occasion.

The return at Pittodrie two weeks later gave Aberdeen the chance to exorcise the final of 1979 in front of another near capacity home crowd. It was also the first time that the new Merkland Stand was opened with a range of new facilities. The traditional King Street end of the ground had been the popular area for the younger element of the support to congregate. These days it is the home of the 'Aberdeen Ultras', the loyal brigade who have added so much to the atmosphere at Pittodrie.

Aberdeen were dealt a pre-match blow when Black failed to shrug off an injury and Ian Angus was brought into the side. With the Dons having the edge following their first-leg win it made for an exciting cup tie as a normally defensive Dundee United side were forced to be more adventurous which meant there were plenty of chances, mostly falling to Aberdeen. In a virtual repeat of the first leg it was another great run by Hewitt down the left that ended with a superb cross converted by Frank McDougall in 68 minutes. McDougall was arguably the finest front-post forward in Britain at the time and many of his goals came from that area. Fabulous Frank got in between Hegarty and Holt to superbly clip the ball past McAlpine, who barely moved to attempt a save. Alex Ferguson stated after the game that McDougall was the best finisher in the country and not many would have argued the point. That goal set up Aberdeen for a comfortable finish to the game, as United were down and out.

McDougall was looking forward to Hampden as he spoke in the *Green Final*, 'I honestly thought I was fated never to play in a final at Hampden. I have lost six semi-finals before with St Mirren and had to watch on last season as Dundee United knocked us out in the Scottish Cup. Now my only priority is getting my hands on the League Cup. The boss has also waited a long time to win this cup, so you can be sure we will go out and win it for him. I came to Aberdeen to play in finals and win leagues. Taking the championship last season was special. Hibernian will be tough, and they have the experienced Alan Rough in goal. They also knocked out Celtic and Rangers; I thought it was only Aberdeen who did that. We will not underestimate them, but we are desperate to win this cup. I have only played at Hampden once and that was for St Mirren in the Drybrough Cup Final and we lost to Aberdeen.'

Aberdeen had qualified for the final in style and had yet to concede a goal; Hibernian would be facing the Dons as rank outsiders to lift the trophy, despite the fact that the Edinburgh side had knocked out both Celtic and Rangers on their way to Hampden. Normally any team who achieved that would expect to win the silverware, but these were not normal times with Aberdeen dominating Scottish football.

Hibernian manager John Blackley was relatively inexperienced, but he had turned around his team's fortunes along with former Don Tommy Craig as his assistant, 'The club was beginning to stagnate and too many people were allowing it to happen. Tommy [Craig] has been magnificent in helping us achieve what we have.' Craig told the *Press & Journal* ahead of the final, 'It looks like we will be taking around 15,000 through and that will be a big help. Aberdeen will be a difficult side as they know how to win at Hampden, and we have a lot of young players.'

The Dons were full of internationals and players who were experienced in big games and they showed that maturity against a starkly contrasting Hibernian side. The game became known as the '12 Minute Final' as that was all it took for Aberdeen to effectively finish the match as a contest by taking a two-goal lead, an advantage they would not surrender at any stage of Ferguson's entire Pittodrie career. Those first two goals were created by Hewitt, who went on to be named the sponsors' man of the match.

The opening goal was a classic Aberdeen move full of pace and movement. McDougall carried the ball across the edge of the

Hibernian box and his reverse pass saw Hewitt latch on to it. His pace brought him between two defenders and as he rounded keeper Alan Rough his cross back across goal was met by Black, who headed home. Minutes later a Hewitt corner was cleared back to the wide man. Hewitt cut inside and on his right foot crossed for Billy Stark, who ghosted into the box to head a second goal. Aberdeen were in imperious mood and totally dominated the final. This was not one for the neutral, hopeful of seeing a keenly contested match. This was one for the purists as they saw Aberdeen in their pomp, showing a swagger and arrogance that came with being the best and most accomplished side in the country.

In the second half the Dons added a third when McDougall and Simpson combined to set up Black to slide in. It was the first and only time that Ferguson won the League Cup and his team had completed the task in style by winning all their ties without conceding a goal.

The side had evolved somewhat from the Gothenburg period and winning at Hampden had become almost routine. Seven of the line-up from Sweden started against Hibernian and their experience was crucial, as a delighted Ferguson said, 'I always felt we had more experience than Hibernian and that proved the case. To go right through the competition and not lose a goal was tremendous and it allowed the players to create their own piece of history.' His counterpart John Blackley conceded, 'The better team won, and Aberdeen deserved to win. When we gave Aberdeen that two-goal lead early in the match it left us with a mountain to climb. It was just great for Hibernian to appear in the final.'

Jim Leighton was delighted to get another winners' medal in what was a quiet afternoon, admitting, 'We started far too well for them and were never in any danger. It's a great feeling to have come through a major competition and not lose a single goal.'

Hewitt, the tormentor in chief in a Sunday stroll for the Dons, said, 'I am playing with a lot of confidence just now because I am getting a regular run in the side. I really should have scored a couple of times but if Aberdeen won the cup that is all that matters. Some people might have thought the game was over when we went 2-0 ahead but I never felt that way. One goal from them would have brought them back into it. The highlight of my career was in Gothenburg, but this ranks as another high point for me.'

Neale Cooper was playing in a three-man defence which was a change for the youngster. He was in good company if he slipped up with Scotland central defensive duo Alex McLeish and Willie Miller looking after him, 'It was a tremendous experience being in that position, and beside Alex and Willie. It's been a long time since I played there but I was quite confident that if I did anything silly, I had those two looking after me.'

The competition had been sponsored by Skol and Aberdeen as winners were to receive an additional £15,500 as they won by three clear goals.

# Aberdeen 4 Celtic 1

2 November 1985
Scottish Premier Division
Pittodrie Stadium, Aberdeen
Attendance: 23,000

| Aberdeen | Celtic |
|---|---|
| Jim Leighton | Pat Bonner |
| Stewart McKimmie | Willie McStay |
| Brian Mitchell | Danny McGrain |
| Billy Stark | Tom McAdam |
| Alex McLeish | Peter Grant |
| Willie Miller | Davie Provan |
| Eric Black | Paul McStay |
| Neil Simpson | Brian McClair |
| Frank McDougall | Tommy Burns |
| Neale Cooper | Alan McInally |
| John Hewitt | Paul Chalmers |
| *Subs:* Paul Wright, Jim Bett | *Manager:* Davie Hay |
| *Manager:* Alex Ferguson | |

THESE WERE heady days at Pittodrie. Aberdeen had just won the League Cup for the third time after beating Hibernian and were challenging for another three trophies. With a European Cup second round second leg against Swiss champions Servette coming in midweek, the Dons welcomed Celtic to Pittodrie. The Glasgow side had once again been challenging Alex Ferguson's men as they did throughout the 1980s. Manager Davie Hay, so often on the end of defeats by the Dons, was in defiant mood as his side travelled north on the Friday, 'We know we let ourselves down in the past so we must show a vast improvement against Aberdeen. This will be our most difficult game of the season, but if we perform the way we can, we are capable of beating Aberdeen.' The record books suggested otherwise; Celtic had only taken one point from their last five visits to Pittodrie.

Celtic were also boosted by the prospect of former Aberdeen and Gothenburg hero Mark McGhee coming back to Scotland. McGhee had joined Hamburg in 1984 but his move to the Bundesliga had been a difficult one with the forward struggling to win over the German support. He was not a regular in their first team and despite his claims that he wanted to see out his contract in Germany, Hamburg were willing to listen to offers with a fee of around £150,000 being mentioned.

Aberdeen had few injury worries ahead of the game of the day in Scotland before an all-ticket sell-out crowd. Ferguson was content, 'It is a huge game in terms of the league race. Celtic are always tough opponents, but we have an excellent record against them. We feel we can take any side on at Pittodrie.' Aberdeen were at the top of the league on goal difference in a season that also saw Hearts and Dundee United in the mix.

There was also some controversy when it was unclear whether Ken Stewart from the SFA would attend the game. It was reported in the *Press & Journal* that Stewart would not have been made welcome at Pittodrie after an argument with Dons directors Dick and Ian Donald at Hampden. The SFA security adviser was at the centre of a row after Aberdeen were fined £1,000 for their part in the controversial clash with Rangers at Ibrox in September. The board were furious at being punished for their part in the game that boiled over with two Rangers players sent off and a brief crowd spillage on to the field. Aberdeen insisted there was no 'ban' on Stewart, but speculation remained.

The game began at the usual frenetic pace and Alan McInally was spoken to by referee Brian McGinlay after a nasty foul on Alex McLeish only 20 seconds in. Aberdeen went with the side that had won the League Cup with the returning Jim Bett on the bench. Celtic began in positive fashion and created a couple of early opportunities, but they could not take advantage. If anybody was going to beat Aberdeen back then, they could ill afford to miss chances when they came their way. Neale Cooper tackled Aitken when the midfielder looked likely to score then Jim Leighton saved from Brian McClair. Driving sleet made conditions difficult as play continued with an orange ball. Dave Provan was then booked after a clash with Neil Simpson near the touchline.

Both sides were keen on attacking at every opportunity. A Provan shot from outside the box went wide before Danny McGrain was cautioned for going in on the back of McDougall. The tackles continued to fly in as Willie Miller was the first Don to be carded when he brought down McInally as he raced clear. Celtic to their credit had been giving a good account of themselves but it was the guile of Aberdeen that was gradually taking control, and the Dons opened the scoring in 27 minutes. Eric Black got clear of McGrain on the right and his cross found Frank McDougall, who headed past Bonner for his 11th goal of the season. Tempers frayed again when several players were involved in a series of clashes in 39 minutes, and Brian Mitchell was the second Aberdeen player to be booked. Just before the break Celtic equalised through Provan, who had been their most likely player to score. His free kick deceived Leighton but there were doubts about the decision as McInally looked to be impeding McLeish as he backed into him.

At half-time two of the Pittodrie ground staff paraded the League Cup, as well as the separate Skol Cup trophy produced by sponsors Skol, as Jim Bett replaced Billy Stark for the second half. Three minutes into that second period, McDougall struck again with another header to restore Aberdeen's lead. McGrain was struggling to cope with the pace and energy of the Aberdeen forwards. The Celtic legend was now 35 years old and clearly feeling the pace, and he had to concede a corner from a clever Bett pass. Hewitt's flag kick was headed back across goal by McLeish and McDougall was alert to beat Bonner from close range.

McDougall completed his hat-trick in 55 minutes as Aberdeen took control and their ruthless approach left Celtic cursing their early missed chances. Celtic were appealing when Neil Simpson challenged McStay in the box but played continued and Bett made a break down the left before his accurate cross found the prolific McDougall to sweep the ball into the net. Bedlam at Pittodrie; Celtic players were arguing with the referee as both Paul McStay and Tommy Burns were booked. In 64 minutes McDougall capped an outstanding performance when he netted his and Aberdeen's fourth goal after a slick move. The hitman started things off by slipping the ball to Hewitt, who in turn found Black free on the right. McDougall again was in the right place to convert Black's accurate cross for the goal of the game. Celtic were clearly stunned as Aberdeen piled on the pressure. The Dons continued to dominate, and Celtic were reduced to some nasty challenges when Aitken and then substitute Willie McStay were booked. In this mood Aberdeen were not the opponents you would like to face and Pittodrie had become a real bogey ground for Celtic in recent years.

As the teams left the field at full time the Dons and McDougall were afforded a prolonged standing ovation.

McDougall was not alone when it came to scoring four against Celtic for Aberdeen. Despite press reports at the time claiming he was the first Don to achieve that feat, he was in good company as on 2 January 1947 George Hamilton had done so in a 5-1 win over Celtic at Parkhead. 'Gentleman' George, as he was known – he was only booked once in his entire career – remains one of the Dons' greatest ever players, making 292 appearance in a career that was interrupted by the Second World War.

McDougall had been signed from St Mirren in the summer of 1984 as a direct replacement for Mark McGhee. In his first season, 1984/85, he scored 22 league goals as the Dons won the Premier Division, finishing as the top scorer in Scotland. His hat-trick in the penultimate game of the season against Hearts at Tynecastle ensured that the title was rubber-stamped. McDougall was a prolific scorer and the goals continued to flow, but his career was tragically cut short at the age of 29 after a persistent back injury forced his early retirement. McDougall played 54 games for Aberdeen, scoring 36 goals.

As Ferguson looked forward to the European Cup tie with Servette he was left with the dilemma of his starting 11, 'I know who will start but both Stark and Bett will play their part. Both were excellent against Celtic. We are now playing well and there is no reason why we can't be positive in front of our own fans.'

It was a busy time for Ferguson as he was also the interim Scotland coach after the tragic passing of Jock Stein during the national team's World Cup qualifier in Cardiff on 10 September 1985. Ferguson had been assistant to Stein and was entrusted to take Scotland to Mexico for the World Cup finals. Balancing the 'day job' at Pittodrie and looking after the Scotland team was a tough ask. News came through that Australia had beaten New Zealand to qualify for a play-off against Scotland at Hampden and the return in Melbourne in a few weeks. It would be the first time a European nation had to travel and play Australia for a place in the finals.

The one disappointment from the Aberdeen game and for McDougall in particular was that it was never televised. A row between the authorities and television companies meant there were no cameras to record McDougall's fabulous display. His fourth goal would have been shortlisted for the goal of the season for certain.

Following a 4-1 win over Dundee a week later, the Dons had begun to take control of the league.

## Scottish Premier Division as at 9 November 1985

|  | P | W | D | L | F | A | Pts |
|---|---|---|---|---|---|---|---|
| Aberdeen | 14 | 8 | 4 | 2 | 31 | 13 | 20 |
| Rangers | 14 | 7 | 3 | 4 | 21 | 12 | 17 |
| Celtic | 13 | 7 | 2 | 4 | 20 | 16 | 16 |
| Dundee United | 13 | 5 | 4 | 4 | 18 | 13 | 14 |

# Aberdeen 2 IFK Gothenburg 2

(First European Cup quarter-final)
5 March 1986
European Cup quarter-final first leg
Pittodrie Stadium, Aberdeen
Attendance: 22,000

**Aberdeen**
Bryan Gunn
Neale Cooper
Ian Angus
Billy Stark
Alex McLeish
Willie Miller
Eric Black
Neil Simpson
Joe Miller
Jim Bett
Peter Weir
*Subs:* Stewart McKimmie, John Hewitt
*Manager:* Alex Ferguson

**IFK Gothenburg**
Thomas Wernersson
Ruben Svensson
Glen Hysén
Peter Larsson
Stig Fredriksson
Roland Nilsson
Stefan Petterson
Tord Holmgren
Tommy Holmgren
Jonny Ekström
Torbjörn Nilsson
*Subs:* Stephan Kullberg, Jerry Carlsson
*Manager:* Gunder Bengtsson

IN AN era when the only advantage gained in European competition was through the simple but fair seeding system, every so often the draw would reveal some intriguing ties. If a team had reached the semi-finals of any of the three major European competitions then they would enjoy automatic seeding for the next five seasons. Aberdeen, by virtue of their European Cup Winners' Cup success in 1983 and reaching the last four a year later, would be a seeded side until 1989 at least. That would mean avoiding the likes of Juventus, Borussia Mönchengladbach and Liverpool, who had eliminated them in 1971, 1972 and 1980 respectively.

It can be argued that the Aberdeen side of 1986 was as good as their 1983 European Cup Winners' Cup champions. On closer scrutiny it is hard to find enough evidence to back that up. Certainly, the team of '86 excelled in cup football, but the dream of a quadruple in 1985/86 was always something that was beyond the Dons, as good as they were. Both domestic cups were won with relative ease, the two Edinburgh clubs given sharp rebukes in those finals as to who which side was the best around. Three-goal victories over Hibernian to claim the League Cup and Hearts to take the Scottish Cup served as harsh lessons for any clubs looking to topple an imperious Aberdeen.

It was again in the European arenas that Aberdeen would ultimately be judged. The obvious target after their Cup Winners' Cup and Super Cup success in 1983 was the European Cup. Alex Ferguson made no secret of that in the latter part of his Pittodrie reign.

Aberdeen had progressed to the quarter-finals after defeating Icelandic champions Akranes and Swiss side Servette. The draw for the last eight could have been kinder but with the likes of Barcelona, Bayern Munich and Juventus all in the bag, the Dons were happy enough coming out against IFK Gothenburg. It would of course mean a return to the Nya Ullevi, scene of their greatest triumph in 1983, but under different circumstances against the Swedish champions.

The first leg in Aberdeen was in doubt right up until 24 hours before kick-off as a hard frost had lingered over the north-east (Pittodrie did not have undersoil heating until 1988), meaning that the game could be postponed until the following week. Conditions eased, however, and there was no requirement for a pitch inspection by German referee Dieter Pauly. Ferguson was pleased with the improvement in the weather, 'There is no problem now, the pitch is fine. Everyone is fit and the side I have chosen will hopefully do the job for us.' Gothenburg had just emerged from a winter shutdown and were real dark horses to go all the way that year. Ferguson knew the pitfalls of playing the first game in Scotland, 'I would have preferred to be finishing the tie at Pittodrie, but it just means we will have to take a lead to Sweden. We were almost caught out in the last round against Servette. Taking a 0-0 draw back to Pittodrie seemed enough but they gave us a real time of it here.'

Gothenburg coach Gunder Bengtsson was targeting a goalless draw as his team arrived in Scotland, 'A no-scoring draw would be a marvellous result for us, but it will be very difficult.' Bengtsson had a very high regard for the Scottish champions and was concerned as to his side's capabilities after their prolonged break, 'Aberdeen are very strong and will give us different problems from Valencia whom we beat when we won the UEFA Cup in 1982. They have good forward players and in Eric Black they have a special player.

*Aberdeen FC 1908*

*Donald Colman*

*Drawing that was in the Aberdeen Daily Journal for the Scottish Cup semi-final in 1908*

*Johnny Miller 1923*

*The Granite Facade at Pittodrie on Merkland Road East, built in 1928*

*Willie Mills 1935*

*George Thomson 1935*

*1937 Cup Final ticket*

*Aberdeen v Celtic at Hampden in the 1937 Cup Final*

*1946 Civic Invite from City Council*

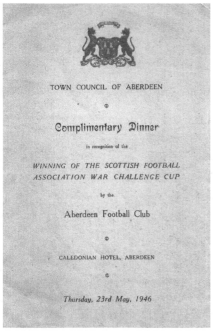

*Aberdeen v Rangers SLC Final Menu May 1946*

*Archie Baird*

*1947 Scottish Cup winners*

*Commemorative glass from 1947*

*Drawing following the 1947 Scottish Cup Final*

*Team line-up from the match programme v Rangers in 1954 semi-final*

*Green Final from the 1955 League win*

*League winners' medal from 1955*

*Fred Martin*

*1955 League Cup winners' medal*

*Aberdeen celebrate their first goal against St Mirren*

*Aberdeen squad before sailing to Canada in 1956*

*Graham Leggat with the League Cup and the jersey he wore on the day*

*1970 Cup Final teams enter the field*

*Aberdeen's 1976 League Cup-winning team*

*Alex Ferguson statue at Pittodrie unveiled in 2022, depicted from his celebration at Easter Road in 1980*

*Bobby Clark with the Premier League trophy 1980*

*UEFA Cup first round v. Ipswich Town, 16 September 1981*

*The Aberdeen team in the dressing-room after their 3-1 victory over Ipswich at Pittodrie in the first round of the UEFA Cup on 30 September 1981.*

*Aberdeen train before the 1983 quarter-final against Bayern Munich.*

*Jim Leighton v Waterschei in the semi-final of 1983's Cup Winners' Cup*

*Waterschei Pennant.*

Miller and McLeish are solid at the back and they have built up a reputation in international football.' Gothenburg had not played a competitive game since November and had taken part in friendlies in Spain and Portugal before a short tour of England in preparation for the Aberdeen tie.

Gothenburg's star midfielder Stefan Petersson was hoping his team avoided a winter freeze like they suffered in their previous campaign, when they had been eliminated by Greek champions Panathinaikos, 'It will be very difficult against Aberdeen, especially as we have not had competitive games. Our winter closedown always creates problems.'

In what was Aberdeen's 66th game in Europe it was also a landmark for captain Willie Miller, who was making his 50th European appearance, a marvellous achievement, stretching back to a UEFA Cup tie against Finn Harps in 1973. Miller, widely acknowledged as the greatest ever Aberdeen player, had been at Pittodrie since 1971 and he would go on to enjoy an incredible 20 years with his one and only senior club. A legend in the true sense.

It was vital that Aberdeen did not concede at home, with away goals back then counting double in the event of an aggregate draw following the second leg. Ferguson would have taken a one-goal lead to Sweden as he was confident in his team's ability and experience away from Pittodrie. In the 32 previous home games in Europe the Dons had kept a clean sheet on 14 occasions and they had won by two clear goals or more 16 times.

The expectation was that the Dons would take at least a two-goal led to Sweden, but European football at the highest level was never an exact science. Despite Gothenburg losing 7-3 to Wimbledon in what they termed as a meaningless result, the Dons would face a club a year out from winning their second UEFA Cup, having also won the competition in 1982. Their pedigree was as strong as, if not superior to Aberdeen's.

There was drama before and at the end of a pulsating tie. Jim Leighton, by now also well established as Scotland's number one, was ruled out at the last minute following an eye infection. His place was taken by Bryan Gunn, a more than able deputy; the Scotland under-21 international was making his European debut and performed well with some crucial saves. Gunn was an understudy to Leighton for the best part of five seasons before he joined Norwich for £100,000 in October 1986. Gunn had a close relationship with Ferguson, who promised to find him a new club after he had been unable to replace Leighton. Gunn used to babysit for the Ferguson, and famously stated that he 'probably did babysitting more than first team games'.

The Dons were left ruing a host of missed chances and a last-minute disaster that was to prove crucial in a 2-2 draw that was harsh on them as they dominated for most of the game. Aberdeen began in impressive fashion and gained the early advantage when Miller celebrated his landmark appearance by opening the scoring in 16 minutes. A Neale Cooper cross found McLeish in the middle and he set up Miller to crack a left-footed shot into the net from 15 yards. Aberdeen piled on the pressure, but the Swedes held firm and gradually began to make their own impact in the game. Gunn was called into action in 35 minutes when he cut out a dangerous cross from Tommy Holmgren and a minute later the impressive Ekström went through before being stopped by Cooper. Aberdeen were having to defend, and Gothenburg were looking more likely as the half progressed. They levelled just before the break to stun the Dons as Tord Holmgren scored after a slick break.

This tie was not going to script as the visitors looked the more likely in the second half, which forced Ferguson to make changes. John Hewitt, the 1983 European Cup Winners' Cup hero, came off the bench to score a second for the Dons in 79 minutes. It proved that despite not being at their best Aberdeen could still find something extra. Gunn was enjoying a marvellous European debut right up until the final minute when Gothenburg levelled for the second time. Ekström beat the offside trap and when McKimmie failed with a last-ditch tackle the Swedish striker rounded Gunn to score. There was little time for Aberdeen to respond as a combination of time-wasting and possession ensured the Swedes escaped from Pittodrie with a result they had not dared to hope for.

Ferguson was defiant and his mind games started early, 'In some ways it is better for us to go to Gothenburg drawing at this stage. The pressure will be on them to attack us and their crowd will be expecting them to win. The incentive is a place in the semi-finals, and they will have to play well to beat us. We could have been going there with a lead but for some suicidal play from us at the end, which left them with a one-on-one position for their lad to score. Peter Weir started to tire in the second half which was not surprising given he was just back from injury.'

Gothenburg's Bengtsson was happy, 'I admit I was pessimistic before the match but after Aberdeen pressed us early, we settled into the game. The tie is only half over, and it will be a different game in Gothenburg. This result is an excellent one for us and I would expect about 40,000 spectators will be at the Ullevi for the second leg. Aberdeen will be hurting and that will make them a dangerous opponent for us.'

Despite a brave performance before a partisan 44,000 crowd in the return the Dons went out after a 0-0 draw in Sweden. Away goals had not been kind to Aberdeen in European ties in the past and so they proved their downfall this time, leading to the disappointment of not making the semi-finals of the European Cup.

Gothenburg defended in depth and their physicality made for a bruising tie. Alex McLeish and Willie Miller were in superb form and limited the home side to very few chances. Ferguson expected Gothenburg to be far more expansive on home soil, but they were happy to sit in and frustrate the Dons, 'The ground was bumpy and sandy which made it difficult for our midfield players to build anything up. There is no doubt though that we lost this tie at Pittodrie, leaving us too much to do in Sweden. I thought we played well enough without creating too many chances.'

Bengtsson was delighted to take his team through, 'Aberdeen were a lot better here than they were in Scotland and we had to defend well to progress. The away goals made the difference.'

It was a harsh lesson for the Dons, who should have had enough experience to deal with the Swedish challenge, but the latter end of the European Cup has no margin for error. The tie in Gothenburg was a bitter disappointment for Ferguson, who had learned from the mistakes against German opposition in the late 1970s and the chastening defeat to Liverpool to turn Aberdeen into European Cup Winners' Cup and Super Cup winners in 1983. The European Cup, though, was to prove elusive.

# Aberdeen 3 Hearts 0

10 May 1986
Scottish Cup Final
Hampden Park, Glasgow
Attendance: 62,841

**Aberdeen**
Jim Leighton
Stewart McKimmie
Tom McQueen
John McMaster
Alex McLeish
Willie Miller
John Hewitt
Neale Cooper
Frank McDougall
Jim Bett
Peter Weir
*Subs:* Billy Stark, Joe Miller
*Manager:* Alex Ferguson

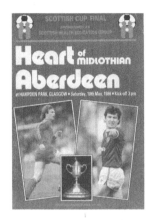

**Hearts**
Henry Smith
Walter Kidd
Brian Whittaker
Sandy Jardine
Neil Berry
Craig Levein
John Colquhoun
Kenny Black
Gary Mackay
Sandy Clark
John Robertson
*Manager:* Alex MacDonald

ABERDEEN COULD do little wrong when it came to the big matches in the 1980s. The team of that era had built a tradition and reputation that was feared at home and abroad. Despite cup final opponents Hearts looking impressive in the closing weeks of the 1985/86 season, the Dons would still enter the fray at Hampden as favourites.

The season was certainly an eventful one for Aberdeen. Under Alex Ferguson they had blazed a trail at home and abroad in all competitions. Although the league championship was gone, Aberdeen had already won the League Cup earlier in the season and had reached their fourth Scottish Cup Final in five years.

In Europe they had an agonising exit in the European Cup, falling to Gothenburg at the quarter-final stage on away goals. Reaching the last eight of Europe's premier competition was a feat but such was the measure of what Ferguson wanted to achieve that the exit to the Swedish champions was still looked upon as a chance missed. It was also a measure of Ferguson's success that the Dons were still strong enough to compete for all the honours after losing several of their great Gothenburg players.

In the Scottish Cup, Aberdeen looked to regain their supremacy in the competition. Winners in 1982, 1983 and 1984, it took a controversial defeat against Dundee United in April 1985 to halt their bid for a record fourth successive triumph in the national competition. In 1986 Aberdeen were on the Hampden trail once more and reached the final after defeating Montrose 4-1 at Pittodrie, Arbroath 1-0 at Gayfield, Dundee 2-1 at Pittodrie after a 2-2 draw at Dens Park, and Hibernian 3-0 at Dens Park in the semi-final. What was unique about that relatively easy run to the final was that Aberdeen did not play any of their matches beyond Dundee and all ties were played on the east coast. The semi-final against Hibernian was as easy as the 3-0 score suggests and the Easter Road side were glad to see the back of Aberdeen that season as it was the Dons who had showed their ruthless streak by disposing of them in the League Cup Final.

Hearts had a tough road to Hampden after beating Rangers 3-2, Hamilton 2-1, St Mirren 4-1 and then Dundee United 1-0 in the semi-final. While that run was impressive, Hearts had contended with the astonishing disappointment of losing the league title only seven days before the final. On the back of an incredible 31-game unbeaten run they had the Premier Division championship within their grasp as they went to Dens Park on the final day. It all went horribly wrong as two late Dundee goals and a five-goal haul for Celtic at St Mirren took the title to Parkhead in an amazing sequence of events. The Hearts party was well and truly stuffed, and questions remained as to whether they still had the nerve to face Aberdeen in the final. It was a huge blow to Hearts' hopes as a generation of Tynecastle supporters had been starved of success and the manner of events at Dens Park that fateful afternoon would leave a long-lasting legacy of failure.

If there was one side that would capitalise on Hearts' misfortune then it was Aberdeen, by now seasoned campaigners at Hampden for the big occasion and they rarely lost when it mattered. Ferguson had instilled a winning mentality that was bringing a rich harvest of silverware to Pittodrie. The Dons were used to winning and that would be a crucial factor in the final. While Hearts were throwing the towel in at Dens Park, a shadow Aberdeen side cruised to a 6-0 win at Clydebank as Ferguson kept his big guns fresh for Hampden. The only injury doubt was Neil Simpson, who played for the reserves against Clydebank but felt a reaction to his groin injury. Jim Leighton looked certain to come back, which was tough on Bryan Gunn who had deputised in recent weeks. Neale Cooper also shrugged off his injury to return to the side.

Aberdeen's preparations were, however, hit by the news that striker Eric Black had told the club that he would be moving to French club Metz in the summer. That infuriated Ferguson, who promptly dropped Black from the cup final squad. Ferguson said at the time, 'Any player is entitled to leave a club at the end of his contract if he feels he can better himself elsewhere. Since the introduction of freedom of contract, that has become normal procedure and we are not the only big club to experience that. However, I feel players should go about it in the proper way. Agents operate secretly and can get up to 20 per cent of the proceeds. Aberdeen as a club will never conduct their business like that.

'We have had no contact whatsoever from the French club and the first I knew about it was when Black told me that he was moving. Aberdeen FC do not deserve this kind of treatment and we are big enough to take a stand on this matter, even if it means leaving Black out of our cup final side. Everyone knows how determined I am to win trophies for Aberdeen, but the line must be drawn somewhere. It is a sad end to the successful association which we have had with Black since he first joined us as a 13-year-old. He had our support when he was out with back trouble and he has repaid us with many valuable goals. It is a pity it has turned out this way, but I feel he has been badly advised. His agent has certainly not done him any favours fixing him up with an insignificant club like Metz. He could have done much better for himself.'

While Black's departure was the only cloud on Aberdeen's horizon, Hearts had to pick themselves up following their disappointment at not taking the championship. That would be a tall order as they had set themselves up as champions, but that dream came crashing down about them and it would be difficult to forget about what happened at Dens Park. While Hearts duo Alex MacDonald and Sandy Jardine had a wealth of experience as players behind them, they were up against the master in Ferguson.

In Willie Miller, Ferguson had an experienced captain who had got used to winning ways. Miller was confident going into the final, 'Aberdeen have a deep affection for Hampden and to be honest we never play badly there. But we have set high standards for ourselves, so most people will think we have had a bad season if we don't win both domestic cups; that is just the way it is, but we are not complaining.'

Aberdeen had boasted about being a big-occasion side while a Hearts trip to Hampden was a rare occasion. The Dons were certainly aware of that and with the disappointment their opponents would be feeling before the game. Crucially, Miller won the toss and elected to play with a strong wind behind him.

Aberdeen went for the jugular from the start, testing Hearts' nerve to the limit. In five minutes Miller sent a through ball to John Hewitt. The striker took control and made his way towards the Hearts goal. As the Jambos' defence backed off, Hewitt let fly with a screamer that flew past Henry Smith into the bottom corner of the net. It was the perfect start and settled an Aberdeen side who took control of the game in an almost imperious fashion.

Hearts seemed to have the Hampden jitters although they did make a fight of it in spells. Leighton looked as though he had never been away with some superb handling while Sandy Clark and John Robertson rarely troubled McLeish and Miller. Goal number two duly arrived four minutes into the second half and it was one that was worthy of winning any cup final. Peter Weir, who had tormented Hearts' defence all afternoon, made his way down the left before Frank McDougall superbly dummied his low cross. Hewitt ghosted in to clip the ball past Smith for an exquisite finish.

At that point there was no way back for a clearly shattered Hearts side, and substitute Billy Stark completed the rout with a well-taken header after another slick attack by the Dons, who were now turning on the style. Again it was Weir who instigated the move. It all got too much for Walter Kidd, who became the first captain to be sent off in a Scottish Cup Final after a moment of sheer madness. Kidd had been given a torrid time of it by Weir and was simply outclassed at every turn. He lost the plot when he initially hit Neale Cooper on the head with the ball after play had stopped. After catching the rebound he threw the ball into Frank McDougall's face, all in front of the referee. That may have been the only time Kidd got near the ball all afternoon, but it was certainly his final involvement as he was rightly sent packing to end his torment.

The 3-0 result was a fair reflection as Aberdeen showed just why they had been so successful and were ahead of Hearts in every department. Miller and his side went on to make the familiar trek up the Hampden steps to collect their fourth Scottish Cup in five seasons. There would be the usual parade down the city's Union Street a day later while Hearts were sent home to lick their collective wounds.

While Ferguson was sympathetic towards his close friend Sandy Jardine after the game, the ruthless efficiency of his side had shown just why he was one of the most sought-after managers in the game. Ferguson, though, would have little time to dwell on his latest success as three days later he was taking the Scotland squad to Mexico for the World Cup finals.

Aberdeen received £15,000 from the sponsors for winning the trophy while Hearts' indiscretions on the field – with three others booked, alongside Kidd's red card – cost them almost half of their prize money.

Ferguson was content after the game but was still unhappy that the Dons had not won the treble that year, 'As far as I am concerned, we should have won the lot. We just lost too many players through injury at crucial times in the league campaign. I suppose two cups in the same season will mean that I am a good manager though!'

The party headed back to Anstruther and an overnight stay before their victory parade through the streets of Aberdeen the following day.

# Aberdeen 2 Rangers 1

22 October 1989
Scottish League Cup Final
Hampden Park, Glasgow
Attendance: 61,190

| Aberdeen | | Rangers |
|---|---|---|
| Theo Snelders | | Chris Woods |
| Stewart McKimmie | | Gary Stevens |
| David Robertson | | Stewart Munro |
| Brian Grant | | Richard Gough |
| Alex McLeish | | Ray Wilkins |
| Willie Miller | | Terry Butcher |
| Charlie Nicholas | | Trevor Steven |
| Jim Bett | | Ian Ferguson |
| Paul Mason | | Ally McCoist |
| Bobby Connor | | Maurice Johnston |
| Eoin Jess | | Mark Walters |
| *Subs:* Brian Irvine, Willem van der Ark | | *Sub:* Stuart McCall |
| *Manager:* Alex Smith | | *Manager:* Graeme Souness |

THE EMERGENCE of Aberdeen as a real force in the 1980s not only upset the 'establishment' in the west but left other provincial sides looking on in envy. Both Edinburgh clubs will always look to make a breakthrough and to their credit during that period Dundee United achieved far more than their status in the game suggested. Nevertheless, it was Aberdeen who sustained a level of success that had not been seen before in Scotland, prompting radical action from bitter rivals Rangers and ultimately Celtic.

Years of mediocrity at Ibrox culminated in the only way the Glasgow club could compete, and that was to invest huge money into their playing squad. The 'Aberdeen Way' of blooding their own youngsters into a side of experienced, streetwise pros and getting them to gel into a team was built over time. After years of decline, Rangers went on a spending spree that dwarfed anything the game in Scotland had seen. It was a policy that the likes of Aberdeen would never follow, even if they could merely struggle to match their rivals in terms of finance and resources.

Following years of looking on as Aberdeen dominated in Scotland and enjoyed success in Europe, it was after the departure of Alex Ferguson to Manchester United in November 1986 that the Ibrox club began to spend big with the appointment of Graeme Souness as manager followed by the signing of several top England internationals. Even some of the clubs down south could not compete, although that was all to change in 1992 after satellite television began to finance the English Premier League.

Aberdeen were not quite done with their golden era. By 1989 the Dons had dispensed with Ian Porterfield – who had the thankless task of following Ferguson, – and Alex Smith and Jocky Scott were at the helm. Aberdeen could still invest in transfers but had to be far more astute than their free-spending rivals. They tapped into the Dutch market and signed several players who were to make a big impact at Pittodrie. Looking at the Netherlands made sense; there was better value and traditionally Dutch players travelled well. The Scottish market at that time was not something Smith was overly keen on as opposition clubs tended to inflate any potential transfer fees.

Aberdeen had taken the likes of Peter van de Ven, Theo Snelders, Hans Gillhaus, Theo ten Caat and Willem van der Ark to Pittodrie between 1988 and 1991. It was, however, an Englishman playing in the Dutch league who was to play such a huge role in the 1989 League Cup Final. Paul Mason left his Merseyside home after becoming disillusioned with the game after spells with Everton and Tranmere as a youngster. He went to the Netherlands to work as a labourer on building sites, at that time a popular route for British nationals in search of construction work. He continued to play in local amateur leagues where he was spotted by Groningen, who offered him a full-time contract. It was while Aberdeen were watching Mason's team-mate Snelders that they then enquired about the right-back. There had been interest from Feyenoord, but Aberdeen got their man with a £200,000 bid.

Aberdeen went into the 1989 Hampden showpiece looking to avenge two defeats to Rangers in the 1987 and 1988 finals. Both games were remembered as classics with the Dons going down on penalties after a 3-3 draw in 1987 and losing 3-2 a year later.

Aberdeen qualified for their third final in a row against Rangers after defeating Albion Rovers, Airdrie, St Mirren and Celtic to get to Hampden. Ian Cameron, a signing by Alex Smith from his old club

St Mirren, scored a spectacular winning goal against Celtic in a tense semi-final. Cameron was a lucky mascot as in his three previous trips to Hampden he had not been on the losing side, 'I am aiming to make it four out of four against Rangers. There is no doubt we are good enough. After my career was going nowhere at Paisley, I was delighted to join Aberdeen. Scoring the winner against Celtic was a highlight for me and we can do the same to Rangers. They are a quality side but so are we. We respect them but they are not superior. The morale at Pittodrie is sky high. We are winning most of the time and not conceding many goals. There is a feeling within the club we should have won at least one, if not both previous finals against Rangers.'

Aberdeen's allocation of 20,000 tickets was taken up as once again they would be well supported in the national stadium. On this occasion 'loadsamoney' Rangers, as they were called, were favourites, and that suited Smith, who told the *Press & Journal*, 'I often feel our best performances come hard on the heels of a disappointment. We have given the players some extra time off this week and I sense they are up for this one. The last two finals have both been classics, but we get nothing for being runners-up. It will be different this time.' The Dons would be without semi-final hero Cameron as he had not recovered from a head knock in his most recent outing, against Hearts.

Rangers went into the final on the back of a 19-game unbeaten sequence in the League Cup and were odds-on to win. Souness was, however, cautious: 'Aberdeen had a bad result last week [losing 3-1 to Hearts] and I expect them to be very dangerous. They are without doubt a very good side with plenty of experience. Both sides have some fantastic players and it should be another tremendous final.'

Aberdeen sprang a surprise with young Eoin Jess given a starting role. The midfielder played his part in what was to be another classic encounter and this time it was Aberdeen who gained revenge over their bitter rivals, Liverpool-born star Paul Mason grabbing the headlines as his two goals overcame the setback of a controversial penalty awarded after the Dons went ahead.

The final began with some tough challenges and Richard Gough was spoken to after fouling Charlie Nicholas. Rangers winger Mark

Walters was always a threat and Stewart McKimmie had his work cut out to keep him quiet. Rangers missed an opportunity in 14 minutes when Maurice Johnston headed into the side netting with Snelders out of position. Referee George Smith seemed to be getting carried away as he booked Bobby Connor for an accidental handball in 19 minutes. Considering the extent of the tackles that were flying in it seemed a poor decision.

Aberdeen took the lead soon after that when a free kick from Jim Bett set up Connor, whose cross found Mason to float a header into the net past England keeper Chris Woods. That goal gave Aberdeen the confidence to take the game to Rangers and Jess went close to a second but just as the Dons were in the ascendancy and the Gers' supporters were growing impatient with their side, in stepped referee Smith to offer them a way back into the game by giving them a penalty in 34 minutes. It was a shocking decision as Ally McCoist was clearly backing into Willie Miller. The striker was getting nothing out of Miller and the decision had the referee surrounded by Aberdeen players. Walters scored from the spot but it only spurred on the livid Aberdeen players.

In the second half both sides had chances to take the lead, but a mixture of bad luck and some great goalkeeping kept the final score level. Snelders had been outstanding and his team-mates took confidence from the big Dutchman. Woods was also called into action to make several saves, including one outstanding stop to deny Nicholas.

Aberdeen had brought on giant Dutch striker Willem van der Ark to replace Brian Grant, and his involvement proved crucial. As the first period of extra time ended his head flick from a Robertson corner set up Nicholas to square for Mason to score a sensational winner.

Not surprisingly Rangers threw everything they had at Aberdeen but when Snelders twisted to save from a McCoist effort it was to be the Dons' day. The Rangers players slumped to the turf at full time as Aberdeen gained revenge.

It was to be the last time that Miller, Aberdeen's own 'Captain Marvel', would raise silverware for the Dons. An injury sustained playing for Scotland in a World Cup qualifier against Norway was to effectively end a glorious career that saw him receive two testimonial games from the club in 1981 and 1990. It was full circle for Miller. His first success as captain was the League Cup Final in 1976; 13 years and ten major titles later the same trophy was again in his safe hands.

In the aftermath of the win, manager Smith was in great demand from the media, 'I would love to be in demand for this sort of thing because it would be a mark of success. It's what we feel like after wins like this that make all the pressure and the hard work so worthwhile. The players were very determined to win the cup, and we were aware that had we lost it would have been three finals against them. That would have been hard to take. It was a tough test against a side that are not used to losing. We showed a lot of character to get over that penalty decision. We were under pressure immediately after that and it was a terrific display of character to go on and win the game. We altered the style of the side because we were short of a striker with Paul Wright's departure. That allowed us to give Eoin Jess a start. He is a special talent and will be a great Aberdeen player going forward.'

Smith also had high praise for two-goal hero Mason, 'Paul is turning out to be a real important player for us; the trip to Holland was well worth it as we picked up Paul and Theo [Snelders]. Mason is a class act, he can pass, dribble and link up with others. He can also play in several positions. I would like to think we can use this success as a launching pad for success in the league and Scottish Cup. We are already in Europe so that is a bonus from winning the League Cup. I cannot speak for other teams, but I feel that when we went out of Europe earlier this season [going out of the UEFA Cup in the first round to Dynamo Dresden], we were virtually kicked out of it. It was nothing to do with skill that beat us this season. We have learned from that painful experience.'

Smith was dismissed in February 1992 after the Dons had slipped to a sixth-place finish in 1991/92. Many observers believed he was never forgiven for the last-day defeat to Rangers in May 1991 that cost Aberdeen the Premier Division title. Smith's record with the Dons remains an outstanding one and the wisdom of his departure split the support.

# Aberdeen 4 Dundee United 0

14 April 1990
Scottish Cup semi-final
Tynecastle Park, Edinburgh
Attendance: 16,581

| Aberdeen | Dundee United |
|---|---|
| Theo Snelders | Alan Main |
| Stewart McKimmie | Freddy van der Hoorn |
| David Robertson | John Clark |
| Brian Grant | Jim McInally |
| Alex McLeish | Miodrag Krivokapić |
| Brian Irvine | Dave Narey |
| Charlie Nicholas | Billy McKinlay |
| Jim Bett | Dave Bowman |
| Paul Mason | Darren Jackson |
| Bobby Connor | Paddy Connolly |
| Hans Gillhaus | Mixu Paatelainen |
| *Subs:* Graham Watson, Willem van der Ark | *Sub:* Hamish French |
| *Manager:* Alex Smith | *Manager:* Jim McLean |

ONE TERM in Scottish football that 'sticks in the craw' of most supporters is something that you will not find much of in these pages: the 'Old Firm', in reference to Celtic and Rangers, the two main Glasgow clubs, who are divided not only by sporting abilities but religious differences that have persisted for generations. Rangers were founded in 1872 and city rivals Celtic in 1888; their rivalry has become embedded in Scottish culture and contributed to religious division and sectarianism in Scotland. From the loyalist conservatism of Rangers (Protestant) to the republican socialism of Celtic (Catholic), deep divisions between the two remain.

Elsewhere the existence of these divisions is meaningless, although the Edinburgh clubs are not entirely free of religious differences. For Aberdeen their go-to song is 'Stand Free', which has become a familiar tone heard around Pittodrie and other Scottish grounds for many years. Free from any religious baggage, it separates the Dons from the rest.

It was back in 1980 when Aberdeen won the Premier League and Dundee United won their first trophy, the League Cup (at Aberdeen's expense), that there was a stirring in the east. Not since the 1950s

239

when several clubs won the league title including Aberdeen and Dundee had there been a swing towards a power shift in Scottish football. It spawned a new term – the 'New Firm', an obvious reference to the old guard in Glasgow. It was lazy and insulting, originating from the media in the west. It was never accepted by Aberdeen but for years the 'New Firm' was never far away from a headline or two and a sub-editor's dream.

On closer examination though there was a stark difference between the success of Aberdeen and their Tayside rivals. The Dons' success at home and abroad was significantly superior to the Tannadice club. Indeed, their first major success was against a leg-weary Aberdeen in a League Cup Final replay in 1979, played in Dundee. The Dons had eliminated both Rangers and Celtic en route to the Hampden final they dominated but failed to score in, forcing the replay. In 1983 United claimed their first and only Premier Division championship. Again, at that time Aberdeen were going for their European Cup Winners' Cup and Scottish Cup double and took their eye off the ball in the closing crucial league games that were packed into a tight schedule. Earlier in the season Aberdeen had hammered United 5-1; the Tannadice club looked like anything but potential champions. The Dons' slip-up allowed them to take advantage.

Comparing United's one league title and two League Cup wins with Aberdeen's haul of the 1980s remains one of the most imbalanced approaches in Scottish football history.

Alex Ferguson, during his spell at Manchester United, referred to the emergence of Manchester City as the 'noisy neighbours' in the early 2010s when City were backed by huge investment. He could easily have used that term for Dundee United who, although situated 70 miles south down the east coast from Aberdeen, were the nearest Premier Division opponents and as such their clashes were perceived as derbies.

Ferguson was also close friends with United counterpart Jim McLean after they met at SFA coaching courses when their playing days were coming to an end. Both evolved into master tacticians, keen to get one over each other. Their rivalry was intense, and many

Aberdeen v Dundee United clashes were described as chess matches with each side often catching the other out. It made for an intriguing period as both clubs were serious in chasing the silverware.

In 1990 under Alex Smith the Dons had once again evolved into a side that was to be successful. Winning both domestic cups in season 1989/90 rounded off a golden decade of success. The one outstanding result against their Tayside rivals came in the Scottish Cup semi-final at Tynecastle. This was no chess game; it was a demolition derby as Aberdeen cruised to the final with a 4-0 win at the Edinburgh ground.

Aberdeen had already won the League Cup earlier in the season and were favourites to make it a domestic cup double for the second time following on from a similar success in 1985/86. In the quarter-finals there were loud noises from Hearts who came to Pittodrie in confident mood, but they were sent packing after a 4-1 win. Aberdeen still had their warhorse Alex McLeish, the Gothenburg veteran who had now taken over the captaincy after a long-term injury to Willie Miller.

Smith looked forward to the tie, 'It is about time we were coming out on top against them. We have clashed in recent years and not had many breaks; we need to change that. Our preparations have gone very well. The players know what is expected of them. There is a quiet resolve about the squad, and I like that. Like most semi-finals it will be frenetic and tense, but we have the experience to deal with that.'

Aberdeen were set to recall Theo Snelders to replace the on-loan keeper Bobby Mimms. Dutch striker Willem van der Ark had recovered from injury and the Dons were looking at his Dutch team-mate Hans Gillhaus to spearhead their attack at Tynecastle. One significant absentee was club legend Miller, who was battling to recover from injury. Smith sent him with the reserve squad to play Dundee United's reserve team at Tannadice that afternoon. Jim McLean was in mind games mode, but the Dons had heard it all before, 'It is fair to suggest that Aberdeen are the favourites, they are the team in form. However, our record at Tynecastle is very good and going into the game the pressure will be off us. I am confident we can win the tie.'

Aberdeen sprang a surprise when David Robertson, their young full-back, was in the starting 11 for his first game since December following a toe injury. United started well enough without creating any chances and it was Aberdeen who struck first in 11 minutes. Gillhaus found Charlie Nicholas on the edge of the box and the Scot sent over a low cross. Brian Grant met it with a full volley, which was saved by United keeper Alan Main. The ball spilled invitingly for Brian Irvine to score from close range. The Dons came close again when Gillhaus just failed to connect from a cross while Main was again in action dealing with a McKimmie cross.

Any fears as to the condition of the Tynecastle surface were dispelled as both teams were able to play on the lush surface; Aberdeen continued to dominate and United were rarely seen in attack and it was no surprise when the Dons went two goals ahead. Constant pressure ended with Irvine forcing an error from Mixu Paatelainen who put through his own net. That goal gave Aberdeen the confidence to express themselves and United were outclassed at times.

The second half was more of the same as Paul Mason came close in the first action of the second period. Then Jim Bett sent in a fierce shot from 20 yards, forcing a third corner in a minute. Just before the hour the Dons were gifted a third goal and their passage to Hampden. Robertson, who had been improving as the game went on, sent in a cross that was sliced by Freddy van der Hoorn over Main to the horror of the United support behind the goal. Aberdeen rounded off the rout in 85 minutes with the best goal of the game. A Grant pass was controlled by Gillhaus on the edge of the box and although being closed by Krivokapić, the Netherlands international rounded the Yugoslav and thundered a shot past Main. By that time large swathes of the United support had left, missing that final goal.

The way Aberdeen beat United was one of their most emphatic semi-final wins. Their only issue ahead of the final was guarding against complacency. It was a good problem for Alex Smith, who also had to deny the latest transfer rumours that came from the west coast media, 'We have been hearing all sorts of rumours that we will be signing Celtic striker Andy Walker. That is simply not true and it's a concern I have to clarify these stories that keep cropping up. Naturally we are delighted to be in the final, but we will be taking nothing for granted. We know Celtic will make it difficult for us and we will prepare in the usual way.' Looking back to Tynecastle, Smith told the *Evening Express*, 'Our midfield was excellent. That was where we won the game, we took control and that gave us the platform to go on and win with ease. Jim Bett and Brian Grant were outstanding, and the defence stood up so well to anything that United could throw at us. That allowed Hans [Gillhaus] to show his class in forward areas – he was all over their defence and unplayable. It was a complete performance from us.'

Aberdeen were looking forward to their 13th Scottish Cup Final, having won the trophy on six occasions in 1947, 1970, 1982, 1983, 1984 and 1986.

# Aberdeen 0 Celtic 0 (aet)

*Aberdeen won 9-8 on penalties)*
12 May 1990
Scottish Cup Final
Hampden Park, Glasgow
Attendance: 60,493

| **Aberdeen** | | **Celtic** |
|---|---|---|
| Theo Snelders | | Pat Bonner |
| Stewart McKimmie | | Dariusz Wdowczyk |
| David Robertson | | Anton Rogan |
| Brian Grant | | Peter Grant |
| Brian Irvine | | Paul Elliott |
| Alex McLeish | | Derek Whyte |
| Charlie Nicholas | | Billy Stark |
| Jim Bett | | Paul McStay |
| Paul Mason | | Dariusz Dziekanowski |
| Bobby Connor | | Andy Walker |
| Hans Gillhaus | | Joe Miller |
| *Sub:* Graham Watson | | *Subs:* Mike Galloway, Tommy Coyne |
| *Manager:* Alex Smith | | *Manager:* Billy McNeill |

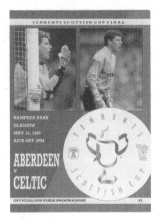

THE SCOTTISH Cup has long been the 'holy grail' for Aberdeen sides through the generations. It was not until the 1970s that more stature was afforded to the league winners; the national cup was the tournament that everyone wanted to win. Traditionally the final domestic game of the season, the showpiece of Scottish football was one of only two games that were guaranteed to be shown live on television every year long before satellite TV was a thing, the other being the annual Scotland v England clash at either Hampden or Wembley.

Aberdeen's last Scottish Cup win was in 1990 when they defeated Celtic in a historic penalty shoot-out – the first final to be decided on penalties. Manager Alex Smith recalled the final with an unusual description of the outcome, 'It was like shooting ducks at the fair. We held our nerve in what was a tense situation but in these types of situations it can go either way. Theo [Snelders] was immense and he showed his class not only in the shoot-out but in the game itself. We will play a lot better than that and lose. But it's all about winning and it was our day. Big Brian [Irvine] was brave enough to stand up and be counted. I don't think he has ever taken a penalty before so all credit to him. We had a few chances but in fairness to Celtic they stood up to us for long spells.'

It was the end of a great era for the Dons, who had enjoyed a decade of success during the 1980s that remains their most productive period. Aberdeen had won the Premier Division in May 1980 and ten years on the Scottish Cup was going north for the fifth time since then. It represented a golden era that not even either of the two big Glasgow clubs could match before the 21st century.

Aberdeen had evolved throughout that period and by 1990 only Alex McLeish remained from the side that won in Sweden in 1983. Alex Ferguson had departed in 1986 to take over an ailing Manchester United; one of only two clubs Ferguson said he would leave Pittodrie for. Ian Porterfield, the Sunderland FA Cup hero of 1973, took over from Ferguson, a thankless task as many managers at Old Trafford have discovered, but Porterfield had spent almost his entire career in England and had little knowledge of the Scottish game.

As Aberdeen were celebrating at Hampden, Ferguson was left frustrated at Wembley as his United side were involved in a thrilling 3-3 draw with Crystal Palace in the FA Cup Final. No sudden-death finish there – Ferguson had to wait to win the replay to become the first manager to win both the Scottish and FA Cups.

In 1988 Aberdeen turned to a co-manager setup with Alex Smith and former Don Jocky Scott taking over. They were also once again the only serious challengers to big-spending Rangers as Celtic were struggling to make an impact.

Aberdeen had beaten Partick, Morton, Hearts and Dundee United to reach the Hampden final. They were going for a domestic cup double while opponents Celtic were staring at a season without a trophy. Aberdeen were the clear favourites and only days before the final they dealt a blow to Celtic's European qualification hopes with a 3-1 win at Parkhead. The victory was not the surprise – but its manner was notable. The Dons rested McLeish, Gillhaus, Nicholas, Mason, Bett, Connor and Grant and a virtual reserve side had eased past Celtic by a comfortable margin. Surely, they only had to turn up at Hampden to win.

Nevertheless, that Celtic team could boast of having six full internationals and were managed by Billy McNeill, who had been in charge at Pittodrie for the 1977/78 season. However, they were up against their former golden boy Charlie Nicholas and Netherlands international Hans Gillhaus. Celtic keeper Pat Bonner described the Aberdeen front pairing as the most prolific in British football at the time. Nicholas had been a marquee signing by Porterfield in January 1988 for £400,000 from Arsenal. Gillhaus was a proven scorer and European Cup winner with PSV Eindhoven when he joined the Dons in 1989 for £650,000.

The game began at a fast pace and Aberdeen looked the more composed side, but Celtic for their part made a real fist of it. Paul Elliott was tasked to man-mark Gillhaus and he stifled the Dons' attacks on several occasions. Over the 120 minutes Aberdeen were the better side but just could not find a way past Bonner. Celtic matched the Dons in passion but Aberdeen carried the bigger threat, and they should have scored on a couple of occasions before Snelders made his first save of the game from former Don Billy Stark in 38 minutes. Aberdeen again took control in the second half but were held by a resolute Celtic defence. Nicholas was playing his final game for Aberdeen before his move back to Celtic in the summer, and when the penalties came around he had the opportunity to defeat his new club and deny his new employers the opportunity to play in Europe the following season. Nicholas, as the professional he was, dispatched his penalty with his usual calmness.

Incredibly 20 players had to go through the pressure of taking a spot kick after Aberdeen won the toss, and the penalties would be taken at the end where their support was housed. Celtic missed their first and last penalties, taken by Wdowcyzk and Anton Rogan. In between Grant, McStay, Coyne, Galloway, Miller, Whyte, Elliott and Dziekanowski all scored.

Aberdeen scored with their first three through Bett, Connor and Gillhaus. Then Brian Grant blasted over the bar followed by success for Nicholas, McLeish, McKimmie, Robertson and Watson before Brian Irvine hammered in the final blow. Snelders pulled off a fantastic save from Rogan that gave Irvine the chance to win the cup for the Dons. The Dutch stopper immediately turned to the Aberdeen support with clenched fists.

Both managers were sporting after the game. McNeill declared in the *Sunday Post*, 'I have already made my views clear about not liking penalty deciders. What we have seen confirms that opinion; and I would feel the same if it had gone the other way.'

Smith thought Aberdeen deserved to win, 'This has been my greatest season ever. First, we won the League Cup, now the Scottish Cup, but we would have liked to have won the match; not on penalties. This augurs well for our bid to win the league next season.' Smith also revealed that his brilliant youngster Eoin Jess might have had to come on as a substitute, 'I had to think of the possibility of penalties and that might have been too much pressure for him. Who knows, if he had missed the crucial one it might have affected his career.'

Alex McLeish felt for Rogan, 'It was a terrible way for them to lose after they battled all the way. I feel sorry for Anton and I told him so after the game.' Celtic midfielder Paul McStay was generous towards the Dons, 'Aberdeen have had a great season and I think it was a good game.'

Irvine scored the decisive penalty, shooting high past Bonner to trigger bedlam on the park and on the terraces. He recalled, 'I know that it wasn't my strength that kicked the ball into the net. God was beside me and helping me.'

For Aberdeen, it was a return to the city and the reception which had become so familiar in recent times following their fifth Scottish Cup win in nine years.

McLeish looked back on their success, 'We were certainly expected to win the 1990 final. Earlier in the cup there had been a great deal of paper talk about what Hearts' "tiny terrors" John Robertson and Scott Crabbe would do to us in the tie at Pittodrie. We let the hype go and, on the day, we swept them aside in a 4-0 victory. I think in the final the same thing happened to us. Everybody told us we would win comfortably but we just didn't get our game together on the day. Celtic played as well as they could, and they fought hard, but we were the better side.

'We didn't have any closely worked out list of penalty takers; we felt it better not to put too much strain on young players in advance. Jim Bett would take an early kick; he was a regular penalty taker and our forwards were asked to go early too. But as it went on, we were looking for volunteers, and I can't remember anyone hiding away as the kicks progressed. When Brian Grant missed, we were really in trouble as we were now going second and having to score. I therefore thought it was up to me, a senior player, to take responsibility. I remember asking the referee if I could place the ball myself and he agreed. I thought it best to take a long run-up. I had seen penalties missed before and usually after a short run-up. I made up my mind where I was going to place the ball. All I could think about was that I was awarded the writers' player of the year earlier in the week and I dare not miss. Paddy [Bonner] guessed right but my shot was too powerful for him. When Theo saved from Rogan, I knew we were going to win it for sure. It was harsh on Rogan as his penalty was a good one. It was Theo's agility and shovel-like hand that turned the ball around the post. It was a marvellous save.'

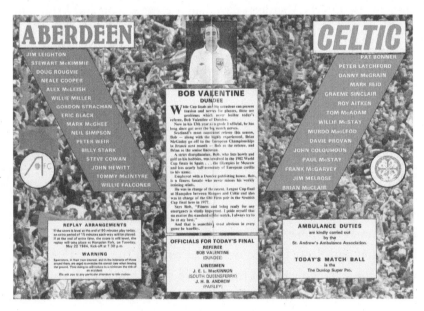

# Aberdeen 2 Dundee United 1

6 May 1995
Scottish Premier Division
Pittodrie Stadium, Aberdeen
Attendance: 21,364

**Aberdeen**
Theo Snelders
Stewart McKimmie
Stephen Wright
Brian Grant
Brian Irvine
Gary Smith
Peter Hetherston
Duncan Shearer
Joe Miller
Billy Dodds
Eoin Jess
*Sub:* Stephen Glass
*Manager:* Roy Aitken

**Dundee United**
Kelham O'Hanlon
Mark Perry
Maurice Malpas
Christian Dailly
David Craig
Grant Johnston
Scott Crabbe
Jim McInally
Sérgio Gomes
Craig Brewster
Robert Hannah
*Subs:* Andy McLaren, Robbie Winters
*Manager:* Billy Kirkwood

THE SUMMER of 1994 was certainly a time of change at Pittodrie. The legendary Willie Miller ended his playing career in 1991 and he became manager in 1992, replacing Alex Smith. Miller was determined to take the Dons back to the top. After two frustrating seasons of being runners-up to Rangers, a huge gamble was taken in that close season.

Alex McLeish, Jim Bett and Bobby Connor left the club as they were winding down their playing careers. All three had played a significant part in keeping the Dons as serious challengers. McLeish was the last of that great side of 1983 to leave the club, accepting the player-manager role with Premier Division rivals Motherwell. Bett and Connor had cost £650,000 in transfer fees from Lokeren and Dundee respectively and both formed part of the Aberdeen midfield for the best part of ten years. Losing such experience was going to be expensive and their departures were perhaps lost on the Aberdeen support as they welcomed new faces to the squad.

Aberdeen splashed out a record £800,000 to sign Billy Dodds from St Johnstone. The Perth club had been relegated from the top flight the previous season but still were hard to deal with when it came to parting with their prize asset. Also coming in was Colin Woodthorpe from Norwich, and Peter Hetherston from Raith Rovers. On reflection they were hardly marquee signings and none of the trio had come from teams who were challenging in their respective leagues.

Dodds apart, the new signings failed to establish themselves in the side and the alarm bells were ringing as early as the opening games. Aberdeen came unstuck against Latvian minnows Skonto Riga in the UEFA Cup. Despite a 0-0 draw in Riga, the Dons could only manage a 1-1 draw in the return and went out on away goals. It was their lowest point in European football.

With only one win from their opening ten league games, Aberdeen found themselves at the foot of the table and struggling to get a positive result. A 3-0 victory over Dundee United in October provided false hope as the team then went on to win only five from 25 matches. The signing of John Inglis from St Johnstone suggested Aberdeen were in a panic as the big money earlier splashed had failed to provide any kind of return. That signalled the end for manager Miller as he cut ties with the club after a lengthy and glorious career. It was a wretched period in club history as their greatest servant left.

The board had been under intense pressure for months. The steady influence of Dick Donald was no longer there after his sad death at the end of 1993. With son Ian and local businessman Stewart Milne at the helm, these were challenging times at Pittodrie. Aberdeen turned to assistant manager Roy Aitken to steady growing anxiety within the club as they faced up to the very real prospect of being relegated for the first time in their history. It all started well enough with a sensational 2-0 win over Rangers but a week later the Dons' fragility was again exposed as they went out of the Scottish Cup at lowly Stenhousemuir, in a result that remained their worst ever in the Scottish Cup until their exit to Darvel in January 2023.

By the end of April, the bookmakers had Aberdeen down as relegation certainties. Cut adrift at the bottom, they had to go to Tynecastle on 29 April 1995 knowing that defeat could mean the drop. The national cameras gathered outside Tynecastle anticipating the supporters leaving the Edinburgh ground if as expected the Dons were going down. The club put on several free buses to take the fans to Edinburgh. A huge following helped Aberdeen muster a real gutsy performance epitomised by Dodds, whose two goals saved them that day. In their time of need the supporters rallied behind the team like never before. As news came through that Dundee United had lost at home to Hibernian, the Dons sensed that an escape was possible.

A full house at Pittodrie the following week was guaranteed as the Dons knew that a defeat would automatically relegate them for the first time in 92 years. A win would almost certainly send their close rivals down. Theo Snelders was recalled for his first game in seven weeks, such was manager Aitken's desire to get the Dutch international back into the side. Aitken told the *Press & Journal* ahead of the game, 'Theo will start. He is a major player for this club. He has been through it all for Aberdeen in the past and is ready to come back and answered our call.'

Improved performances of late indicated that the players had at last realised the gravity of the situation and they had the appetite to scrap for the points that would secure the Dons' status. Aitken continued, 'The difference with us and United is that we have been living with this pressure for weeks; everyone has said we are going down. My players have handled that and shown character. We know what it's all about. We now have the chance to get off the bottom of the league.' Aitken was correct as Aberdeen were now looking like a side that was fighting for everything; United, in contrast, were in freefall and had been dragged into the relegation mire after a series of poor results.

## Scottish Premier League as at 6 May 1995 (bottom three)

|  | P | W | D | L | F | A | Pts |
|---|---|---|---|---|---|---|---|
| Hearts | 34 | 11 | 7 | 16 | 41 | 48 | 40 |
| Dundee United | 34 | 9 | 9 | 16 | 39 | 53 | 36 |
| Aberdeen | 34 | 8 | 11 | 15 | 39 | 45 | 35 |

United manager Billy Kirkwood was banking on Craig Brewster being fit for the relegation clash. Faced with a hostile Pittodrie and with

United's Premier Division existence on the line, Kirkwood admitted he needed all the experienced players he could get. Kirkwood had taken over from Ivan Golac and had won just one game in five, 'We could go to Pittodrie and go for the draw which would mean we would get another opportunity next week against Celtic at home, but three points against Aberdeen will certainly put us in the play-offs. That is all we have prepared for all week. We will go all out to win the game.'

Interest in the match meant several ex-Dons players keeping an eye on the events at Pittodrie. Gothenburg hero Gordon Strachan could not understand the Dons' slump, 'I keep in touch with some of the guys and all we talk about is Aberdeen. We are at a loss to explain what has happened although we have all shared one thing in common, not one of us wants to see Aberdeen relegated after spending so many years at Pittodrie. But there is nothing we can do because it's down to Roy and the players to come out on top against Dundee United. If they want it badly enough, they can make it happen.'

Dodds and Duncan Shearer made sure Aberdeen's battle against relegation would go to the last day by scoring the goals that earned a crucial 2-1 win which took the team off the bottom of the table for the first time since 8 April. For United it meant that they were virtually doomed, having to rely on other sides and hope to beat Celtic in their final game. It was a forlorn task. Dodds put Aberdeen ahead in a highly charged game with a unique atmosphere. United crumbled and six of their players were booked in an explosive clash. Dodds also set up Shearer for his goal in 68 minutes, and although United substitute Robbie Winters (later to play for the Dons) pulled a goal back three minutes from time Aitken's men were pulled through by their fantastic support, who had provided incredible backing throughout. The players received a standing ovation at full time and openly embraced each other. This was high-stakes football not seen at Pittodrie before or since.

The opening goal, in 37 minutes, had arrived after Shearer and Jess combined on the right. The winger crossed to the front post where Dodds latched on to the loose ball to score from close range. The second goal came when Peter Hetherston played the ball wide to Dodds on the left. Dodds squared for Shearer, who drilled his low shot past O'Hanlon. It was a well-deserved win for Aberdeen who had plenty of chances during a frenetic 90 minutes.

One player rejuvenated under Aitken was Hetherston, who was outstanding against United. The midfielder had been frozen out by Willie Miller and considered walking away from Pittodrie, 'I would have left the club then. At that time, I wasn't getting a game at all for Aberdeen. The manager was picking the team he thought was right and that was up to him. But I got the vote of confidence from Roy who said he would give me a chance. He has come into the dressing room in the last couple of months and changed things. He got the players going again, believing we will not go down.'

As Aberdeen went into the final game of the league season, they knew that a win might have kept them clear of the dreaded play-off place. Once again the club laid on free buses to take an 8,000-strong Red Army to Brockville. Tickets for the away sections arrived at Pittodrie when the Falkirk chairman delivered them personally in what was an end-of-season financial boost for his club. The 2-0 win was all they could do but with Hearts surviving against Motherwell it meant a first Premier Division play-off against First Division Dunfermline. Pars manager Bert Paton never for one minute thought his side would face Aberdeen in such circumstances but his team were blown away in front of a packed Pittodrie in the first leg. Again, the stadium was a cauldron for what was a survival battle. The Dons' 3-1 win was followed by a similar score in the East End Park return. Even by Houdini standards this was a great escape and one that the club vowed would never be repeated.

The rapid decline in fortunes from finishing runners-up in 1994 to almost being relegated 12 months later was as surprising as it was unexpected. The side that played Dundee United in that crucial season-defining game included no fewer than seven players who were full internationals at some stage of their career.

# Aberdeen 2 Dundee 0

26 November 1995
Scottish League Cup Final
Hampden Park, Glasgow
Attendance: 33,096

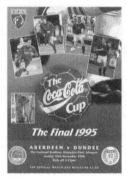

| Aberdeen | Dundee |
|---|---|
| Michael Watt | Michel Pageaud |
| Stewart McKimmie | Jim Duffy |
| Stephen Glass | Tom McQueen |
| Brian Grant | Roddy Manley |
| John Inglis | Morten Wieghorst |
| Gary Smith | Neil Duffy |
| Joe Miller | George Shaw |
| Duncan Shearer | Dušan Vrťo |
| Paul Bernard | Paul Tosh |
| Billy Dodds | Jim Hamilton |
| Eoin Jess | Neil McCann |
| *Subs:* Hugh Robertson, Peter Hetherston | *Subs:* Ray Farningham, Gerry Britton, Iain Anderson |
| *Manager:* Roy Aitken | *Manager:* Jim Duffy |

THE INTRODUCTION of three points for a win came into force in 1994 and the immediate effect on Aberdeen was almost disastrous. The Dons' proud record of never having been relegated came under serious threat in 1995 but the club and fans answered the call in the closing weeks to preserve their status at the expense of rivals Dundee United, who took the drop to the First Division.

During the summer of 1995 the Dons made improvements to their squad and the general opinion was that they had to re-establish themselves to their rightful position in the game. That came in the League Cup in 1995 as the Dons won the competition for the sixth time.

Aberdeen had started their cup campaign with a comfortable 3-1 win over St Mirren at Pittodrie. It was their opening game of the season and renewed optimism was the key. Scott Booth was among the goals, his second coming courtesy of a dreadful blunder from St Mirren keeper Campbell Money.

Falkirk were beaten 4-1 at Brockville four days after the Dons had won 3-2 there in the league. After the Bairns' keeper Parks had been sent off for handling outside of the box, the Dons ran riot in the cup tie. A tough quarter-final then went into extra time against Motherwell at Fir Park, the Dons eventually winning 2-1. Michael Watt had replaced Theo Snelders, who was on paternity leave, and kept his place in the side.

That set up a semi-final against bitter rivals Rangers. Eoin Jess was in majestic form and with Paul Bernard looking every bit a £1m player, it was in midfield that Aberdeen controlled proceedings. It was at Hampden that Jess performed his famous 'keepy-uppy' routine as the Dons defeated a Paul Gascoigne-inspired Rangers 2-1.

Preparations for the final had gone well with the squad leaving for Glasgow at Saturday lunchtime after a light training session. Snelders was a doubt, but Watt had been an able deputy. Roy Aitken was looking forward to bringing silverware to Aberdeen, 'We will be ready. If we play to our capabilities, we are a match for any team in the country.' The manager had been on a spying mission earlier in the week looking at strengthening his squad. With more than £1.5m still available to spend following the club share issue, Aitken was looking at several options.

Opponents Dundee had not won an honour for 22 years and were desperate to get their hands on the silverware. Manager Jim Duffy was still playing and appearing in his first Hampden final at the age of 36. Chairman Ron Dixon had been coming under criticism as he had not been near Dens Park for more than 13 months. The Canadian-based businessman did, however, make the trip to Scotland ahead of the final. He was full of praise for Duffy, who he claimed was the best young coach in the game. However, the thrifty nature of life at Dens Park came to light when it emerged that the champagne ordered for the final was based on a sale or return basis. There was also chaos with potentially hundreds of supporters being stuck at home because of a postal strike north of the border. The Scottish League announced that any fans who had not received their tickets through their postal application should not go to Hampden as no replacements would be available on the day. They would have to be returned so that a refund could be made. With the BBC and Sky TV taking the game live, it was a small consolation for those who missed out.

The Hampden final was going to be the last major occasion to be played in front of the old South Stand. Opened in 1903 of all years, the same year that Aberdeen were formed, it was due to be demolished for redevelopment.

Aberdeen had a long and distinguished history in the League Cup and were the first winners of the competition in 1946. Success followed in the 1955, 1976, 1985 and 1989 finals, and not for the first time the Dons went in against Dundee as hot favourites. The Dens Park side were in the First Division back then and Aberdeen recorded an impressive 2-0 win, backing up their status. Scott Booth failed a last-minute fitness test and Duncan Shearer was given a starting place up front alongside Billy Dodds, whose two goals saw off Rangers in the semi-final. In the final, Dodds opened the scoring in the first half and when Duncan Shearer headed a second early in the second half there was no way back for Dundee.

The opening goal came in 34 minutes. Stephen Glass went down the left and his cross fell to Shearer, whose intervention knocked Pageaud off balance. The keeper could only deflect the ball as far as Dodds, who scored from close range for his fifth goal of the tournament. Joe Miller then went close as Aberdeen began to turn on the style. Dundee held out until half-time but seconds after the interval the second goal came to effectively finish the game as a contest. In front of the massed Aberdeen support, Glass set up Shearer to head in at the near post.

Dundee could barely get out of their own half as Aberdeen dominated for long spells and never looked in danger of giving anything away. Dundee were a decent team with captain Jim Duffy still around and the emerging Neil McCann their biggest danger. McCann, however, came up against the experienced Stewart McKimmie and was never given the opportunity to pose a threat to the Dons. Glass was voted man of the match by the competition's sponsors, Coca-Cola, and his 'reward' was a mountain bike. The Aberdeen support took up most of the ground and the Hampden stands were a sea of red and white as the Red Army celebrated a sweet success given the troubles the club had endured in recent months.

*Neil Simpson's close range shot for the first goal for Aberdeen during the European Cup Winners' Cup quarter-final second leg against Bayern Munich at Pittodrie, 16 March 1983. The Dons beat Bayern 3-2, winning the tie 3-2 on aggregate.*

*The victorious Dons celebrate beating Real Madrid in 1983's European Cup Winners' Cup Final.*

*Alex Ferguson holding the European Cup Winners' Cup in 1983*

*John Hewitt nets the winner against Real Madrid*

*1983 Scottish Cup Union Street*

*1983/84 Aberdeen v Hamburg European Super Cup second leg at Pittodrie*

*Mark McGhee on the ball against Celtic in the 1984 Scottish FA Cup Final at Hampden Park*

*Willie Miller celebrates his goal, that gave Aberdeen the Scottish League championship title. Aberdeen v Celtic 1985*

*Glasgow Rangers striker Ally McCoist slides in to tackle Aberdeen's Stuart McKimmie with Brian Mitchell looking on during the match at Ibrox Stadium in Glasgow, 28 September 1985. Aberdeen won 3-0.*

*The Dons celebrate defeating Hibernian in the Skol League Cup Final, at Hampden Park, Glasgow, 27 October 1985.*

```
EUROPEAN CUP QUARTER FINAL 1ST LEG
ABERDEEN    V    I.F.K.
F.C.        GOTHENBURG


KICK OFF              WEDNESDAY 5TH
7.30 P.M.               MARCH 1986



SOUTH  STAND      £6.00
  ENTER BY APPROPRIATE TURNSTILE

    NUMBER 02236 / 97916
```

*Aberdeen v
Gothenburg EC
1986 Ticket*

*Aberdeen v Hearts in Scottish FA Cup Final on 10 May 1986. Ferguson was content after the game, but was still unhappy that the Dons had not won the treble that year, 'As far as I am concerned, we should have won the lot.'*

*Ticket for the 1989 League Cup Final against Rangers*

THE SKOL CUP
**1 9 8 9**
FINAL TIE

HAMPDEN PARK, GLASGOW
SUNDAY, 22nd OCTOBER, 1989
Kick-off 3.00 p.m.

*J. Farry* Secretary

Patrons are requested to be in their seats not later than 30 minutes
prior to the advertised time of kick-off.

In the event of a draw after normal time, extra time of 30 minutes (i.e. 15 minutes each way) will take place and thereafter, if necessary,
kicks from the Penalty Mark in accordance with the Rules laid down by the International Football Association Board.

| SOUTH WEST STAND TURNSTILE F | PRICE £12 | | Row Seat No. HH 29 |
|---|---|---|---|

TO BE RETAINED — SEE BACK FOR PLAN AND CONDITIONS
INVALID UNLESS PRESENTED IN FULL

*Alex Smith manager for the League Cup Final in 1989.*

*Alex Ferguson, Martin Buchan and Jim McLean (manager Dundee United) after being presented with the Promotion and Teaching of Football Service Award 1985 from the Scottish Football Association.*

*Manager Jimmy Calderwood acknowledges the supporters after their UEFA Cup Group B match against FC Copenhagen at Pittodrie on 20 December 2007*

*The 1983 side at the 25th team reunion against Manchester United in July 2008*

*The Dons line up before facing Copenhagen at Pittodrie in the UEFA Cup in 2007.*

*16 March 2014. Scottish League Cup Final between Aberdeen and Inverness Caledonian Thistle at Celtic Park. Aberdeen won 4-2 on penalties.*

*Action from the Europa League game against Rijeka*

Aitken reflected on the latest success in his long career and he pledged to bring more silverware to Aberdeen, 'Having taken the club through the relegation battles of last season, I wanted to get Aberdeen back to winning ways. I felt if we played at all we would be too strong for Dundee. Jim Duffy did enough to make it difficult for us, but we had the quality in vital areas. I said at the start when I accepted this job it would be important for us to get back challenging for honours. This club was brought up on success and hopefully this is the start of far bigger things.

'A lot of people wrote Aberdeen off six months ago. As far as I am concerned, they have answered their critics in the best way possible. The fans showed today what this club means to them. The expectations are high at Pittodrie. I am looking to consolidate our position in the league and there is a long way to go. I want us to get challenging for all honours. This is the first cup final we have won and now we can look at the remaining two competitions. This club has been brought up on great European nights and it is important to get back to that. That is something we can look forward to again next season.'

Dundee-born youngster Glass was delighted to be nominated as the man of the match and his stock was rising, 'I was a wee bit nervous before the game. Maybe it was the big occasion and I am not used to that. But to play well and win was a great feeling.'

The Aberdeen party returned to the city for a celebratory reception with their wives that night. Details of a civic reception giving fans the chance to salute the side would be announced on the Monday morning.

Scott Booth, who missed the final due to injury, was the subject of some more mischief-making from the west coast media. It was never rare to read such stories which would normally emerge before big Aberdeen games in Glasgow and elsewhere. It was a common trait that the club had got used to and usually scoffed at, given the nature of these 'sources'. On this occasion it was reported that Celtic were looking at offering £2.5m for Booth, who was beginning to establish himself in the Scotland setup. Former Parkhead captain Aitken was not used to such stories emerging, but this was nothing new for the club. He dismissed the report out of hand, 'Anyone thinking Scott is going to Celtic has to be joking. Scott has been secured on a two-year contract and will be going nowhere. In fact, I will be adding to the squad and not selling off our best players.'

It was announced that the squad would parade down Union Street the following Sunday on an open-top bus. Aitken concluded, 'This cup win is for the fans as much as it is for the players. The supporters have shown a passion and fervour for Aberdeen FC that many people claimed didn't exist. They have stuck with us during the difficult times, so it is pleasing to see them celebrate a cup win.'

# Aberdeen 2 Rangers 0

20 May 2007
Scottish Premier League
Pittodrie Stadium, Aberdeen
Attendance: 20,010

| Aberdeen | | Rangers |
|---|---|---|
| Jamie Langfield | | Allan McGregor |
| Michael Hart | | Gavin Rae |
| Richard Foster | | Nacho Novo |
| Scott Severin | | Alan Hutton |
| Zander Diamond | | Barry Ferguson |
| Russell Anderson | | David Weir |
| Jamie Smith | | Kevin Thomson |
| Barry Nicholson | | Saša Papac |
| Steve Lovell | | Charlie Adam |
| Lee Miller | | Ian Murray |
| Darren Mackie | | Kris Boyd |

*Subs:* Karim Touzani, Andy Considine, Craig Brewster
*Manager:* Jimmy Calderwood

*Subs:* Chris Burke, Steve Lennon
*Manager:* Walter Smith

EUROPEAN FOOTBALL has been vital for Aberdeen. Ever since they played their first European tie in 1967, the club have been defined by their exploits on foreign soil. It is the yardstick by which all Scottish clubs are judged, from Celtic becoming the first British club to win the European Cup, in 1967, through Rangers winning the European Cup Winners' Cup in 1972, to Aberdeen's double success in 1983 of the Cup Winners' Cup and Super Cup. Success in Europe is something that clubs in Scotland can be proud of in comparison to other countries. While the finance that has been poured into English football since 1992 has taken their game to another level, it is in Europe where the likes of Aberdeen can at least grab some national attention.

Any prolonged breaks from competing in Europe have always piled the pressure on Aberdeen managers through the years. Ever since they were successful in the 1980s, European qualification has been a minimum requirement for everyone who has followed Alex Ferguson. That expectation was tested to the full in 2006/07. Aberdeen had been out of European action since 2002, when they had played their 100th match in Europe, against Hertha Berlin. As the historical significance of that waned over several years under Jimmy Calderwood, the club did qualify for a return to Europe in the final game of the season. The stage was set for a dramatic finale. It was exactly what the authorities were hoping for when they introduced the controversial split in the Premier League in 2000 after the competition had been increased from ten to 12 clubs. The top six would break after 33 games to decide champions and European places, while the bottom six would sort out the relegation issue.

Calderwood arrived at Pittodrie in 2004 after a successful period with Dunfermline. He took over from Steve Paterson after a disastrous spell that saw Aberdeen again finish in the lower reaches of the league. The days of lavish spending under Ebbe Skovdahl were long gone so a more structured approach was taken with Willie Miller as director of football at the club.

Season 2006/07 promised much but disappointing cup exits to Queen's Park and Hibernian had put the pressure on Calderwood to deliver European football to Pittodrie. Investment in the squad was substantial compared to previous years. Barry Nicholson, Jamie Smith and Steve Lovell had been brought in to join Scott Severin, the Hearts captain who signed in 2004. Consistency in the league did not materialise until after their Scottish Cup exit. When it came to the final day the Dons' task was clear: defeat Rangers and a place in the UEFA Cup would be secured. Hearts were playing Kilmarnock at Rugby Park and their chances depended on them winning and Aberdeen slipping up, so the Sky cameras took in the game in Ayrshire. Aberdeen had secured a 1-1 draw against Hearts in Edinburgh on 6 May when a last-minute goal from Barry Nicholson set them up for their chance to qualify in their final game of the season.

Calderwood was confident going into the clash against Rangers, 'We had to go to Tynecastle and face Hearts without Russell Anderson, so we had to change our tactics. We dominated the first half and I thought we were excellent; I could not believe we went in at the break a goal behind. We did continue to press and although we left it late, we got a deserved equaliser. It would have been an injustice had we not taken something from the game. We had to win one of our last two fixtures and with them being against Celtic and Rangers it would be a difficult task. In midweek we were unlucky to go down [2-1] at Celtic. I have never been with a side there that created so many chances. We should have taken something from Parkhead. Now it is down to the Rangers game; they will be smarting from going down against Kilmarnock last week. I would expect Walter Smith will have his side fired up even though the league has gone for them. If you had offered me the chance to go into the last game knowing a victory would take us into the UEFA Cup, I would have taken it.'

Aberdeen went into the game protecting a good home record against the Ibrox club, having won both Pittodrie encounters the season before. The all-ticket crowd anticipated another nervous, highly charged encounter.

The kick-off was delayed for several minutes to allow for the pitch to be cleared of streamers from the away support, housed in the east corner of the South Terrace. Steve Lovell was first to show when he had the first effort on goal in four minutes. Mackie was then stopped by Papac before a Nicholson cross was scrambled clear of the danger area. Lee Miller then won a free kick as Scott Severin tried his luck, but the ball was blocked. Richard Foster stopped what was Rangers' first attack, before Anderson had to react against Kris Boyd and conceded the first corner of the match. Aberdeen continued to press, and a long Severin throw was eventually cleared by the visitors.

Aberdeen took a sensational lead in 21 minutes. A cross into the box was cleared by Weir and the ball was picked up by Severin, who from 25 yards out hit a volley that gave McGregor no chance. Pittodrie erupted with the home support behind the goal in the Merkland Stand.

Severin was a great signing after joining from close rivals Hearts where he had been their captain. It was a real show of intent from the Dons that had been missing in recent years. In his five years at Pittodrie, Severin made 166 appearances and became captain after Russell Anderson joined Sunderland in 2007. Severin played 15 times for Scotland and was capped during his spell with the Dons. In 2009 he agreed a move to Watford before returning north for brief spells with Kilmarnock and Dundee United. Injury in 2011 ended his playing career.

Aberdeen were piling on the pressure and there was a clash when Lovell chased down a through ball, and McGregor left his area to clear and took Lovell out at the same time. The striker squared up to Weir as tempers frayed. Both were booked while McGregor somehow escaped punishment. Severin then went close with another effort as he was fouled by Thomson before Lovell again caused chaos when his effort came back off the bar.

Aberdeen scored again in 32 minutes. Rangers switched off as a through ball to Lovell saw the forward clip the ball over McGregor and into the net. Lovell celebrated in front of the fans who filled the west side of the South Terrace.

Lovell had been signed from Dundee in the summer of 2005 after the Dens Park club were relegated. Born in Amersham, Lovell started out with Bournemouth and Portsmouth before moving to Scotland. He made 74 appearances for the Dons, scoring 24 goals, one of which was against Bayern Munich in the Allianz Arena in Germany. Lovell eventually joined Bournemouth in 2010, where he teamed up with his half-brother Eddie Howe.

Aberdeen were clearly on top and it looked as though Rangers were simply not up for the battle. Both Anderson and Severin were spoken to by referee Thomson as they went in with some crunching tackles as the home side continued to dominate.

The second half was more of a containment exercise for the Dons. Having got their lead, they never looked like giving anything away although Rangers did continue to fight as hard as they could. Several decisions from referee Thomson bemused those in red as plenty of challenges from the visitors went unpunished. When Gavin Rae flopped in the box in theatrical style it compounded a miserable day for Rangers, who were simply well beaten by a side with more desire and passion.

Once the away support was escorted away from the ground, the Dons' players returned to the pitch for a walk around to enjoy the moment with the home fans. Far from wild celebrations, after all it was only a European qualification that was achieved, but given the turmoil of previous seasons a return to Europe was something to celebrate.

Calderwood was as relieved as he was proud, 'It was a great day for us and at last we gave something back to the supporters. We deserved the win for sure, we were looking forward to this one and we had the right attitude. When this place is full and the fans are like that, it makes a huge difference for us and no team will like coming here. We now have the summer to assess the squad and make a few improvements, so we are ready to go back into European football. That was one of the reasons I came here; to sample the European atmosphere and challenge myself and my staff against the top European sides.'

For Aberdeen it was the end of a tough period in their history. Their centenary in 2003 had been celebrated in the right way but on the field the Dons were struggling. The era of Ebbe Skovdahl, their first foreign manager, ended after significant investment failed to improve things. The appointment of Steve Paterson, who had done exceptionally well at Inverness, proved disastrous as his off-field problems culminated with him leaving Pittodrie in the boot of a car to escape the media. Calderwood to his credit brought stability, which was exactly what the club needed most at the time. It was now the time for further progress.

## Scottish Premier League 2006/07

|  | P | W | D | L | F | A | Pts |
|---|---|---|---|---|---|---|---|
| Celtic | 38 | 26 | 6 | 6 | 65 | 34 | 84 |
| Rangers | 38 | 21 | 9 | 8 | 61 | 32 | 72 |
| Aberdeen | 38 | 19 | 8 | 11 | 55 | 38 | 65 |
| Hearts | 38 | 17 | 10 | 11 | 47 | 35 | 61 |
| Kilmarnock | 38 | 16 | 7 | 15 | 47 | 54 | 55 |
| Hibernian | 38 | 13 | 10 | 15 | 56 | 46 | 49 |
| Falkirk | 38 | 15 | 5 | 18 | 49 | 47 | 50 |
| Inverness Caledonian Thistle | 38 | 11 | 13 | 14 | 42 | 48 | 46 |
| Dundee United | 38 | 10 | 12 | 16 | 40 | 59 | 42 |
| Motherwell | 38 | 10 | 8 | 20 | 41 | 61 | 38 |
| St Mirren | 38 | 8 | 12 | 18 | 31 | 51 | 36 |
| Dunfermline | 38 | 8 | 8 | 22 | 26 | 55 | 32 |

# Aberdeen 4 Copenhagen 0

20 December 2007
UEFA Cup Group B
Pittodrie Stadium, Aberdeen
Attendance: 20,446

| Aberdeen | Copenhagen |
|---|---|
| Jamie Langfield | Jesper Christiansen |
| Michael Hart | William Kvist |
| Richie Byrne | Michael Gravgaard |
| Scott Severin | Mikael Antonsson |
| Zander Diamond | Oscar Wendt |
| Andy Considine | Libor Sionko |
| Jamie Smith | Hjalte Bo Nørregaard |
| Barry Nicholson | Rasmus Würtz |
| Lee Miller | Atiba Hutchinson |
| Sone Aluko | Marcus Allbäck |
| Chris Clark | Jesper Grønkjær |
| *Subs:* Chris Maguire, Richard Foster | *Subs:* Michael Silberbauer, Aílton, Morten Nordstrand |
| *Manager:* Jimmy Calderwood | *Manager:* Ståle Solbakken |

THE DRAW for the UEFA Cup could have been far kinder to the Dons when it pitted them against Ukrainian side Dnipro. After waiting for so long to return to the European arena the Dons had to negotiate a tough first round to qualify for the new UEFA Cup group stage, which had been introduced in 2004. As Aberdeen were unseeded there was always the chance they would come up against tough opposition. Dnipro were experienced campaigners and had hammered Hibernian 5-1 in 2005 so they were no stranger to followers of Scottish football. A 0-0 draw at Pittodrie was a fair result; Aberdeen were keen to take a lead to Ukraine but the visitors were a class act and gave little away in a tense clash before a packed Pittodrie. Just about everyone had written off the Dons' chances of going through. Dnipro were almost invincible at home and had built a formidable reputation on the back of it.

It took a heroic performance in Ukraine to see Aberdeen to the group stage, however. Darren Mackie scored the decisive away goal. His header from a Foster cross was described as the 'million-pound goal'; a reference to the money that Aberdeen would make in the group stage.

The 1-1 draw put Aberdeen through on away goals. On reflection it was one of their finest defensive performances on foreign soil, right up there with some of their greatest nights in Europe.

Progression meant at least an additional four matches in the group stage, not played on a home and away basis but with two ties at home and two away. Aberdeen would face Lokomotiv Moscow and FC Copenhagen at Pittodrie, with trips to Panathinaikos and Atlético Madrid. It was a tough ask to get through such a hard group but if they finished even in third place they would progress.

The game that did capture the imagination of the Aberdeen support was in Madrid. With plenty of time to prepare there was huge fan interest in attending. The initial ticket allocation was sold in quick time but the club managed to secure an additional allocation from Atlético. The Spaniards were an emerging side and on the threshold of further success. The fact that the match was in Madrid had that special attraction for many Aberdeen fans, who would take the opportunity to visit the Santiago Bernabéu Stadium, the home of Real Madrid, conquered by the Dons in 1983. The Vicente Calderón Stadium, home of Atlético back then, was greeted with an 'Invasión Escocesa' as the locals described the 8,000-strong Red Army that descended on the Spanish capital. Atlético beat Aberdeen 2-0 with Sergio Agüero and Diego Forlán spearheading their attack. As the group progressed it all came down to the final round of games. Aberdeen had to defeat Copenhagen to qualify, while the Danes would only need a draw to progress.

Aberdeen had a lengthy affiliation with Denmark; in the 1960s they signed three Danes who were amateurs at the time and went on to play in the first team, most notably Jens Petersen. Aberdeen also had their own 'Great Dane' in the form of the imposing Henning Boel, a cult figure at Pittodrie and part of the 1970 Scottish Cup-winning side. More recently, Ebbe Skovdahl became the club's first foreign manager in 1999.

The Dons' incredible European run peaked with a marvellous 4-0 win over Copenhagen on a night that brought back memories of the club's golden era. They swept into the last 32 after two goals from Jamie Smith helped secure third spot in qualifying Group B.

Copenhagen were on top before the break, but Smith's superb volley from 25 yards put the Dons in front after 47 minutes. Smith then shot home from the edge of the box, Mikael Antonsson turned the ball into his own net following a Lee Miller cross and Ricky Foster fired a fourth.

Smith joined Aberdeen in 2005 from ADO Den Haag after he began his career at Celtic. He had European experience at Parkhead, and he proved to be an inspired signing by Calderwood, whose links with the Netherlands and Dutch football were strong. Smith left Pittodrie after 85 appearance in 2009 and joined Colorado Rapids, later recalling that night, 'I thought we were too conservative in the first half and did what we could to deny them the opportunity to create chances. They were organised, full of experienced internationals, what we expected. I felt we were not taking enough risks, I decided that the first chance I get in the second half I was going to have a pop and see what happens. When Lee [Miller] flicked the ball on early in the second half, I do not think their defenders anticipated what I was going to do as they never closed me down. The ball sat up and I just went for it! After the game the stadium was buzzing, all the background staff, the folk that worked in the stadium. To play a small part was just fantastic. Aberdeen is a great club with loads of history, and I loved my time there.'

In the end it was a thoroughly deserved first victory in Europe that season for the Dons, who had initially qualified on the away goals rule and then only drawn one of their other three group games. Copenhagen had been peppering the Dons' goal early on with long-range efforts and Atiba Hutchinson was closest with a drive that flew just over from 20 yards.

Former Chelsea winger Jesper Grønkjær, who had been missing for a month with a hamstring injury, returned for Copenhagen and fired straight at goalkeeper Jamie Langfield from a difficult angle after a quick and incisive break.

A last-ditch challenge from Richie Byrne was required to thwart Libor Sionko as the former Rangers winger escaped the Dons' offside trap and Grønkjær drove another chance into the side-netting. However, that was all remedied three minutes after the break, with the Dons seemingly under instruction to loft high balls towards the centre of a fragile Danish defence.

Copenhagen were slow to react to a Langfield punt which sat up nicely for Smith and he lofted his volley over the stranded Christiansen from 25 yards.

Lee Miller delivered the high ball eight minutes later and Smith took his time before drilling it low across the face of Christiansen and into the far corner of the net from 18 yards to make it 2-0.

Smith then had an easier chance to complete his hat-trick but found the side-netting after being put clear following Michael Hart's superb run and through ball. Aberdeen's third eventually came after 71 minutes, when Miller did superbly to beat his marker and turn the ball across goal, where Antonsson deflected it into his own net. Ailton fired against the woodwork but any hopes of a late comeback were dashed after 82 minutes when Foster fired home from close range following a low cross from fellow substitute Chris Maguire to complete a night of celebration at Pittodrie.

When the euphoria had calmed down, Jimmy Calderwood took time to reflect, 'It was an amazing night. The atmosphere in there was something else. I came here to get this team back into Europe, so it was so pleasing to see how we managed the game against more experienced opposition. I thought we played a cautious game in the first half but considering what was at stake and the opposition, that was understandable. We were OK in the first half without being too threatening in the last third. It was vital we made a breakthrough early in the second half and Jamie came up with that wonder goal. That set the tone for us and the crowd urged us on to get that vital second goal. From that point on I thought we were magnificent. Our defenders stayed focused and the midfield worked so hard to contain their flair players in there. They [Copenhagen] are experienced in Europe but I doubt if they will have had to withstand what we threw at them in the second half very often. We have so much to look forward to here.'

Aberdeen progressed to the last 32 and as fate would have it, they were drawn against Bayern Munich, who they eliminated on their way to European Cup Winners' Cup success in 1983. When the ties came around it had been 25 years since the sides last met. It was a marvellous draw for the Dons and the first leg was a fantastic occasion.

Pittodrie was once again full and echoes of 1983 could be heard as Aberdeen were unlucky not to take a lead to Germany for the second leg after a pulsating 2-2 draw. Bayern were more used to the Champions League with lush pitches and plentiful, plush surroundings. Pittodrie, more than 100 years old, on a north-east Scotland February night, a stone's throw from the North Sea, is an unforgiving place. The away dressing room is small, almost spartan, not much room for coat hangers let alone the more luxurious surroundings a team like Bayern would come to expect.

To put into perspective how much of an achievement it was for Aberdeen to qualify, most of their group opponents went on to impress in Europe the following season.

Panathinaikos qualified for the Champions League and finished top of their group ahead of Inter Milan and Werder Bremen before going out to Villarreal in the last 16.

Atlético Madrid also reached the Champions League after a strong finish in La Liga and went on to progress from their group, going out on away goals in the last 16 to Porto, while Copenhagen were eliminated from the 2008/09 Champions League at the qualifying stage but went on to reach the last 32 of the UEFA Cup, losing to Manchester City.

# Aberdeen 0 Inverness CT 0 (aet)

*(Aberdeen won 4-2 on penalties)*
16 March 2014
Scottish League Cup Final
Celtic Park, Glasgow
Attendance: 51,143

| Aberdeen | Inverness Caley Thistle |
|---|---|
| Jamie Langfield | Dean Brill |
| Shay Logan | David Raven |
| Russell Anderson | Daniel Devine |
| Mark Reynolds | Josh Meekings |
| Andy Considine | Graeme Shinnie |
| Barry Robson | Marley Watkins |
| Ryan Jack | Ross Draper |
| Willo Flood | Greg Tansy |
| Jonny Hayes | James Vincent |
| Niall McGinn | Richie Foran |
| Adam Rooney | Billy McKay |
| *Subs:* Cammy Smith, Scott Vernon | *Subs:* Nick Ross, Aaron Doran, Ryan Christie |
| *Manager:* Derek McInnes | *Manager:* John Hughes |

BY 2014, 19 years had passed since Aberdeen's last major trophy. Since the end of the Second World War in 1945 their longest period without success was between 1956 and 1970, and after winning the League Cup in 1995 they had rarely threatened to end that run to add to their honours despite reaching both domestic cup finals in 2000, only to lose them both.

Although under Jimmy Calderwood the club did gain respectability and some positive results in Europe, domestic success in the cup competitions remained a black mark on the manager's report card. The harrowing defeat to Queen of the South in the semi-final of the Scottish Cup in 2008 was a result Calderwood never truly recovered from.

It was not until the appointment of Derek McInnes in 2013 that Aberdeen's fortunes changed. It is perhaps a harsh reflection on the McInnes era that the 2014 League Cup was the only success under him. A level of consistency in the league was arguably matched in the cups with several semi-finals and finals being reached but the 2014 success could not be repeated.

Aberdeen were up against Inverness Caley Thistle, surprise finalists after their stunning comeback against Hearts in their semi-final when they had been reduced to nine men but went through on penalties. The Highland side were admitted to the Scottish leagues in 1994 after Inverness Caledonian and Thistle merged. The perception from outside of the north and north-east was that any Aberdeen v Inverness clash was the 'north derby' on the assumption that both clubs were in reasonable proximity to each other. Sky Sports promoted these games as such which brought ironic humour from the Dons' support. Anyone who has dragged themselves up the A96 and the 103 miles from Aberdeen to Inverness would argue it is anything but a 'derby' fixture. For context, no fewer than ten senior clubs in Scotland are nearer to Aberdeen than the Highland capital.

While Inverness qualified in dramatic circumstances, it was more of a stroll for Aberdeen against St Johnstone at Tynecastle. The Perth side had been making plenty of pre-match noise about upsetting the Dons but in one of the most emphatic semi-finals the 4-0 result was more than justified. The Dons were backed by a huge support, selling out their allocation and taking over three of the Tynecastle stands. They helped Aberdeen put the pressure on from the outset, Adam Rooney coming close in the opening minute. St Johnstone appeared hesitant and the Dons took full advantage to open the scoring in three minutes through Jonny Hayes. When Peter Pawlett burst through the Perth defence in 32 minutes to score past keeper Banks the Dons were in control and on their way to Celtic Park.

The Glasgow venue was chosen due to Hampden being prepared for the Commonwealth Games. Neil Doncaster, the SPL chief, explained, 'We lost Hampden as a result of the Games this summer. We were left with two venues to consider; Ibrox and Celtic Park. We had a full consultation with both clubs, Police Scotland and the broadcasters. Celtic Park will provide a great venue which has a tradition of hosting huge games.'

There was the usual sniping from the west coast media who questioned the choice of venue and concerns as to the attendance being well short of capacity. Doncaster told BBC Scotland, 'Certainly with it being the first major final Aberdeen have been in for some years and the first ever for Inverness, we are anticipating big interest from both teams and looking forward to a great final.'

Those concerns were taken for what they were in the north, simple mischief-making. The demand for tickets from the Aberdeen support was unprecedented. More than 43,000 of the Red Army would head to Celtic Park, the ground being dubbed 'Park Red'. Such was the interest that Aberdeen were refused additional tickets on safety grounds by Police Scotland. The additional 7,000 seats behind the Inverness support were never allocated.

It is impossible to establish if that 43,000 fans was the highest number to follow Aberdeen to a major final. Looking back, only the 1937 and 1967 Scottish Cup finals would come close to matching that amount. Reports from 1937 suggested about 30,000 travelled from Aberdeen, but reference to those from outside the city could not be estimated. Further, these finals were not made all-ticket.

There was no doubt the pressure was all on Aberdeen, as favourites and going so long without success, as captain Russell Anderson recalled, 'Every day we were coming back from training and we saw queues of supporters buying tickets and it was a bit surreal. I think because neither Celtic nor Rangers were involved, a lot more families came through for the game. It had been such a long time since the club had won anything so there was an expectation level and a great opportunity.'

Aberdeen prepared for the final in St Andrews, which proved to be a relaxing week as McInnes wanted: light training with plenty of relaxation.

Midfielder Barry Robson remembered, 'When you came out and saw our huge support, you thought this is a big deal. More so for me, as an Aberdeen boy, knowing what it is like and the expectation. It was a huge build-up and I was nervous, but once I was over that line, it felt great.'

The teams entered the field to a wall of noise from the huge Aberdeen support that dwarfed the 7,000 who came down from Inverness. The Highland club have often been criticised for their poor core backing but with so much acrimony over the amalgamation in 1994 it would probably take the next generation to gauge their true levels.

There was a shock for Aberdeen in the opening seconds as Hayes went down awkwardly and injured his shoulder. It was a hammer blow as with Peter Pawlett out injured, Hayes was probably the Dons' most creative player. After treatment he tried to carry on but was replaced by Cammy Smith after only five minutes. Despite having the bulk of the possession, the Dons struggled to seriously threaten the Inverness defence. Aberdeen created an opportunity in 12 minutes when Rooney set up Smith before the ball went out to the left. Considine crossed for Smith, whose header went just over the bar. It was a nervous Aberdeen who were mindful of the pressure on them, while Inverness were happy to sit deep and try to hit the Dons on the break. Robson was the most creative player on the park and with Inverness filling the midfield areas, any good football was at a premium. Aberdeen had a claim for a penalty in 34 minutes when Shay Logan advanced and his cross was met by Rooney, who was brought down by Meekings. Referee McLean had a look but decided that it was no penalty.

Anderson saw his shot go just over as the Dons started the second half in positive mood, and at last the game became far more open but there were still very few chances created. Niall McGinn and Rooney combined well to create an opening but there were no takers from Rooney's cross. In 69 minutes Aberdeen replaced substitute Smith with Nicky Low, which allowed Robson a more central role, and he was having more of an influence as the game moved into the latter stages. Ryan Jack then had an effort saved by Brill and Rooney just missed the rebound. Aberdeen got a fright with three minutes to go when Inverness were claiming for a penalty before the Dons should have broken the deadlock. Rooney and Robson combined to set up McGinn, who blazed the ball over the bar to the frustration of his team's supporters.

Aberdeen continued to put the pressure on in extra time, following on from what was a hugely disappointing 90 minutes. This was no game for the purist; the nerves and what was at stake made for the inevitable penalty shoot-out. It was certainly not what Aberdeen had wanted but probably what Inverness had hoped for.

The decision on which end the penalties would be taken at had been agreed beforehand, and in front of the Inverness support the noise came from all three sides of Celtic Park as the outcome was down to what happened from 12 yards. Inverness forward Billy McKay was first up, and his effort was brilliantly saved by Jamie Langfield. Robson held his nerve to score the first Aberdeen spot kick. Advantage Aberdeen and you could feel the tension. There was joy for the Dons when Tansey stepped up and put his effort over the bar, then Low showed no nerves as he sent Brill the wrong way and Aberdeen were getting closer to victory. Nick Ross scored for Inverness before Scott Vernon also sent Brill the wrong way, and substitute Doran kept the pressure up by scoring a second penalty for Inverness. It all came down to Adam Rooney, the former Inverness striker who Aberdeen had taken back to Scotland from Oldham. The Irishman had been the Dons' regular penalty taker and he made no mistake to send the players, staff and supporters into ecstasy.

Aberdeen, at last, had been successful, and the scenes afterwards will remain part of Pittodrie folklore.

Defender Mark Reynolds revealed afterwards he was keen to take a penalty, but his manager thought otherwise, 'I was the last choice to take one. At the end of extra time the gaffer asked us who wanted it, and I said I would happily take one and I think he blanked me. The manager had always said he was a big believer that penalties are not luck, a shoot-out should be skill and I was confident knowing the players were coming up to take them. Barry Robson was one of the best penalty takers we've ever had and loves the big occasion. Nicky Low was second and he thrived in that environment. Scott Vernon never let us down and then we had Adam Rooney, whose penalty record was unbelievable.'

It was a special moment for Jamie Langfield, 'For the first penalty I was walking towards the goal with Inverness forward Billy McKay and I wasn't nervous. I had a smile on my face – I was so confident I was going to save it. When Adam [Rooney] scored the winner, I sank to my knees and felt myself go a bit. Coming back from my illness [Langfield had suffered a brain seizure several years earlier] and how much it meant to my family was a special moment.'

Barry Robson got stung for paying for the after-match drinks on the coach home, 'I was never late in my career, but one day a couple of weeks earlier I had read the time wrong and was late for a team meeting. So as a punishment I said I would buy all the booze if we won the cup. Sure enough we did and, on the way back, we stopped at a supermarket and the young boys gathered bottles of things I had never even heard of, think I got a bill of about £400. It was a ridiculous journey home; probably the best few hours of my life. I was walking about the bus with a microphone and I would get the next person to sing a song. The bus was actually rocking.'

Mark Reynolds joked, 'We absolutely battered Robbo's bank card. I think at that point he wasn't caring because he was so happy, we won the cup. It was just wild. I don't know if the manager planned it that way, but it gave us the chance to be together. With 40,000 Aberdeen fans trying to get up the road at the same time it took ages, but it was incredible.'

A week later the team paraded through the streets of Aberdeen and a reported 100,000 turned up to pay tribute to the League Cup winners. The Red Army also adapted a rendition of the Human League hit from 1981, 'Don't You Want Me', and changed the lyrics to 'Peter Pawlett Baby'. The song was so popular that it entered the iTunes charts among the top five downloads.

Chairman Stewart Milne spoke on BBC Radio Scotland after the game. 'Nineteen years, 120 minutes and now f*****g penalties,' he exclaimed as he got carried away with emotion. Milne had been at Pittodrie soon after his company was behind the construction of the £4.5m Richard Donald Stand in 1993. He had overseen some tough times through the club's centenary and beyond, all the time carrying the burden of the longest post-war period without success.

# HNK Rijeka 0 Aberdeen 3

**49**

16 July 2015
Stadion Kantrida, Rijeka
UEFA Europa League second qualifying round first leg
Attendance: 10,275

| Aberdeen | HNK Rijeka |
|---|---|
| Danny Ward | Ivan Vargić |
| Shay Logan | Ivan Tomečak |
| Graeme Shinnie | Marin Leovac |
| Ash Taylor | Marko Lešković |
| Andy Considine | Mirai Samardžić |
| Paul Quinn | Josip Radošević |
| Jonny Hayes | Filip Bradarić |
| Peter Pawlett | Marin Tomasov |
| David Goodwillie | Moisés |
| Ryan Jack | Anas Sharbini |
| Niall McGinn | Bekim Balaj |
| *Subs:* Willo Flood, Adam Rooney, Kenny McLean | *Subs:* Zoran Kvržić, Roman Bezjak, Ivan Močinić |
| *Manager:* Derek McInnes | *Manager:* Matjaž Kek |

UNDER DEREK McInnes the Dons had gradually been improving and appearances in the European arena were frequent. The manager was keen on taking his team to the next level and beyond the additional preliminary ties that seemed to become so difficult for Scottish clubs to negotiate. Scotland's co-efficient in the UEFA rankings had taken a battering in recent years but certainly Aberdeen more than did their bit to redress the balance. They had come through some difficult ties in the last few seasons, their 2014 win in the Netherlands against Groningen being their standout victory under McInnes. Qualifying for the new Europa League competition's group stages, however, had still eluded the Dons.

To illustrate how much European football had changed over the years, if Aberdeen were to qualify just for the group stages alone they would have to negotiate four opponents and eight matches, the same amount the club played to get to the semi-final of the European Cup Winners' Cup in 1983. With UEFA opening borders and getting many more teams involved, the earlier rounds in European football are now fraught with danger for Scottish clubs.

The impressive win over Groningen was to be welcomed, but in 2015 that result was surpassed with a sensational victory over

HNK Rijeka. The Croatians had not lost at home in their previous 12 European ties and had an impressive pedigree both domestically and in Europe.

The only completive action Aberdeen had seen so far in 2015/16 was the two ties against KF Shkëndija from North Macedonia. They went through on away goals after two tough games which were ideal preparation for the trip to Croatia.

Aberdeen had a new keeper, a young Danny Ward on loan from Liverpool, experiencing his first involvement in European football. McInnes went with a back three though the wing-backs Shay Logan and Jonny Hayes could tuck in to make it a back five. As expected, the home side came at Aberdeen from the kick-off and Tomasov came close with a volley before the same player saw his cross cleared by Shinnie. Hayes set up the Dons' first attack, but his final pass eluded McGinn and the chance was gone. Rijeka should have taken the lead in nine minutes when Tomasov hit the post from close range despite it looking easier to score. At that stage the Croatians were piling on the pressure and were creating good chances, Ward doing well to hold a powerful strike from Radošević. Aberdeen then broke clear and caused havoc in the Rijeka penalty area after a slip by Vargić, before Balaj tested Ward again. The new keeper was certainly showing his promise with a commanding and confident display.

The searing heat was not something that the Aberdeen players were used to. Despite the kick-off coming at 9pm, the temperature hit 30ºC and in a first for the Dons a water break was called by the referee after 24 minutes. Aberdeen came more into the game although the home side were enjoying the bulk of the possession. There were few chances created, but the Dons were starting to look more dangerous on the break and they scored a vital away goal in 39 minutes. A corner from McGinn found Andy Considine free in the box and his header opened up a vital lead. Aberdeen grew in confidence as the half ended and were unlucky not to score a second after a superb move ended with Pawlett scoring with a header, but the goal was disallowed for a marginal offside decision.

Rijeka made a change at the break as Kvržić replaced Tomasov, who had missed a couple of chances in the first period. Sharbini was arguably the home side's most dangerous player but he was guilty of going down far too easily on occasion, causing frustration even among his own team's support. Aberdeen took full advantage in 52 minutes by scoring a second goal as Shay Logan crossed for Pawlett who netted with a diving header. Ward then produced a couple of superb saves as Rijeka, clearly stung by Aberdeen's clinical finishing, tried to get back into the tie. Aberdeen rounded off a superb evening by scoring a third in 75 minutes. Kenny McLean, who had replaced McGinn, was on the end of a pass from Goodwillie to slam the ball into the net from 12 yards.

Rijeka were stunned but there was a realisation within the ground that Aberdeen had a lot more about them than they had been given credit for. The Croatian press had dismissed the Scots on the back of the Dons not 'having a strong European presence'.

Aberdeen then had to stand up to intense pressure at the end as the desperate hosts tried everything to get back into the tie and at least take one goal to Scotland for the return leg, but they had been beaten by a tactical masterclass from McInnes, his finest hour in Europe for the Dons. The 300 or so away supporters were urging their team on throughout and as the final whistle blew, they were in immediate party mood. Credit to the Rijeka fans, who gave the Scots a warm round of applause and appreciation for a gutsy performance and an incredible first-leg lead. The Stadion Kantrida was in a beautiful setting, facing a huge rock along one side of the pitch, and it provided a fantastic atmosphere for European ties. The first Aberdeen goal was met with jeers by the home support, the second by silence and the third by a grudging appreciation of opponents who had cut through Rijeka's defence in what was their record home defeat in Europe.

The water break that came midway through the first half proved more significant in terms of Aberdeen gaining a foothold in the game. Up until that point they had been under the cosh and lucky to still be on level terms. Andy Considine recalled, 'We were backs to the wall for the opening period and they had hit the woodwork a couple of times. Once the break came the manager changed the midfield, which helped us settle and reduced their chances. When we managed to score, that was a huge moment for us.'

McInnes made it clear Aberdeen would need to do a professional job to see out the tie at home despite that impressive win. McLean was preferred to Pawlett in the starting line-up as an indication that the manager was as keen to keep a clean sheet in the return as he was to add to their aggregate lead. David Goodwillie was once again the lone striker with everyone in a red jersey apart from him quick to get back into a good defensive shape whenever Rijeka were in possession.

As a result the visitors, who had made the group stages for the previous two years, often ran into dead ends when they tried to find the space in a first half in which the Dons had managed the game brilliantly, but suddenly after an hour it was game on. Two quick goals for the visitors showed just how much quality they had in their side and Pittodrie became very nervous. After a sterile opening period Rijeka threatened a miracle recovery from their 3-0 aggregate deficit when Marin Tomasov scored with a sublime strike and substitute Zoran Kvržić netted with the aid of a deflection.

However, that Aberdeen side was made of stern stuff. As well as having real quality they had the mental strength to cope with those situations and minutes after the second goal McGinn popped up to score with a great strike. Pittodrie erupted. The tie was safe, and the Dons made sure of their passage into the next round when the outstanding Goodwillie set up Jonny Hayes, who had missed a great chance at 1-0.

Rijeka were a class act on and off the pitch; they showed great humility after the game and were respectful of Aberdeen, who clearly rattled them in the first leg and had the guile to come through strongly at Pittodrie.

There was no doubt the result in Croatia is one of the best achieved by Aberdeen away from home in Europe. When you consider that Alex Ferguson claimed his great team of the 1980s was confident enough to go anywhere in world football and get a result, the class of 2015 had certainly created their own piece of history.

# 50

# Hearts 1 Aberdeen 3

20 September 2015
Scottish Premiership
Tynecastle Stadium, Edinburgh
Attendance: 16,702

| Aberdeen | | Hearts |
|---|---|---|
| Danny Ward | | Neil Alexander |
| Shay Logan | | Callum Paterson |
| Andy Considine | | Błażej Augustyn |
| Ash Taylor | | Alim Öztürk |
| Paul Quinn | | Igor Rossi |
| Graeme Shinnie | | Jamie Walker |
| Kenny McLean | | Miguel Pallardó |
| Niall McGinn | | Prince Buaben |
| Peter Pawlett | | Osman Sow |
| Ryan Jack | | Juanma |
| David Goodwillie | | Gavin Reilly |

*Subs:* Ryan McLaughlin, Adam Rooney, Jonny Hayes
*Manager:* Derek McInnes

*Subs:* Billy King, Sam Nicholson
*Manager:* Robbie Neilson

WHEN DEREK McInnes took over from former Scotland manager Craig Brown as Aberdeen manager on 25 March 2013, he joined a club in dire need of improving. He wanted to help the city of Aberdeen to 'fall in love' with the football team again. McInnes had been manager at St Johnstone before a spell with Bristol City ended as financial cutbacks took effect. Until his disappointing departure from Pittodrie in March 2021 there can be no doubt that under McInnes the club certainly regained their pride. Apart from that League Cup win in 2014, the McInnes era will be remembered for a consistency that had been missing from previous Aberdeen sides. It brought regular European football, a mandatory requirement that the Aberdeen support had craved. Although the group stages were never achieved, there were some remarkable scalps added under McInnes. Wins in Groningen and Rijeka were standout results which would have compared well with that great Aberdeen side of the 1980s.

On the domestic front Celtic were the dominant force in Scotland and with the likes of Rangers and Hearts spending considerable time outside of the top flight it was down to Aberdeen to provide a credible challenge. Despite the gulf in finances the Dons did on occasions suggest they would be able to make the breakthrough. In season 2015/16 they pushed Celtic all the way. Two Pittodrie wins over the Glasgow club in the league had the supporters in raptures and the championship race went all the way into the final two weeks of the season. It was a gutsy effort for Aberdeen that was to fall just short. Had the club been more active in the January transfer window it could have been very different.

It was not only Pittodrie that provided McInnes with his finest hours. On the road the Dons had become a potent force and it has been accepted by most observers that their finest 45 minutes of football under the manager came against Hearts at Tynecastle on 20 September 2015.

Tynecastle had often been a tough venue for the Dons. Traditionally both Hearts and the Dons have laid claims to being the worthiest of challengers outside of Glasgow, but on closer scrutiny it has been Aberdeen who have down the years been more successful. British clubs are invariably defined by how successful they have been on the European stage. In Scotland such success has Aberdeen, Celtic and Rangers as trophy winners; for Aberdeen their European Super Cup victory puts them in the elite 'two stars' category, something even the two Glasgow clubs have not achieved. Beyond those three, no other Scottish club has achieved similar success in Europe.

It was also at Tynecastle that Aberdeen clinched the Premier Division in May 1984, and 11 years later it was a very different cause as their 2-1 win over Hearts almost certainly saved them from a first relegation. While Aberdeen's no relegations are well known, for Hearts it has been a more common occurrence ever since the inception of the Premier Division in 1975.

Aberdeen have been blessed with many great combinations through the years, and under McInnes they could boast of McGinn, Rooney and Hayes as a potent front three that would serve them well. The Irish-born trio all played a major part in the McInnes era. Niall McGinn was signed by Craig Brown on 12 July 2012 after a short spell with Celtic where he made only 28 appearances in three seasons. After making his debut against his former club, McGinn was injured in his first game at Pittodrie. The Northern

Ireland international recovered well enough to pick up as he became the Dons' top scorer that season and was shortlisted for the PFA Player of the Year award. McGinn also turned down interest from several Championship clubs in England to stay loyal to Aberdeen. He was among the goals in the Dons' European ties and his strike in Groningen helped earn a memorable victory. After a short spell with Gwangju in 2017, McGinn returned to Pittodrie in December of that year. McGinn went on to make 279 appearances for the Dons. He was also a regular in the Northern Ireland side and went on to gain 72 caps for his country, his most memorable occasion being his goal against Ukraine in the 2016 European Championship finals.

Republic of Ireland under-21 international Adam Rooney joined Aberdeen from Oldham on 23 January 2014 following spells with Inverness, Birmingham and Stoke City. A prolific scorer, he formed a great understanding with McGinn and Jonny Hayes. He returned to haunt Inverness by scoring the decisive penalty in the 2014 League Cup Final, and later that year he became only the third Aberdeen player to score a hat-trick in Europe as the team eased past Daugava Riga. By 2017 Rooney had signed a four-year extension to remain at Pittodrie and he notched his 100th goal in March 2017 in a 7-0 rout of Dundee. In the 2012 Scottish Cup semi-final against Hibernian at Hampden, Rooney scored after 12 seconds as the Dons progressed to another final.

Jonny Hayes was also signed from Inverness in May 2012 and went on to become a firm favourite. His first goal came against Manchester United in a testimonial game for Neil Simpson at Pittodrie. Arguably the best goal Hayes scored for the Dons was on 25 February 2014, a sensational 30-yard drive which beat Celtic keeper Fraser Forster, who had not conceded a goal in domestic football for 13 games. It was later voted Scotland's goal of the season. After joining Celtic in a £1m deal in 2017, Hayes returned to Aberdeen for a second spell in June 2020. He made four appearances for the Republic of Ireland in 2016/17.

Aberdeen travelled to Edinburgh looking for their eighth win in succession after a sensational start to the season. They had defeated Hamilton in midweek and McInnes made four changes to the side, including Peter Pawlett coming in for the suspended Hayes. Hearts had been in decent form, more so at Tynecastle, and after wins over St Johnstone, Motherwell and Partick they were confident of success against the league leaders. The visiting Red Army sold out their 1,400 tickets in just two hours; there would have been plenty more had their allocation been increased.

Hearts by tradition were always a tough, physical side and were always keen to mix things up. On this occasion it was a classy Aberdeen who imposed themselves all across Tynecastle with a whirlwind first half that saw them go in three goals to the good and out of sight. Despite Hearts trying to press early on, Aberdeen opened the scoring in nine minutes. McGinn's superbly placed free kick was met by David Goodwillie, who scored from six yards. That goal quietened the home support but even they were in admiration when McGinn scored an incredible individual goal in 23 minutes. He latched on to a Ryan Jack ball near the corner, swivelled and teased his way past two challenges down the touchline, leaving defenders in his wake before dropping the shoulder and sending a fierce drive from a tight angle to score one of the finest goals seen at Tynecastle.

Hearts were still trying to force their way forward but Danny Ward in goal was rarely tested, and the game was effectively over when Goodwillie scored the Dons' third just before half-time. Hearts had the opportunity to get the ball into the box but Graeme Shinnie was on hand to send the ball clear. The lightning quick break was a joy to behold; McGinn raced away, leaving a defender before squaring to Goodwillie to score. It was a classic move and typical of how the team was set up away from home.

Derek McInnes's eight-year spell at Pittodrie will always be defined by a solitary League Cup success in 2014. While semi-finals, finals and European games were frequent, it will be a period in which the Dons just came up short. Some great players had emerged in the McInnes era; the aforementioned Irish trio of McGinn, Rooney and Hayes apart, the likes of Ryan Jack, Graeme Shinnie, Kenny McLean and Scott McKenna all flourished and went on to play for the Scottish national team. Aberdeen also had some excellent loan signings during the McInnes reign, most notably a young James

Maddison and Danny Ward, who have both progressed to become regulars in the English Premier League.

It is European competition, however, though that remains all-important to the club. Under McInnes pride was certainly restored as Aberdeen qualified for the Europa League between 2014 and 2020 during his tenure.

Since McInnes's departure on 8 March 2021 the Dons have still been searching for the level of consistency that he took great pride in. The balance between winning domestic cups and qualifying for Europe through a high enough league position is a fine one. In the modern era so much emphasis has been placed on league football, certainly more so down south in England where the financial rewards dwarf anything that is available in the Scottish game. The more cynical would suggest that in Scotland the fact that the championship is essentially shared by the two Glasgow clubs means a greater emphasis is placed on the league.

Aberdeen, more than any other, have been the one club to challenge that duopoly over the years and for that one glorious period under Alex Ferguson they not only competed but conquered. The two stars are shining bright over Pittodrie.

# Acknowledgements

IT WAS back in 1978 that the publication of the first book on Aberdeen FC history began a lifelong passion for the club's history. Reading through Jack Webster's excellent review of the first 75 years of the Dons prompted an interest that has gathered momentum through the years. As this is now my fifth book on Aberdeen, it remains a pleasure to research and write about our great club.

The excellent resources that I have used to complete this book include:

Webster, Jack, *The Dons: The History of Aberdeen Football Club* (Stanley Paul, 1978)

MacLeod, Ally, *The Ally MacLeod Story* (Stanley Paul, 1979)

Leatherdale, Clive, *The Aberdeen Football Companion* (John Donald, 1986)

Crampsey, Bob, *Aberdeen: Final Edition* (Keith Murray Publishing, 1990)

Ferguson, Alex, *A Light in the North* (Mainstream Publishing, 1985)

Stirling, Kevin, *Aberdeen: A Centenary History 1903–2003* (Desert Island Books, 2002)

Turnbull, Eddie and Hannan, Martin, *Having a Ball* (Mainstream Publishing, 2006)

Begg, Ally, *Aberdeen European Nights* (Polaris, 2021)

Other resources that formed part of my research included the BNA Archive, the fantastic Aberdeen FC website, and my own personal archive which has grown over many years. My collection of old copies of the *Aberdeen Press & Journal* and *Evening Express* provided excellent sources for quotes from players and managers alike.

My personal thanks to Joe Harper for writing the foreword for this book. Joe is of course an Aberdeen icon. As a young boy growing up and going to Pittodrie in my formative years, Joe became my hero, idolised by a generation of supporters who were fortunate enough to see him play for the club.

The first time I came across Joe was after a game at Pittodrie in 1969 when his Morton team-mate Joe Mason passed on my autograph book on the bus before it was leaving Pittodrie after a 2-2 draw. Joe was soon to be signing again some weeks later but this time his signature was to confirm him joining Aberdeen as a player. Joe went on to become the club's record scorer and earn legendary status at Pittodrie in his two spells. He is still around at Pittodrie on matchdays and one of the most popular ex-Dons around. Thanks, Joe.

For a more current perspective I turned to Malcolm Panton at Aberdeen FC. Mal has become a good friend ever since he joined the club in September 2001. For the past 24 years I have been involved in the historical content of *Red Matchday*, the official club programme. Malcolm takes a lot of pride in what has become the best programme in Scotland for more than 20 years. He also offered me a more recent perspective on club history, to save me getting too wrapped up in the Dons' historical glories.

Thanks also to Ally Begg, one-time boy band member (Bad Boys Inc) and proper Aberdeen supporter who has written two excellent books on the Dons and currently produces an insightful club YouTube channel called AllyBeggABTV. Ally and Mal keep this older scribe relevant so for that I am eternally grateful. Thanks also to Scottish football historian Andy Mitchell, whose knowledge has no equal.

Many thanks to all at Pitch Publishing for being patient with me as personal circumstances delayed the completion of this book.

To all the Aberdeen supporters everywhere who make this club so unique and special, I thank you.

To my son Kevin who still comes with his father to all of the Dons' home games, it is appreciated. Finally, thanks to my loving wife Bernadette, who has always been there for me for many years and put up with my dedication to supporting Aberdeen that has often taken me away from the family.